The world has lived under arms since it has memory to remember or imagination to invent its past. "Why should we moderns, or at least some of us, be so anxious to make it alter its ways? Salvador de Madariaga answers this question brilliantly. He has discussed armies and navies and causes of war humorously, lucidly, profoundly, and analyzed the possibilities of world disarmament.

The result is a book that is enlightenment to the layman, and a handbook to statesmen. No book that has ever been published is so wise a study of the subject, so aware of facts and practical political difficulties, so sensible to the psychology of nations, and yet so full of foresight and potent imagination about future wars and their consequences to the health and happiness of all nations and races.

Salvador de Madariaga, professor of Spanish Studies at Oxford University, was for five years Chief of the Disarmament Section of the League of Nations Secretariat. He is a frequent contributor to THE ATLANTIC MONTHLY and other magazines.

DISARMAMENT

DISARMAMENT

by

SALVADOR DE MADARIAGA

PUBLISHED IN NEW YORK BY
COWARD-McCANN, INC.
IN THE YEAR 1929

Printed in the U.S.A.

Contents

PART I—CRITICAL

PART II—HISTORICAL

Preface

THIS book is the outcome of six years' experience of international affairs, acquired while the author was an official in the Secretariat of the League of Nations. The League Secretariat is an international civil service. Its members are expected to divest themselves of any national bias and to serve the world as the world, not as a field for the unlimited development of their own nation at the expense of the others. The book is therefore written from the point of view of the world citizen. The author has no ax to grind. He would in any case consider ax-grinding as a most unseemly occupation for a man devoted to the cause of disarmament. However, he adds to this first cause for disinclination toward ax-grinding, yet another one born of an innate intellectual tendency not to interfere with the things that be and must be. Hence a double guarantee of impartiality: on the one hand, the reader is asked to bear in mind that since the book is written from the point of view of the world, it cannot be expected to lead to exactly the same results which his own national point of view might suggest; on the other, since events and trend of history are considered with intellectual detachment, the author claims to have remained cool enough to judge what is likely to happen even when most deeply convinced of the desirability of what should happen.

Ultimately, the world-citizen's point of view is sure to prove the best even for the interests of any one nation. Such a conviction stands at the basis of the author's ability to feel like a world-citizen at all. In criticizing national policies from the point of view of world policy, he is therefore confident that he is using the best method for upholding the truest interests of the nations criticized. He may, of course, misuse the method. But the method is the best.

The right to criticize is inherent in world-citizenship. For world-citizenship means world solidarity which in its turn implies world interest. To put it at its simplest, the world has reached such a degree of interdependence that decisions taken in any one country may bring about grave and even tragic consequences in other lands. Nothing but the sluggish pace of men's mental evolution can justify the citizens of a particular nation in considering themselves as privileged exclusively to control a government whose activities react on other countries with almost as much effect, if not with more, than in their own. At the outset of his work, the author wishes to assert his right to criticize other governments than that of the country in which he happened to be born.

In so doing, he knows that he is running counter to at least two of the most deeply set national currents of our era. The first is the tendency to resent the slightest censure coming from a foreign source. It is a kind of awakening of the herd instinct which scents the strange species in a newly-arrived beast. But there is another tendency more dangerous perhaps and certainly more objectionable. I refer to that deplorable aberration of patriotism which leads people, out of what they imagine to be "public spirit," to abdicate all right to criticism in matters of foreign policy. It is obvious that when the nationals give up their right to speak out, the stranger, who raises his voice, however friendly and well-meaning, does so at his own risk.

Well, the risk must be taken. But it must be taken with a pure heart. The foreign critic can only claim a right to criticize if he endeavors to keep on the plane of world interests, free from the slightest trace of national bias, and if, moreover, he tries to enter into the life and spirit of the nations he criticizes and to understand them with insight and sympathy. In fact, the true world citizen should be able to feel the national patriotism of the nation he studies. These are high standards which the author may have failed to reach. But he has tried to come as near them as his own weaknesses permitted.

Such an aspect of the question is, however, but a minor point. It finds a place in these preliminary remarks as a kind of ceremony for exorcising evil spirits. Let them be gone and we shall be free to turn our attention to the subject itself. It is a kind of subject the novelty, complexity and vague limits of which allow a considerable variety of treatment. In this particular case, the treatment was dictated by the author's own approach to it, i.e., through direct personal experience. The subject is therefore discussed in its human essentials rather than in its technical accidents. This is no historical treatise on disarmament from prehistoric times till the present day; no thesis on the place of disarmament in international law; no disquisition on the strategic and tactical strength of the several nations which vie with each other in their eagerness to disarm without loss of military power. It is rather an endeavor to stimulate the layman (or, as Mr. Bernard Shaw would say, the intelligent woman) to think for himself the whole problem afresh, free from the overgrowth of largely irrelevant technical material which has been allowed to smother the essential issue.

This book is, in fact, an experiment. Is it possible through the medium of literary expression to convey the vital element in experience? The "facts" about disarmament can be found in files, books, official documents and technical treatises. But, what about the facts behind the "facts"? What about the tendencies? What about the interplay of the human moods which the intimate observer of "facts" can see, guess and even scent around him as the "facts" pass before his eyes on the screen of time? Is it possible for such an observer to convey that elusive spiritual wealth to the laymen and intelligent women who happened to be absent from the play?

This book must therefore be considered, not as a perfect though passive repository of information, but as an active though imperfect source of suggestion and inspiration. Not a photograph but a picture, its standards are less scientific than esthetic. Nor should it be thought less accurate for that. When the iron bar of a "fact" is needed to keep up one of the limbs of the statue in its right position, the reader will find the iron to be of the very best metal. But no time has been wasted in the alignment of minutiæ without any significance; and due freedom has governed the arrangement of the material in order to obtain a suggestive and vital, not an informative and so-to-speak, statistical effect. In one word, information has been given not merely when it led to knowledge but when this knowledge was necessary to the understanding of the subject. For understanding and not mere knowledge is what is needed if the problem of disarmament is to find a solution.

The author is convinced that such a solution exists; moreover, that the solution is one which every man and woman can understand. It is his belief that the issue has been confused by an undue admixture of political and technical arguments and counter-arguments, born not of disarmament itself but of armaments speaking under the guise and mask of disarmament. He thinks that, once all this overgrowth is cleared away, common sense suffices to point the path; but he believes also that though this path is clear to our common sense, it is a difficult one to follow for men and women whose innermost texture has been woven with prejudices, traditions and feelings inimical to human coöperation. The difficulties of detail, organization and procedure—which are great—are as nothing when compared with the psychological difficulty. Hence the justification of the treatment, chosen a priori for other reasons; for it is evident that if the main obstacle is in the mind and soul of men, we must try to reach the mind and soul by the most direct approach, i.e., through man's sensibility to events conveyed in vital form by esthetic means.

A few simple yet bold assumptions underlie the whole work. The first is that author and readers mean what they say. This claim, elementary as it may seem, is almost startling in political circles. From them, born, bred and baked in insincerity, insincerity gradually penetrates the masses through the all too ready medium of the press. Let it be understood then between the author and his readers that we are using words in their plain, honest meaning and therefore, when we express abhorrence of war or when we denounce the gospel of power, we mean it.

It follows—and it will be our second assumption—that we cannot admit that a thing and its contrary are compatible and can be simultaneously maintained by serious-minded men. We are sufficiently conversant with psychology to realize that many, if not most, people live and thrive amidst the most atrocious cacophony of inward contradictions; and we know that life is complex and must carry along all kinds of waters in its troubled stream. But once we begin to study a problem of life, such as disarmament, an elementary law of mental discipline binds us to single-mindedness. Things may be quicker or slower, lighter or darker, but they cannot simultaneously go backward and forward.

Insincerity and muddled-headedness are undermining men's faith in themselves. By a process which cannot even claim the merit of novelty, the men of prey are quickly adopting the vocabulary of the men of good will while keeping their claws as sharp and crooked as heretofore. Our third assumption shall be that we mean to judge by deeds. *Obras son amores y no buenas razones*, says the Spanish proverb, and the Gospel: "By their fruits ye shall know them."

But, while the Gospel lies open before us, let us paraphrase that word in it which fits our subject as to the manner born: "Peace on earth to men of good will."—Yes, but to men of good will only.

S. de M.

Part I

CRITICAL

Introduction

WHY DISARM?

THE world has lived under arms since it has memory to remember or imagination to invent its past. Why should we moderns, or at any rate some of us, be so anxious to make it alter its ways? The question may at first sight appear idle. Yet there are at least two reasons why it should be answered. The first is that, despite appearances, most people don't seem convinced that disarmament is necessary; the second, that in the investigation of the motives for disarmament we may find higher necessities still and higher aims than the mere discarding of destructive weapons.

The existence of armaments in the world is a formidable loss and a formidable danger.

ARMAMENTS A LOSS

A rough and ready method of calculating the material loss involved in armaments is to add up the "defense" budgets of all the nations of the world. This sum amounts nowadays to about 3,856 million dollars. Yet, a figure in itself speaks less eloquently to the mind than a comparison of figures. Now, if the total obtained by adding up the "defense" budgets of all the

Members of the League for one year only was set aside, even neglecting the interest accumulated on the unspent sums (no small concession indeed) the capital thus secured would suffice to meet the present expenses of the League of Nations (including the World Court and the International Labor Office) for about six centuries. This means that the world (even if the United States, Russia, Mexico, Turkey, Ecuador, Egypt and Afghanistan are left aside) is nowadays spending in preparing for war six hundred times the sum which it devotes to preparing for peace.

What becomes of these sums? They are spent in men and in material. Now this material is the most expensive in the world. While we grudge the quality of the material we grant our schools, hospitals, astronomical observatories, we lavish our best steel, our choicest woods, our finest optical appliances, our purest chemicals, on the soldier, the sailor and the airman who ask for them. And these costly guns, these expensive aeroplanes, these extravagant battleships, how long do they last? The life of an aeroplane engine is measured in hours; the number of shots a gun can shoot is smaller than the number of dollars it costs. The life of a battleship can be represented by a number of years smaller than the number of millions of dollars which went to its making. All the skill, patience, attention, devotion, all the precious human life which goes to the making of these destructive machines is not only directed to wrong uses, but to flitting uses. The objects thus created, as if cursed by their own destructive destinies, are self-destructive and live but short lives.

Save vice, nothing is as wasteful in the world as war and the preparation for it. The factories erected and maintained at full swing, the workers employed are often mentioned as arguments in their favour—mere fallacies hardly worth refuting. The "defense" expenditure is so huge that it would suffice to pension off all workers employed in war industries and yet would leave a substantial surplus for the nations' treasury. But of course the real argument is quite different. The release of taxation which disarmament would bring about would increase the purchasing capacity and reduce industrial burdens to such an extent that production would be stimulated in general by disarmament infinitely more than it would be paralyzed in its armament branch.

As for the men, considered now from the strictly material (i.e., economic and financial) point of view, the armament system implies of course huge sums spent in food, clothes and salaries for soldiers, sailors and airmen, that is to say, for unproductive services. Yet the material loss is even greater. For these men are all diverted from productive occupations, so that to the yearly sum represented by their salaries must be added the value which their labor would have reached in the market, indeed the whole value of the goods and services which, left to live a productive life, they might have created.

Nor is that all. These men, thus diverted from creative occupations, are made to learn a trade which, in all coolness of mind and with no wish to offend, it is impossible to describe otherwise than as organized, disciplined, systematic and wholesale murder. True, the military profession calls forth many a fine quality in man: courage, self-denial, to mention two of the most prominent virtues of the soldier. But the point is that such splendid gifts are put to a destructive and repulsive use, so that to defend soldiering on account of the virtues which it breeds is tantamount to justifying commercial frauds on the ground that they call forth great proficiency in arithmetic and stimulate quick wits. Were military training the only way to attain such virtues, the case for armaments would still have to be made on other counts. But it is not. It is evident that the virtues usually associated with war and with soldiers can be bred without having to pay for them as expensively in blood, treasury and spirit as the war system makes us do.

The fostering of a spirit of distrust is inherent in such a system. Armaments cannot be justified except on grounds of dire necessity, and such necessity must rest on mistrust. During the press campaign which preceded, accompanied and followed the Naval Conference known as the Coolidge Conference, an English visitor complained to an American Admiral in Washington of the abuse which could be read daily in the American press at the expense of the English nation. The Admiral answered, "Don't mind it. We need it in order to get our Naval Bill through." Thus armaments and mistrust are linked together by one of those cause-and-effect connections of which, as in the case of the hen and the egg, it is idle to enquire which is the cause and which the effect. Now international mistrust is in its turn one of the greatest causes of material, intellectual, moral and spiritual loss in the world.

Materially, it tends to foster artificial economic systems by lending some plausibility to the theory that a nation must be self-supporting. Examples of such economic folly abound in our day. During the preliminary stages of the work of the Preparatory Commission for the Disarmament Conference, a question was put by the Polish Delegation as to whether regional disarmament could be envisaged by drawing out regions (i.e., groups of adjoining nations) constituting self-supporting units. The Commission of Experts to which the matter was referred reported that the only self-supporting region in the world is the whole world. And so it is, of course. Yet, both before and after the findings of that Commission, the self-support will-o'-the-wisp dances in the otherwise sober head of many a statesman, and the map of the planet is anxiously explored for oil, rubber, gold and other sinews of war.

Nor is this the only economic absurdity which armaments and their moral equivalent, mistrust, impose on our distracted world. For military and naval reasons warp, distort and even subvert economic loss at every turn. Spain is, and will probably remain for ever, the victim of an over-zealous general staff which, fearful of French invasions, forced the Government in the middle of the nineteenth century to lay out Spanish railways on a gauge nearly one foot larger than the normal European size. The economic loss of this well-meant stupidity is incalculable. Great Britain has turned down the Channel tunnel scheme time and again, the last time under a Labor Government, on the mere unfavorable advice of its Committee of Imperial Defense. The decisions of general staffs are wont to be inscrutable, but that which denies England and the Continent the immense benefits of a prompt and convenient land connection by rail and road must be put in a class apart for its egregious absurdity.[1]

A similar case arises in connection with aviation. Commercial aviation is kept going by military protection. But this protection is the reverse of a blessing in disguise. It is a curse in disguise. It prevents a clear and unprejudiced case for aviation being made on its civil merits only. Further, it maintains a kind of tutelage on civil aircraft construction, thus hindering the free development of civil aircraft design by imposing on it military specifications. As against these evils, it is sometimes argued that without the Great War, the present development of aviation would have been impossible. But without in any way denying that the unlimited supplies of life and money which the war

[1] During one of the first sittings of the temporary Mixed Commission (a League Disarmament Commission which worked from 1922 to 1924) in which I acted as secretary, M. Viviani, its president, made a speech commenting on the fact that, despite the peace, all nations were possessed of mistrust, all were peeping over each other's frontiers anxiously watching what was being prepared behind. Lord (then Robert) Cecil answered, correcting the president's statement, which, he said, applied perhaps to some but certainly not to all nations. Lord Cecil quoted at least two which, he said, did not seem particularly afflicted by either fear or mistrust of their neighbors: Spain and Great Britain. The president had asked me to give him the gist of what Lord Cecil was saying, and when I came to this, M. Viviani turned to me and asked: "Did he mention Great Britain?" "He did." "Are you sure?" "I am." He feverishly grasped a piece of paper and a pencil, scrawled: "Why doesn't Great Britain let us build the Channel Tunnel?" and handed it to Lord Cecil.

squandered allowed a quicker pace of progress on the then newborn invention, it is evident to any one conversant with the enterprise of air inventors and pilots both before and after the war that the military claim here is simply preposterous.

Needless to say, the economic and financial evils of armaments and mistrust are much greater than those accruing out of a few economic fallacies and of a fair number of hindrances to the normal and free development of the world. The very fact that armaments are kept acts as a deterrent on enterprise. What if the state of armed peace was to degenerate into armed war? This sword of Damocles hangs over the world community and prevents it from pursuing its occupations in all peace of mind.

But the greatest loss of all is in the realm of the spirit. For the existence of armaments is a permanent blot on mankind. That in our present stage of civilization, twenty centuries after the divine teachings of Christ, five centuries after the all but divine creations of Leonardo, four centuries after the splendid achievement of Shakespeare, mankind should still be treasuring, piling murderous weapons in its arsenals, divided against itself, its soul still blackened by fratricidal passions and its hands still soiled by human blood, is an appalling thought on which no mind can rest that is worthy of the name of human.

ARMAMENTS A DANGER

Yet, even a waste can be met with more work, and even shame can be borne in silence. But armaments are not only a waste and a shame, they are also a danger. It has become the fashion to minimize it. There is a certain type of fanatical pacifist who, by insisting on armaments as the sole cause of *all* wars, has brought discredit to the view that they can be the cause of *some* wars, and that they are in any case *one* of the causes of *all* wars. Yet this view could hardly be denied. The matter need not be discussed documents in hand. A historical proof, if one is to judge by recent events, is one of the most fickle of human documents. Novels are more interesting and at times truer than so-called history. Fortunately, this question of how far the existence of armaments may contribute to bring about wars is one which can be discussed on its merits by the mere use of the mind unaided, nay, undisturbed, by "documents."

Two points offer themselves for consideration.

The first concerns the relations between the armament industry and war. Let us repeat that we need not refer to any definite events. We need not rake up the history of this or that press campaign, the underground relations between fighting departments, armament firms and newspapers. We do not know. We do not need to know. What is the position? Armaments presuppose armament firms. There are no armament firms in the world which are established on the principle of pure and disinterested patriotism. They are all industrial enterprises which have in common with every other industrial enterprise in the world that their aim is to manufacture dividends. They only differ in that the intermediate products wherewith they manufacture dividends are guns and battleships instead of motor cars or cheese. Now an industrial enterprise is essentially interested in its market. There is no mystery about that, no villainy. It is all above board. Let us print it in capitals, for it is blatant, open and obvious, in fact it is a platitude: ARMAMENT FIRMS ARE INTERESTED IN FOSTERING A STATE OF AFFAIRS WHICH WILL INCREASE THE DEMAND FOR ARMAMENTS.

This assertion cannot be gainsaid. There may be firms who refrain, but there may be firms who do not. The natural tendency of the trade is to foster the production of situations which may increase their market. Other causes may act against this tendency, but so far as they are concerned, armament firms are more likely than not to let the world drift if not actually to push it towards international unrest. That they may deliberately force the world into war is more doubtful. The question whether a war may or may not be *ultimately* beneficial to even an armament firm is perhaps, particularly after the experience of the last war, too problematic, and the responsibility entailed too heavy perhaps even for the most unscrupulous business man to shoulder; but that armament firms are more likely than not to keep a state of mistrust and international unrest endemic in the world is a conservative view of the situation which could hardly be disputed. And it follows that from such a state of international unrest war may spring at any moment.

The second point is even more important. Armaments are not held by a nation in an inchoate form. Men and material are organized into a force, and put under the leadership of a general staff. The general staff, composed as it is of soldiers or sailors, has, as is traditional in the fighting profession, a high sense of honor. The military branch of any administration may therefore be expected to give full value to the state in exchange for its salaries and privileges. Now, what can a general staff do three hundred and sixty days a year at the rate of six hours a day but prepare for war? Here again, the facts are above board. There is no mystery. Every important nation keeps a fully manned and fully endowed general staff which is expected to be fully occupied.

Very well. But strategy is not a pure science. It is an applied art. It must be exercised on a definite hypothesis. The first thing a general staff does, therefore, is to set up before its eyes a concrete hypothetical adversary. Nor is this adversary chosen capriciously. In most cases, there exists a series of circumstances—historical, geographical, traditional—which clearly single out a particular nation for such a distinction. The same set of circumstances, acting in the opposite direction with equivalent effects, make the general staff of the second nation choose as its hypothetical adversary the nation whose general staff chose it. Then begins the usual rivalry. Armaments closely watched, policies uncharitably discussed, statesmen's speeches microscopically scrutinized by anxious leader writers, the public gradually aroused from indifference for the affairs of the adversary to interest in them; from interest to misgivings; from misgivings to fear; from fear to hatred; from hatred to fury. And one day, the spark flies through the air and death rides rough-shod on the horses of folly.

That this is not the whole picture is obvious. This book would not be written if it were, since its main purpose is to show that disarmament pure and simple is impossible, because disarmament pure and simple is not self-consistent. That "preparedness" is a folly would have been more widely understood had the advocates of the pacifist view taken greater care to show that preparedness cannot and should not be abandoned without putting something in its place. But, that granted, and the "something" in question left moreover for discussion in subsequent pages, it is necessary to nail to the counter the fallacy of *si vis pacem para bellum.* Nail it and nail it again. Its vitality is incredible.

"If you want peace, prepare for war." That is, if you want something, get ready for the reverse of it. Such is the slogan generally opposed to disarmament efforts. Now, there was a time when circumstances may have given some practical justification to this theoretically untenable position. Nations small and sparsely distributed over unorganized territories, small armies, simple weapons, little or no international faith, unstable compacts, personal influence on international policies, may have made the method of preparedness the cheapest, safest, and most practicable, nay, the only one available. To-day, the situation is the very reverse. The world has grown small for our power and resources. Only one opinion and only one market cover the face of the earth. Wars absorb the whole population of the countries which engage in them, exact all their resources and consume all the raw materials which human ingenuity has wrung from the recesses of the earth. In this condition, preparing for war means securing indefinite stocks of food and raw materials of all kinds and/or absolute control over the sources of supply and communications. Short of that, preparing for war is a worthless slogan or a misleading falsehood.

Preparedness leads therefore to the scramble for raw materials and territories, and thence to increasing causes of friction and possibilities of war.

Moreover, an armed nation cannot prepare for war. It can only prepare for *a* war. For no self-respecting general staff is going to prepare for abstract and vague events. The numbers, composition, formation, tactics, armaments, transportation arrangements and even uniform of the troops, as well as the plans, numbers and equipment of men-of-war and naval stations, depend on definite and concrete war hypotheses. The hypothetical adversary commands the armaments of the nation which has chosen him, just as the consumer commands the offer of the producer.

Thus, owing both to the general conditions prevailing nowadays and to the technical reasons inherent in the existence of organized armies and navies, preparing for war may be said to be a highly dangerous system of preparing for peace.

A waste of money and life; a shame and a blot on mankind; a danger for peace, armaments were the first evil which the drafters of the League Covenant sought to secure. The Article enjoining on all the Members of the League a reduction of armaments to the minimum compatible with their national security and with the adequate fulfillment of their national obligations, is the eighth in the Covenant. The seven first Articles deal with the constitution and organization of the League. Disarmament may therefore be considered as the first task entrusted to the League by the drafters of its Charter. Yet this task, the importance of which is thus emphasized, from its very inception is perhaps that in which its efforts have proved least effective.

Numerous obstacles make progress slow and agreements laborious and precarious. It may be convenient to deal with the most important of them, grouping them into two categories:

General obstacles, being those of a greater or less degree, are met with in every walk of international life.

Special obstacles are those more specifically attached to the work of disarmament.

In the second category, we shall have to distinguish outer obstacles, being difficulties that arise, so to say, on the outskirts of the problem of disarmament, and finally the inner obstacle, the very kernel of the difficulty which this problem opposes to men and peoples of goodwill.

Chapter I

GENERAL OBSTACLES

1. SLOW RHYTHM OF THE LEAGUE

IT is a well-known fact that the League works on the principle of unanimity. The alternative to such a principle is a super-state, since on the day a nation could be bound by decisions taken by an international body against its own vote, its own sovereignty would have been transferred to the international body in question. The rule of unanimity implies a technique radically different from the majority rule. Under the majority rule, the aim is the outnumbering of the adversary, and the means his outwitting. The technique is not unlikely that of war. Surprise, strategy, ambush, are useful and often resorted to. Results are relatively rapid. Under the unanimity rule, numbers do no longer count. One "no" beats all "ayes." Surprise and victory are impossible. Persuasion is necessary and patience indispensable. Full warning, plentiful information, readiness to explain, to argue and to compromise are the necessary ingredients, and the Master Cook is Time.

Such is the main cause of the slowness of the rhythm of the League. Yet, built on compromise, the League has applied its spirit to its procedure, and by way of compromise between the rule of unanimity on the one hand, and the requirements of time on the other, it has admitted the majority rule in all but its executive bodies—Council and Assembly. Thus, its Advisory Commissions can speed up work by applying the majority rule to their debates and findings. It must not, however, be imagined that such a liberty enables them to adopt the methods often observed in majority-governed assemblies, for in the end the decisions taken in an advisory capacity by the majority of a Commission must be passed by the unanimous vote of executive bodies in which the same nations are represented. Yet, there is no doubt that, so far as it goes, the application of the majority rule to Advisory Commissions does speed up the work of the League.

Or at least it makes it less slow. For slow of necessity it must be. The periodical movements which compose it may be summarized as follows:

(1) The Assembly decides that a particular work must be put in hand and informs the Council to that effect. (Theoretically, the Assembly might decide to put it in hand, but the habit has set in that the Assembly allows the Council a free hand as to the choice of the moment when action has to take place.)

(2) The Council resolves to put in hand the work in question and sets up a Commission to study the matter.

(3) The Secretariat circulates the Council's decision to the Governments concerned, and the names of the members of the Commission are asked for and sent to Geneva.

(4) The Commission meets. Possibly a delegation may bring a paper as a basis for discussion. If the

matter is important, the first session is never sufficient, for the several Governments must have time to study the proposals that are being made and to form an opinion on them.

(5) The results—final or temporary—arrived at by the Commission are formally sent before the Council. This implies distribution to the fourteen Members of the Council, i.e., to the fourteen Governments in their fourteen capitals, some of which, such as Tokyo and Santiago, lie at several weeks' or months' distance from Geneva.

(6) The Council may agree or adjourn, in the hope of later agreement. The Council meets every three months. If it agrees, the matter goes before the Assembly. The Assembly meets once a year.

Such is the beat of the League's pulse. It will be found much slower than Napoleon's (forty-five a minute) yet much more sparing in human lives. It is foolish to find fault with it. An immense "living thing" having the whole earth for its mighty body, the League cannot move with the ease and swiftness of a flapper in jazz. When we are about to study its activity, we must begin by realizing the fundamental law of its life. Its speed is not our speed. Its years are centuries.

2. COMPLEXITY OF NATIONS. INSTABILITY OF POLITICAL SITUATIONS

In all that precedes, nations have been considered as strongly individualized units. Yet this assumption, made for the sake of argument, is unwarranted, indeed belied by experience. Nothing is further removed from reality than that melodramatic view of international affairs which imagines them as a kind of detective story in which "France" does this, and "England" counters with that, and "America" insists on a particular thing, while "Japan," lurking behind distance (what a wall distance can be), prepares for something else. In point of fact, France and England, America and Japan are infinitely complex units: divided horizontally into layers of greater or lesser education or knowledge of foreign affairs, and vertically into parties animated with a different spirit, widely divergent tendencies, conflicting ideas. Thus, the policy of every particular nation is but the more or less broken line which joins successive decisions taken as the result of successive states of equilibrium among a considerable number of national forces, all variable. If, in practically every case, the existence of well organized foreign offices, with a tradition and a political memory, provides a minimum of continuity in the foreign policy of each particular nation, the fact remains that decisions to be taken, as time brings problems in its flow, are dominated by such things as the political bias of the Government in office, an impending general election, the temperament and ability of the foreign secretary, and such like factors, not necessarily connected with what might be considered to be the theoretical policy of the nation concerned.

It follows that the rhythm of the League, which we know to be slow for international reasons, is made slower still owing to the complications arising out of the instability of national executives. It often happens that a Commission reaches a unanimous conclusion after a considerable time and effort, through much self-denying and conciliatory sacrifices on the part of many of its members, only to find that when the document thus arrived at reaches this or that Government, the party in office have changed, and the efforts to meet that particular point of view prove vain. A case in point occurred in connection with disarmament. During the years 1922-1923, the temporary Mixed Commission worked under the leadership of Lord (then Robert) Cecil. His intellectual distinction, his capacity for work, the great prestige which he deservedly enjoyed in Geneva, overcame all obstacles, and the Commission set up the famous Treaty of Guarantee. Lord Cecil was not an official British representative, yet who could reproach the French for believing that when they compromised with him on some important point, they were compromising with England? When the Treaty arrived in London, the Conservative Government had gone out of office, and the Labor Government were in the saddle. Mr. Macdonald, Prime Minister and Foreign Secretary, rejected the Treaty. It must have been a matter of melancholy satisfaction in Paris when the letter in which Mr. Macdonald explained his opposition to the Treaty contained passages, which a wary reader could trace back to French memoranda, criticizing Lord Cecil's proposals from the French (and military) point of view. But that is by the way. Mr. Macdonald, having rejected Lord Cecil's Treaty, went to Geneva and he, the Prime Minister and Foreign Secretary of Great Britain, laid down the principles on which an international instrument should be drawn. Very well. Geneva took down notes and drafted the new instrument; and in order to remain on the safe side, two British Cabinet Ministers—Mr. Henderson and Lord Parmoor—were kept in direct charge of the work. The work was done with remarkable rapidity in 1924. Geneva was very proud of it. It was the famous Protocol. Though sent posthaste to London, it had been preceded by another no less famous document, the Zinovieff letter. Mr. Macdonald resigned, and on the two chairs once occupied by him sat now Mr. Baldwin and Sir Austen Chamberlain. The Protocol, drafted to please the British Government, was rejected by another British Government. Our path is strewn with tombstones.

Is this written in reproach? Far from it. Lord Cecil was sincerity itself. Mr. Macdonald could not be more sincere. Nor could Sir Austen Chamberlain. Three British statesmen: three views on disarmament. Yet the world goes on talking about "Great Britain" or "England" as if she were a young woman with a steel helmet on her head and ideas as solid as the helmet under it. But these abstract words and these concrete pictures contain and conceal an infinite variety of opinions, each of them not only different from the neighboring one, but different from what it was itself yesterday, and from what it may become to-morrow. Thus the difficulties inherent in the slow rhythm imposed on the League by the number and distance of its Members are multiplied *ad infinitum* by the fact that each of these Members is itself a world of its own, made of a great number of different and fluctuating opinions. By its constitution, the League is like an orchestra of fifty-five musicians which must seek perfect unison. When this has been secured after infinite patience, one or two of the musicians are withdrawn and replaced by new artists with new instruments and new ideas about the tune to be played.

3. DIFFERENCES IN NATIONAL PSYCHOLOGY

Yet, even if we were to assume a perfect national consistency and continuity by every one of the League Members, the work of international organizations would remain extremely difficult, owing to differences in national psychology. The difficulties which beset a given international problem fall under two heads: objective differences inherent in the problem, and subjective differences due to the way in which the problem and its objective differences are seen by the men and nations called upon to tackle them. Of the two, the former are, of course, the more substantial, but the latter are more bewildering. The former are the fortress to be stormed; the latter the barbed wire inextricably woven around it. Let us imagine an international question theoretically soluble; an open fortress. The barbed wire of psychological differences would still remain to be crossed.

For think of the composition of an ordinary League Commission. The discussions carried on in several dozen varieties of French and English are fed by intellectual waters coming from all climates and lands—white, yellow, and brown, Catholic, Protestant, orthodox, Moslem, Buddhist, atheist, old tradition and new progress, the abstract, the empirical, the impatient, the traditional, the skeptic, the enthusiast, the obvious and the enigmatic; the soloist who commands the powerful blasts of French eloquence; the virtuoso who performs on the violins of Italian dialectics: the master who controls the fifes and drums of English persuasiveness and the perfect artist who plays impeccably on the wide and subtle registers of Japanese silence.

In order to illustrate this difficulty, it is not necessary, however, to seek wide contrasts of race and continent. Two peoples closely allied by ties of race and language, whose long intimacy of peace and war might have been expected to develop an accurate mutual knowledge, will offer us an unrivaled illustration of the psychological obstacles which beset all international work. France and England have been for six years the almost exclusive leaders of the League of Nations. They bid fair to remain its most important Members for a long time to come. Now France and England are often in Geneva at loggerheads. Not that their interests cannot be made to agree. As national differences go, their differences are more often than not bridgeable in themselves, given a little time and goodwill. Thus it is not altogether impossible to bring the French and the British delegates to see eye to eye. Only their eyes are so different. . . .

It has been my privilege to attend in the closest possible way the Anglo-French discussions on disarmament ever since Lord Cecil submitted to the second Assembly the draft resolution which, with the collaboration-in-opposition of M. de Jouvenel, became the famous Resolution 14. Since then, both in private discussion and in public debate, I have observed many a case of that permanent discordance between the French and the British mentality which is the true source of their misunderstandings. Time and again I have seen the French nonplussed at the illogical and empirical vagueness of the English, and the English shocked and irritated at the unseemly yet unreal clarity of the French.

The whole difficulty comes from the particular region in which the center of gravity of their respective psychologies is situated, which in the Frenchman is above, and in the Englishman below, the neck. The Frenchman thinks with his head, and with nothing but his head; the Englishman thinks—or rather, as he himself says, "feels somehow" with everything but his head,[1] and, provided he does not allow his head to meddle with it, he is generally right. The Frenchman, trusting thought, is apt to distrust life, and therefore he endeavors to imprison future life in present thought by foreseeing every case and regulating every action in advance; while the Englishman, who trusts life but mistrusts thought (his own and still more so the Frenchman's) refuses to foresee, and is content to cross the bridge when he comes to it—even at the risk of

[1] Readers whom this point may interest are referred to "Englishmen, Frenchmen, Spaniards," Oxford University Press, 1928, in which a parallel between the three national psychologies is developed at length.

having to ford the river on finding there is no bridge at all.

The history of the Franco-British dialogue on disarmament and security—for it was mostly a dialogue between two protagonists—is but the working out of this psychological contrast between the English and the French characters. The Frenchman said: "We are all agreed about principles; therefore, please sign this paper in which our agreed principles are set forth and developed to their logical conclusions." And the Englishman answered: "True, we are agreed about principles, but there is no need to sign anything at all. When the time comes to apply them, we shall do so in the light of the circumstances, and since we are agreed on principles, there is no doubt but that we shall agree as to their application." Then the Frenchman was taken aback and went home full of misgivings: "He does not want to sign, therefore he does not really believe in the principles," he suspected. While the Englishman went home muttering: "He wanted to pin me down for ever. I wonder what he had up his sleeve." Thus does misunderstanding arise, and even mistrust is bred out of a mere difference in character.

In a greater or lesser degree such a subjective discordance arises between any two nations in Geneva. Thus a complex set of subjective discordances is interwoven with a no less complicated set of objective conflicts in the problem in discussion. Such is the maze through which the one positive force has to act—goodwill.

Chapter II

SPECIAL OBSTACLES

I. Special Obstacles of an Outer Nature

1. TROUBLED STATE OF THE WORLD

WHETHER disarmament appeals to a feeling of international trust, the existence of which it implies, or is in itself the indispensable condition for such a feeling to develop, it cannot be doubted that the present state of the world is not particularly favorable for either disarming or even discussing disarmament schemes.

Europe has been left by the war in a state of profound division. A trained eye can perceive in it several lines of cleavage along which the European crystal is ever threatening to split. The Rhine remains what it always was, the most important line, the very axis of European politics and one on which are still at work forces which, if made to coöperate, may build up a strong and healthy Europe, but which, if left to antagonize each other, may finally disrupt the civilization of the continent. The eastern frontier of Germany is another line of cleavage for European statesmen to watch. Hungary, reduced to a (for her, unbearable) minimum, broods in discontent amongst uncomfortable neighbors; Italy asserts her youthful forces northeast towards Belgrade, northwest towards Paris, southeast towards Asia Minor and southwest towards Africa; and Russia, self-isolated and self-encircled in her uncompromising dogma, remains a mystery or a bogey for her neighbors and an irritating problem for nations farther afield.

Nor is Asia more favored. The war, seen as a world event, was lost by the white and the Christian. The self-appointed superiority of the western race and of the western religion can hardly be expected to strike the easterner with much respect when whites and Christians drift into such orgies of bloody and ruthless destruction as the late war let loose. Moreover, by some irony of fate, the east loses its respect for the west at the moment when it undergoes the effects of certain western influences to which it had remained impervious in earlier times. Thus nationalism, a purely western spirit, agitates Turkey and Persia, India and China; while an eastern British Isles seems to rise in Japan, foreboding the development of an eastern British Empire.

If we turn from Asia to America, things can only seem rosier to the uninformed or to that type of debonair optimist who looks away from what he fears to see. Several conflicts divide between themselves American nations born of the same race; Colombia and Venezuela are at loggerheads on the question of the traffic on the Orinoco; Brazil and the Argentine Republic are entering the path of rivalry which has been shown them by older nations; Chile and Peru have invented in

Tacna and Arica an American Alsace-Lorraine; the Monroe Doctrine, unilaterally defined, is less a defense than an offense to nations who have outgrown (or to those which want to outgrow) the period of infantile development which made its proclamation possible and perhaps necessary in the past. The United States have built the Panama Canal less as a life artery for the world than as the axis of their naval power. Every one of its interventions in the Caribbean Sea may have been inspired by the higher and most disinterested motives, but every one has left behind exactly the same result—a naval base.

Finally, Australasia—that immense sea with but one important territory on its unlimited waters—raises a thorny question on that very territory. The Australian people hold the continent, possessed of one of the narrowest racial prejudices which history has known. And where can we find a more disquieting factor in international politics than racial prejudice?

Such is, briefly told, the state of the world to-day. It can hardly justify high expectations.

2. DIFFERENT STAGES IN IMPERIAL EVOLUTION

If, weary of the present, we tried to fathom the future, our hopes are not to rise much higher. The present holds the future as the egg the chicken. The tendency of to-day becomes the act of to-morrow. Now, to-day, we see nations that hold their own by the side of nations whose grasp is weakening, and of others whose hands are fidgeting, empty and vigorous. The question of disarmament is closely dependent on that of imperial evolution.

There are empires which blossom no more; their crop is of the past. Thus, for instance, Sweden and Spain.

There are empires which are ripe and in full vigor. Thus, for instance, England or Holland.

There are empires which are just on the edge of over-ripeness. Their crop is just as much as they can bear without bending. Such is the case, for instance, of France and Belgium.

There are empires which are frankly over-ripe, such as Portugal.

There are empires which are green. Their crop is in the future. Thus, for instance, Italy, the United States of America and Japan.

The idea of giving up armaments cannot appeal equally to all these empires. For some of them, youthful and cynical, it sounds like a hypocritical appeal to stop gambling in the name of virtue made by a winning gambler when he has wiped out the green table with his lucky hands.

3. PRESTIGE

Then there is prestige. As nations become more and more related to each other through the general shrinking of the world, brought about by the improvement in communications, they acquire a keener consciousness of relative values—those values which we might call "social" by comparison with the world or society of men. Rank, appearances, "show," prestige, all the characteristics of "society" as we know them in a collectivity of individuals, tend to appear in the world of nations. This tendency is particularly noticeable in the realm of naval disarmament. I had occasion to observe it at close quarters during the meetings of the Naval Sub-Commission of the Permanent Advisory Commission of the League which met in Rome in 1924, in order to extend the principles of the Washington Treaty to non-signatory powers. This meeting deserves further comment. For our present purpose the important rôle which prestige played in its failure should be emphasized. The three nations represented in the Commission, which were also signatories of the Washington Treaty, i.e., Great Britain, France and Italy, wished other powers to limit the tonnage of their warships to certain figures. Arguments were endless and involved, but there ran under them a current of feeling which could be best interpreted by means of a parable. A nobleman, the scion of an old and powerful family, has fallen into narrow straits and keeps a small establishment. He, whose ancestors were surrounded with swarms of servants, is now reduced to three or four of them. Other neighbors who have, on the contrary, risen to fortune, seek to make an arrangement to the effect that each of the dwellers in the street is to limit his establishment to the number of servants he happens to keep at the time. The nobleman refuses. Why? He knows he shall never be able to afford one single servant above that figure. But he does not want to sign his own downfall. Theoretically, he is a many-servanted man.

This parable illustrates one of the most formidable obstacles on the path towards a definite convention on disarmament.[1]

In the absence of a definite agreement implying reciprocal obligations, each State feels itself free to maintain a force which is a compromise between the ambitions of its fighting departments and the sobering influences of its exchequer. This internal compromise is relatively easy, because there is a free future in which to revise it. If and when a definite engagement of an international, solemn and binding character, is envisaged, such a freedom threatens to vanish and then three sets of forces come into play, all tending to increase the figure to be "offered": the tendency to reserve a margin against possible contingencies in international negotiation; prestige; and the necessity to provide a margin for discussion with the national exchequer. Such is the explanation of the warning often heard in League disarmament discussions to the effect that a conference for the reduction of armaments may well result in all-round increases.

4. OVER-LIVING FORMS OF THOUGHT

Nor is it possible to blame Governments which take a conservative view in this respect, since the world still tends to estimate nations according to their military power. There is a curious feature of the human mind, a kind of laziness, which makes it keep on empty shells

[1] We shall see that such a convention is neither a necessary nor a sufficient condition for disarmament to take place.

of thought already dead, just as railway carriages kept—some of them still do—the curve of the old coaches cut out to give room for the wheels, long after the wheels which made it necessary had become smaller and disappeared under the carriage floor. The forms of our dead ideas still linger in our thought long after we have discarded the ideas themselves. Numerous examples could be given. Two may be quoted, because they refer to the two greatest apostles of disarmament and of moral force.

In a speech delivered by President Wilson at the Peace Conference (31st May, 1919) on Minorities questions, there occur the following words: ". . . And back of that lies this fundamentally important fact that when the decisions are made, the allied and associated powers guarantee to maintain them. It is perfectly evident, upon a moment's reflection, that the chief burden of their maintenance will fall upon the greater powers. The chief burden of the war fell upon the greater powers, and if it had not been for their action, their military action, we would not be here to settle these questions. And, therefore, we must not close our eyes to the fact that in the last analysis the military and naval strength of the great powers will be the final guarantee of the peace of the world. . . ."

Lord Cecil speaking on the criteria on which parties should be granted permanent seats in the Council (14th May, 1926) said he did not want to discuss at length whether the principle of permanence for the great Powers was a reasonable principle or not. M. Fromageot had given an excellent exposition, if he would allow him to say so, of the idea which was in the minds of the framers of the Covenant, namely: that the great Powers were those which were always interested in every subject that was likely to be discussed by the League and therefore ought always to be present at the Council. There was the other argument, which had been very admirably put by M. Paul-Boncour, that so long as force played a part in international relations—and it was foolish, indeed exceedingly foolish, to deny that force did still play a part in international relations—it was important to have on the Council those Powers which were best able to assist in realizing the decisions, or rather the objects, of the Covenant and carrying out the provisions contained in it, such as those of Article 16.

These two examples are typical, coming as they do from two men so closely connected with the effort towards establishing international life on moral as distinct from physical forces.

But there are other cases in which beliefs and opinions thus overlive their utility. Since I am writing in English, let me quote two, referring each to one of the two Anglo-Saxon peoples. England, as a whole, still believes in the supremacy of the British Navy, as the panacea for all her international ills. That it has been a panacea for about three centuries no one could deny. That it played its last scene in this magnificent rôle during the Great War no one can deny. But that it was the *last* scene is apparent to every one outside England and to those clear-sighted Englishmen who do not allow the glow of the past to interfere with the light of the present. No more brilliant illustration of this fact could be wished than the astounding speech delivered by Lord Jellicoe at the "Coolidge" Conference held in Geneva during the summer of 1927. The gist of this speech was that since England, with one hundred and fourteen cruisers (plus all the cruisers of her formidable allies) had nearly gone down on her knees when attacked by a few German auxiliary raiders, it was evident that she needed seventy cruisers for the security of her food communications. The logic of this speech has a peculiar British flavor, unlikely to be appreciated outside the boundaries of the old country; but the burden of the message is obvious. The British fleet is no adequate solution for British security. Yet the dogma and the cult overlive their god.

A similar case occurs in America. Some one has vaguely remembered that Washington once said there were not to be American tanglements in Europe, and it matters little that it was not Washington, but Jefferson, who said it; still less that he meant something else; even less still that circumstances have changed; that the small, struggling sapling of a nation has become a gigantic tree; that the colony for European capital and enterprise has grown to be the banker of the world; that the American wealth invested in Europe is equivalent to that of seven or eight American States; that while several European wars can be imagined which would not affect some European nations, no single European war can break up without direct important losses for the United States; nothing sensible matters but this idea (?), this sentimental fossil whose empty shell lies encased in every loyal American brain.

5. DIFFERENCES IN MILITARY TRADITION

Every discussion on disarmament reveals keen differences in military tradition underlying differences in technical or political interests. The most notable of these is that which lends much of its animus to British pacificism, or rather anti-militarism, i.e., the deep-rooted feeling of the Briton against standing armies, contrasted with the Republican tradition of universal service which takes root in France under the French Revolution. Here again, the protagonists are England and France. In England, the prejudice, for it amounts to a prejudice, takes its origin in the nation's traditional distrust of the crown. Men and money are only granted the executive for one year, and with watchful eyes. While the Navy is a permanent service, the Army lives from year to year. Curiously enough, this hostile feeling which, in view of the political evolution of the English people, is in itself also a fossil, an over-living form, leads to paradoxical results. It would seem but logical to guard against the executive by setting up a strong citizen army; yet the British nation prefer a small and efficient army of professionals. For in fact, the strongest psychological element amongst those which determine this question is the reluctance of the average Briton to submit to military discipline. A good fighter, if he must fight, the Briton is not a soldier. Nothing is more odious to him than the barracks.

In France, on the contrary, soldiering for a couple of years in one's youth is considered as one of the duties of the citizen. The dogma of equality is as sacred to the Frenchman as that of the immaculate conception to the Catholic—equally absurd as they both may look in the eyes of third parties. The idea of limiting military service to a few men, still worse that of entrusting the custody of the sacred territory of the country to professionals who would do it for money, is far more abhorrent to the Frenchman than the idea of barracks to the Englishman. But the Englishman, who hates standing armies, i.e., citizen armies organized on compulsory service, attributes to them all sorts of evil effects, since nothing save love stimulates the imagination as much as hatred; and that explains why England should direct the best of her disarmament efforts towards abolishing standing armies. Yet, nations whose democratic and peaceful feelings are beyond doubt, Switzerland, for instance, are resolutely in favor of citizen armies, and the bulk of that part of French public opinion which stands by genuine disarmament favors an evolution of the French army which, by the gradual reduction of periods of service would make the Swiss army of to-day the model of the French army of to-morrow. Ultimately, the problem must be solved according to international standards, but it is well to emphasize here that in all internal discussions, the differences in military traditions add further discordances to the all too numerous discordances which the subject presents in itself.

A further point to be mentioned in this connection is that armies and navies can hardly be compared statistically, for they are living collectivities with peculiarities of their own; each united to the life of the country by a kind of biological alliance, a symbiosis which evades all generalization. Thus, the navy in the British Empire is a kind of *growth*, deeply inserted in the body and soul of the nation; it is the ubiquitous presence of the whole empire in every far-flung part of it; it is like the imperial consciousness circulating through all the veins and arteries of the mighty body—in every one of which vital values it has no equivalent with the navy of, say, France or the United States. Thus, again in Spain, the army is a political force, one of the elements of the system on which the Restoration has been built and stood for the last fifty years, and therefore its size and budget are matters, not only of international but of national concern. Thus, again in the United States, owing to its peculiar constitution, the army provides the federal administration with experts which it would otherwise lack—for instance, doctors and civil engineers. We may have to recall these and similar other cases when dealing with the problem of the possibility of wholesale and immediate disarmament.

Chapter III

SPECIAL OBSTACLES (*Continued*)

II. The Inner Obstacle

WE have so far reviewed the obstacles which lie on the outskirts of the problem. The main obstacle, however, is in the very core of it. Nothing can better illustrate its central position than a method consisting in attacking the problem from a series of different angles, and showing how all the avenues of approach lead to the same conclusion.

1. THE PACIFIST POINT OF VIEW

For the purposes of this study, we understand as the pacifist point of view that which considers that armaments are the cause of wars. We have already set down some, at any rate, of the reasons which militate (if the verb be allowed in such a context) in favor of this view. We accept, therefore, within the limits then defined, that armaments *in themselves* are a danger of war. The conclusion would appear to be that armaments must be discarded.

The time has come, therefore, to discuss the possibility of total and general disarmament. The proposal has been made by the Soviet Delegation at the Preparatory Commission for Disarmament in Geneva (December and March sittings). We shall see in due time why in our opinion Soviet Russia should have been the only nation able to propose such a drastic change in the habits of the world. We shall then be in a position to add theoretical reasons why general and immediate disarmament is not possible. But we can give at once practical reasons which lead to the same conclusion. The first is that which we have occasion to mention in connection with the different characteristics of armies and navies to be found in nations. What Soviet Russia seems to forget—in this as in home affairs—is that thought cannot be immediately applied to life without provoking grave results. Doctors who know their business are fully aware of the dangers which beset a sudden change in the habits of a patient who has injured his health by years of ill advised diet or even drugging. Were it theoretically proved that armies and navies could be abolished wholesale, nothing could be more dangerous than their immediate disappearance. Long-lived tradition, feelings, political ties, social growths have to be adjusted. The operation is in the nature of a half surgical, half medical intervention on a patient. To quote a famous Spanish parliamentary taunt, it requires something more than mere daring.

But the possibility of a complete abolition of armed forces has not been proved. I confess but little sympathy with the view that nations must remain armed in order to meet their obligations under the Covenant. If a nation, Member of the League, chooses to reduce her armaments to a limit which makes her internationally disarmed, I fail to see in such an action any but good results, so far as the Covenant is concerned. For, to begin with, that nation is off the map of possible aggressors, and so far, so good; then, should she be involved in a scrap, it will be obvious that she is not the party to be blamed for actual hostilities (whatever her attitude may be in the aspects of the conflict other than its military side); should her record be also good on the civil side of the conflict, the Members of the League are undoubtedly bound to defend her, disarmed or not; obviously she would re-arm in such a case. But the idea that a nation that disarms foregoes her right to be defended if attacked always appealed to me as one of the most arrant pieces of nonsense put forward in Geneva. Moreover, the argument is purely theoretical, for no nation is likely to disarm who sees trouble even in a very far-off horizon. As for the argument that she ceases to count as a co-worker in sanctions, it is not quite correct, since the disarmed nation remains available for economic and financial sanctions, and even—after re-arming—for military sanctions. On the other hand, in my opinion, the fact of disarming is infinitely more useful for the peace of the world as an example, and owing to the increased facilities which it provides for the disarmament of others, than the fact of keeping armed forces would be as a help for a hypothetical case of aggression. No argument against disarmament drawn from the Covenant can ever have any sense, since the Covenant was written in order to make disarmament possible.

Yet, the possibility of immediate general and complete disarmament is not proved. Some armaments will have to remain on two counts: as elements of national order and stability and as elements of an international police force. It will readily appear that both these requirements would have to be met even if a considerable measure of disarmament was accepted; both, moreover, raise matters of delicate import. Under cover of police forces, nations might keep forces amounting to real armies. There are indeed nations—Spain one of them—in which the gendarmerie is at least as efficient a force as the army. An international authority would appear to be necessary in order to guard against any complications that might arise out of this situation. Moreover, the requirements of an international police force would need careful adjustment by an international authority. The fact remains, therefore, that even if we admitted the possibility of an immediate and drastic wholesale reduction of armaments to the level required by police duties, the problem would have to be tackled by an international authority.

But as a matter of fact we do not admit such a possibility. For in a wholly disarmed world, the smaller nations would be still more at the mercy of the big ones than they are at present. Nations industrially and economically powerful would, in such a world, be able to re-arm with ease and rapidity. Nations not so favored would lie helpless before them. While all would have destroyed the eggs of armaments, some powerful countries would still retain the hens. The argument is sometimes put forward—it was put to me by Mr. Litvinoff—that small nations are at the mercy of the big ones in any case. This argument overlooks the imponderabilia which in politics, contrary to all etymology, carry great weight. Small nations are armed, and if necessary can show a fight. Now, a fight between a big and a small nation kills people on both sides, and that gets into the press. But, moreover, in most cases matters would not happen that way. Nations would not re-arm. They would exert some kind of quiet economic pressure which would force the small recalcitrant nation to bow before the strong. And then the situation is even more complex than that. The fact is that the world is still surrounded by "outlying" political problems; it is as a town well planned and built in its central districts, but girded by waste zones in which the architect, the sanitary engineer and the builder have not entered yet. The words Manchuria, China, Pacific, Monroe Doctrine, Africa, Arabia, suggest a host of problems which would suffice to block all disarmament. Unless they are tackled on a coöperative basis, how can we hope to disarm?

What is our conclusion? That no general disarmament is possible in the absence of a well organized World-Community. Such a community would solve outlying problems; it would guarantee small disarmed nations against undue pressure exerted by the strong, and moreover, if the conflict developed into hostilities, would put at the service of the victim the combined economic power of the world, transformable if necessary into military power.

2. THE REALIST POINT OF VIEW

We shall understand as realist the opinion which holds that armaments are not the cause, but the effect of wars. The remembrance of past wars and the fear of future wars are undoubtedly the strongest springs which make people maintain their armaments in spite of the heavy expenses involved. It follows that, according to this doctrine, the remedy for armaments lies in the abolition of wars.

Two possibilities have been put forward: one of them is to search for the causes of wars and to seek to put an end to them; the other is to outlaw war. Let us examine them successively.

a. Causes and cures of war.—There are as many causes of war amongst nations as there are of quarrels amongst individuals. We should be wasting our time if we were to venture into a complete analysis of the political, historical, psychological, geographical, economic and what not causes which have made people fight in the past and may still make them fight in the future. There would appear to be a swifter and more fertile method of approach. Let us attempt to reduce all possible causes of war to one general law covering them all.

At any given time the world presents a certain network of facts recognized as law. Frontiers are defined, obligations and rights laid down, zones of influence recognized, debts acknowledged, limitations of sovereignty accepted, occupations of territory admitted; in fine, a system is established which constitutes, so to say, a zero of history, a starting point, not for history which has none, but for our own thoughts. Then, life flows on and every day something happens, some change takes place which gradually makes the world of facts and forces move away from the world of law. This nation grows weaker; that nation stronger; this territory, once uninhabited, grows to be an important center of population; new national feelings appear where careless and self-ignorant masses were once herded together by a foreign power; the nation yesterday subjected grows stronger than its subjector; economic and financial currents are reversed. Between the static set of law and the dynamic set of forces there appears thus a set of conflicts. At every point in the world disruptive forces begin to act. This may be said to be the normal state of the world considered as a whole.

Since life is the true cause of the trouble, the more life flows in the channel of time, the stronger trouble will grow. There are two ways of dealing with such a situation; either to let it drift, or else to take it in hand.

If left to drift, the set of conflicts will never be considered *as a whole.* Here and there, one or other of the difficulties will be handled by the States more directly concerned, and it will be "solved" normally on lines satisfactory to the most powerful, therefore through trouble and the sowing of more trouble. Sooner or later, either through the incidence of one of these local conflicts involving too many nations or from the very tension of all the disruptive forces accumulated, the explosion occurs, and considerable parts of the world—or the whole of it—are caught in the conflagration.

Such is the way in which things have been happening. The masterpiece of this—we can hardly call it method—is the Great War. And the Covenant is inspired in the feeling that the other way is worthier of men grown up to full manhood.

This way consists in taking the matter in hand as a whole. Wars are due, we know, to the tendency inherent in life to produce a set of conflicts as the dynamic set of facts moves away from the static set of laws. The problem cannot be solved by piecemeal methods; it must be tackled in its entirety. This implies that the problem cannot be solved from the point of view of any one nation, but that it must be handled by the World-Community organized for the purpose, and from the point of view of the World Community.

Let us then summarize our argument. Armaments are due to wars. The cause of wars is the tendency of life to create a set of conflicts. Such a tendency can only be dealt with successfully by the World-Community organized to that end. Therefore, along this second avenue, our conclusion is the same as when we followed the first. The solution of the problem of disarmament lies in the organization of the World-Community as such.

b. The outlawry of war.—But on the same assumption, i.e., that armaments being the effect, and not the cause, of wars, wars must be struck off human history, there has appeared another school, no longer intellectual as the preceding one might be described, but psychological. The school claims that wars exist because men accept them as eventual methods for regulating conflicts. If, therefore, it argues, men committed themselves to the opposite course of action, officially declaring that on no account would they resort to war in order to settle their differences, war would be wiped off the map of possibilities; people would stop preparing for them and both wars and armaments would cease to exist.

Let us examine successively:

The assumption implied in the very word outlawry;

The value to be attached to the optimistic theory that wars would cease if nations solemnly outlawed them;

The conditions which would be necessary to induce the nations of the world to enter into such an undertaking and to give it substantial value.

(a) Assumption implied in the word outlawry.—

The outlawry of war means the driving of war out of the law. What law? Evidently, since war is an international phenomenon, it can only be an international law. An international law implies an international legislator. And therefore, this theory of disarmament leads direct to the organization of the World-Community.[1]

(b) Value to be attached to a declaration of outlawry.—

[1] The authors of this theory admit as much, but would limit the organs of the international community to a court having jurisdictional powers. This point, i.e., the actual scope of the World-Community organization, will, however, be discussed on its merits later.

The first criticism which this optimistic theory calls forth is that it seems to put excessive faith in the value of a declaration of outlawry. Let us transfer the question from the world of nations to the world of men. How long is it since murder was outlawed by civilized units? And yet how many crimes are committed every year in, say, the city of Chicago, in which the outlawry of war theory was born? It seems therefore wise to provide for possible lapses in the observation of the undertaking. If that is so, it seems necessary to provide for some organized international system to foresee and guard against such lapses, and if they actually occur, to deal with them. The methods whereby this might be done will be discussed anon. All we wish to put on record at this stage is that on this count also the outlawry of war theory presupposes the existence of an organized World-Community.

(c) Conditions which would be necessary to make the outlawry of war an acceptable and substantial proposition.—

The undertaking implied in this theory could not be a practical policy, nor could it be considered as more than a mere pious declaration, unless certain conditions were fulfilled.

To begin with, no nation is going to give up its right of self-defense. The advocates of this doctrine used to be vague when this question was raised. Yet it is crucial, and the matter had to be cleared up in unmistakable terms when it emerged on the plane of actual politics with the Kellogg proposals. Though unwilling at first, Mr. Kellogg had to recognize explicitly that his proposals reserved the right of self-defense. But indeed the fact is so obvious that we would not have labored it were it not all-important, and moreover, apt to be blurred by the "outlawists" who stoutly resist being drawn into the inevitable conclusions which flow from their premises.

This point established, it is evident that no outlawry of war declaration is going to be worth the paper and ink if it leaves to each and every State the sole right of defining when it is fighting a defensive war. Every State will in good or in bad faith maintain that the particular war which it has set its heart to fight is purely defensive. Nor should bad faith be too readily assumed in this matter. Indeed, bad faith is an incomparably smaller danger in international relations than is generally supposed. The real danger is failure to see things objectively, i.e., from the point of view of the World-Community. After all, the frontier between what is defensive and what is not is far from being a hard and precise line. Feelings and emotions move it to and fro as much or more than dispassionate ideas. The very State which has put forward the proposal for the outlawry of war as an instrument of national policy is simultaneously waging a war which it considers defensive, while many good and true men in America and out of it consider it indefensible. Such a fact is significant. For it is evident that the State in question thinks that the marines killed in Nicaragua are dying in a defensive war, while it is no less evident that such is not the view of international public opinion. This does not mean that public opinion is right, and the Government of the United States of America wrong. But it does mean that, unless a proper international organization is set up to deal with such cases, any Government can do anything and call it defensive. To outlaw war purely and simply does not mean anything. It adds absolutely nothing but words to the already excessive number of words written on worthless papers in the files of the World-Community.

It follows that the condition which is going to make the outlawry of war something more than a mere slogan is the engagement to abide by the considered opinion of the adequate organs of the World-Community as to what is and what is not defensive war. Now, in actual fact, no great State which has entered the warpath is going to withdraw on being told that it is in the wrong. Such a self-denying behavior the great powers expect from the small (cf., the attitude of Greece in the Greco-Bulgarian case); but they themselves give us no hope that they would be willing to rise to such a level of international morality. In the circumstances, therefore, the only way in which the principle of the outlawry of war could be made to mean anything would be to adopt it as a companion of another and more important principle; the undertaking to solve all the conflicts by peaceful means recognized on a permanent basis by the World-Community, so that the adequate organs of the World-Community could have a say before conflicts degenerated into hostilities.

The outlawry of war therefore, from whichever angle considered, leads to the same conclusion: the problem of disarmament cannot be solved except through the establishment of an organized World-Community.

3. THE TECHNICAL POINT OF VIEW

Let us now examine the question from a technical angle. We have so far accepted the aim in view without attempting to define it. But what is it exactly that we mean when we say "Disarmament"? We know now that we do *not* mean complete immediate and general disarmament. What is meant is general reduction of armaments arrived at by common agreement and consent.

This sounds simple enough; yet its simplicity is most deceptive. We can only reduce that which we can measure. The temperature of a sick man, the balance in a bank account, are types of notions which can be reduced, because they are measurable: i.e., they can be expressed in terms of quantity. But what is the common measure of armaments or, put in a different way, what is the quantity or measure of armaments of a nation?

The answer again *seems* simple enough. So many men under arms, so many tons on the water, so much horse power in the air. Yet that is not enough. For it is evident that if the British Empire and the Duchy of Luxemburg had each an army of 100,000 men, no man in his senses would say that they were equally armed; the general view would be that the Duchy of Luxemburg was armed to the teeth while the British Empire was but moderately garrisoned. It is clear therefore that the notion we are seeking is essentially relative: it may be understood as a relation between two terms: war power, on the one hand, the requirements which this war power has to meet, on the other. We might even put it in the form of a fraction, and say that the measure of armaments of a nation equals its war power (the numerator) divided by its requirements (the denominator).

We now have transferred our difficulty to each of these two terms. As for war power, far from being an easy notion to define, it reveals itself as a combination of many elements, some of which are altogether rebellious to measurement. They are such imponderabilia as the patriotism, the religious faith, the national cohesion and solidarity, the physical and moral courage, the general and technical intelligence, the tradition and strength of institutions and such other qualities of the nation and its inhabitants. There is no way whatsoever by which such notions can be compared. At this stage of our enquiry we might as well wind it up with a robust non-possumus. Since these imponderabilia play perhaps the predominant, or at any rate, a most important rôle in war power, it is evident that the measure of armaments of a nation cannot be defined.

Yet we must persevere, if only because the advocates of a definition of armaments, taking the word in its strict technical sense, can make a very strong case. But before discussing their view, mention must be made of another important element in war power, i.e., that which came to be known after a name in which the author of this work has perhaps some responsibility, *war potential.* It is obvious that no adequate idea can be formed of the war power of a nation unless due account is taken of the forces which the nation can transfer from peace to war aims. Thus, to put an example dear to English delegates, the trained reserves of France are a first-rate addition which could be made to her actual war power after war was declared; or again, to recall an instance no less dear to French delegates, the trained seamen of all ranks which England occupies in her merchant marine are a formidable potential strength on which England can rely in time of war.

It will be seen that, through this opening, the vista of war power, at first limited to men in uniform and to destructive material in service, stretches away from the actual fighting organizations until it covers the whole nation, till far away on the horizon of our now enlarged view, the young mother, peacefully feeding her tender baby at her breast, is transfigured from an idyllic picture of motherhood into a grim amazon, pouring sinews of war into a recruit ready to take up a rifle on the twentieth year of the hostilities.

We shall have to refer again to war potential. Here, mention is made of it only because it contributes to illustrate the complexity of the idea of disarmament. Let us however leave it aside in our calculation, as we have left other weighty imponderabilia, and for the sake of argument limit our definition of war power to the three elements of armed forces which would appear to be the least rebellious to statistical handling: men, material and money.

It is obvious that there exists no satisfactory standard of comparison for men. English soldiers, professionals enlisted for a long period of service; French soldiers, ordinary citizens made to serve for eighteen months under compulsory service; Swiss soldiers, citizens called upon to serve a very short number of days for a long number of years, and the Dutch, the Norwegian, the Russian and other types constitute wholly heterogeneous units which cannot easily be reduced to a common standard, even when their psychological differences have been left aside.

A comparison of material is no less difficult. One hundred machine guns in the hands of a nation economically and industrially powerful, which can therefore provide an ever-flowing supply of ammunition, and moreover, replace the machine guns themselves at short notice, are by no means equivalent to one hundred machine guns in the hands of a nation dependent upon foreign supplies for its arms and ammunition.

Finally, money is equally available in its actual value to the nation, according to whether the nation can dispose of ample home reserves and credit and enjoys good credit abroad, or, on the contrary, lacks such advantages. This very sketchy and rapid outline of the position as concerns the three most tangible elements of war power shows that the first term or numerator of our fraction, i.e., the armed force of the nation, is wholly rebellious to any objective standard of comparison.

As for the second term, i.e., the estimate of the requirements which the armed force of the nation may have to meet, it is purely subjective. When I took office as head of the Disarmament Section of the League, the Council had addressed a circular to all the Members, requesting them to set down the reasons—political, geographical and others—which made it necessary for them to maintain the armed forces at the figure stated in the League statistics. The answers were couched in all styles, forms, lengths and languages. Yet the gist of them all could be interpreted in one and the same sentence: "I am anxious to disarm, but my armaments are already as small as I can safely afford. I am a peaceful nation, but I am surrounded by bellicose countries." Thus every nation in its own eyes was a lamb, and every other nation a wolf. There is no way of fighting against this failing, but time and mutual education in coöperation. Meanwhile, the fact remains that every nation is going to use its right to estimate its own requirements in the most extravagant manner.

Let us sum up the position. This notion, which seemed so simple, the measure of armaments of a nation, reveals itself to be in the manner of a fraction, the numerator of which is not measurable by any objective standards, while its denominator is purely subjective. The technical method therefore breaks down.

If, then, we cannot hope to bring nations to agree on some statistical standard, enabling them to reduce their armaments by common consent, can we devise some such standard in other than statistical fields? There is such a standard. It flows from the principle which inspires disarmament. Why disarm? In order to establish peace. Then let us agree that armaments must be reduced if they have an aggressive nature. Our standard shall be the capacity for aggression.

The problem is thus transferred from the notion of disarmament to the notion of aggression. Such a notion is not statistical or abstract, but concrete and organic. For in effect a nation's forces, whatever their number, may be organized as a shield or as a spear. Theoretically, at any rate, it might be possible to study each case from the technical point of view, and to pronounce whether the armed forces so studied could be considered as offensively or as defensively organized. In actual fact, however, the question cannot be solved on technical grounds.

Let us, for example, consider the case of two nations, A and B, the forces of which are in the following relation:

Actual armed forces of A bigger than those of B
Potential armed forces of A smaller than those of B

If A maintains a strictly defensive establishment, it will be at the mercy of B, should B suddenly reverse its normally peaceful policy and spring a war on A with but a very short warning. The only hope of safety in such a case is to maintain an establishment allowing her a lightning offensive, a short war and a crushing victory, before B has had time to draw on her potential strength, for if A allowed the war to last, she would be bound to be defeated owing to B's superiority in potential strength.

Hence the possibility of an aggressive organization

of armed forces in a nation sincerely attached to a defensive policy.

Thus, in transferring the matter from the notion of disarmament to the notion of aggression, what we have really done is to transfer it from the technical to the political field. The stick which a man carries in his hand is an offensive or a defensive weapon, according to the intention which the man harbors in his breast. The standard of aggression is a standard of policy.

But who is to judge policy? Evidently some organism outside and above the nation. We come, therefore, to our now familiar conclusion: the question of disarmament, when examined technically, leads to the conclusion that it is necessary to set up a system whereby the World-Community as such can authoritatively have a say in the happenings of the world.

CONCLUSION

It will be seen, therefore, that the inner obstacle which has so far stood in the way of disarmament lies in the very substance of the problem. It may be put in the following terms: The solution of the problem of disarmament cannot be found within the problem itself, but outside it. In fact, the problem of disarmament is not the problem of disarmament. It really is the problem of the organization of the World-Community.

The task before us now is to explore the consequences of such a conclusion. But before admitting it, we must present the matter under yet a new light which may prove to be the most illuminating of all.

Chapter IV

THE INNER REASON OF THE INNER OBSTACLE

SO far we have considered the question of disarmament as a problem in itself. Convenient as it may be, such a view cannot be upheld otherwise than as an abstraction for the sake of study or argument. Disarmament is but one of the ways of looking at the only problem there is in international life, i.e., that of international life itself. Naturally enough, life has claimed its rights and every time we have shouted "Disarmament" before its hills and dales, its dales and hills have echoed back "World-Community."

Let us now go a little more closely into the matter. Let us ask ourselves what is exactly the rôle of armaments in international life. Are we not simplifying such a rôle a little too naïvely when we visualize it exclusively under the "glorious" and "grim" features which it takes in actual war?

Are armaments nothing but instruments for carrying out actual hostilities? Evidently not. The fact is that armaments are more useful in time of peace than in time of war. The normal wielders of armaments are not the soldiers, but the diplomats. The gun that does not shoot is more eloquent than the gun that has to shoot and above all than the gun which has shot. There is a Spanish light comedy in which a man is made to agree with a particular course of action by the liberal exhibition of a revolver before his frightened eyes, and as the victim is asked by a third party whether he has at last been convinced: "Yes. He brought me round by means of a 5-bullet argument." Yet no shot had been fired. The diplomacy of the great powers is carried out not exclusively, not always openly, not even always consciously, but always nevertheless on such a principle. The foreign secretary of this or that nation may be the most conciliatory man on earth; yet the minimum which will be granted to him by his adversaries will be considerably the higher for the fact of his armaments. At their lowest, therefore, armed forces are one of the most formidable tacit elements in international policy; at their highest, the most formidable indeed, the determining factor. All this, be it understood, in time of peace.

Of peace? But can we call peace our peace? The fact is that our wars are but acute states of the permanent war in which the world lives. Just as a cough is not a cold, but merely a fit of acute symptoms of a disease which afflicts the patient before and after his coughing fit, so what we call wars are but fits of hostilities in a disease which is the real war, a state of open rivalry, of jealousy, of grab, of fear of our neighbors' progress. Let us take economic life, for example. What do we see? A wholly militant, if not military, attitude dominates the field of economic relations. The style of economic and financial specialists lags far behind that of their military cousins in point of warlike spirit. While military experts affect a pseudo-scientific attitude and study the methods for murdering a million people with the cool detachment of an astronomer calculating an eclipse, our economic and financial expert will speak with bellicose ardor of *conquering* markets, of a *defensive* commercial policy, of rate *wars*, of *vanguard*, *pioneer*, *campaign*, *attack*, *outposts*. Nor are they the only soldiers in mufti in our modern nations. For the spirit of rivalry has worked itself into us with such devastating effects that it has infected even our intellectual and artistic life; and the time has come when we must look behind a poem in case it conceals explosive feelings and disentangle mathematical theorems in search of propaganda goods. The war spirit is permanently with us. Now and then it bursts into military hostilities which we call wars in a technical and narrow sense. But strictly speaking, we are permanently at war.

The true head of the army and navy is the foreign secretary. For the army and navy are but the military wing of the nation's diplomacy. In normal times the foreign secretary carries on the war. The stronger his military and naval wing, the easier his task, the less he has to water down truth, the higher can his reputation soar. A war, i.e., a fit of hostilities in the permanent world war, occurs when the foreign secretary has to own up a failure, and to hand over the army and navy to generals and admirals. It is not as fine a day as is generally supposed, for generals and admirals are human beings, and admirals particularly, however brave they may be, hate to risk their ships.

Under this light, armaments appear to us as instruments of policy. They are indeed the most important instrument of policy, together with financial power—a rarer thing. It is evident, therefore, that no disarmament is possible as long as no alternative instrument of policy to armaments is devised, and no reduction of armaments is possible as long as the utility of armaments as instruments of policy has not been reduced.

As an illustration of this assertion, let us come back to the proposals for wholesale and immediate disarmament made by the Soviet delegation at the Geneva meeting (December, 1927, and March, 1928). Why should Soviet Russia be the first nation to be ready to disarm? Simply because they are the first to have evolved an alternative instrument of policy. For in effect the Soviet Union, being a Church-State, their only foreign policy consists in the spreading of the communistic gospel. Their foreign policy being one, needs but one method everywhere, and this method, the fostering of a communistic revolution in every nation, has no need of Russian armaments, and would fare better without foreign ones. Such is the reason why the Soviet delegation was free to present their disarmament proposals, and why, in my opinion, they were sincere in doing so.

Now, since the only way to secure a reduction of armaments lies through the discovery of methods for reducing the utility of armaments as instruments of policy, it is obvious that the solution of the problem of disarmament depends on the solution of the world permanent war. We must, in one word, replace rivalry by coöperation.

There was a time when nations were small and far

between in a wide world. Rivalry, free national enterprise, adventure had space enough to develop, and even if they led to a scrap now and then, what did people care or even know about things that happened at the other end of their valley? Nowadays the world is small and crowded with nations all packed together. Raw materials and markets are jealously watched. Land has been divided up. The very seas have lost their solitude and the ocean roads are as crowded with ships as land roads with cars. The world is one. It must be thought of as one, governed as one, kept in peace as one. And if it goes to war, it goes to war as one—i.e., against itself.

And so we come again to the same conclusion: disarmament cannot be successful, unless a new policy is evolved which will no longer need armaments for its instruments. This policy is that of coöperation.

This conclusion implies one important consequence bearing on international conferences and commissions on disarmament. Since, in the absence of a well-organized World-Community, armaments remain indispensable as instruments of policy, disarmament conferences can never hope to succeed substantially, even though they may succeed in appearance—and particularly in the manufactured appearance which is made for them by the press. For in effect every delegation goes to the conference determined to secure an increase in the *relative* armaments of its own nation, even though the conference may lead to an all-round reduction of *absolute* armaments. What matters for the expert is: (a) the national standing power in relation to that of the nation's potential adversary; (b) the national potential power (power for expanding armaments) in relation to that of the nation's adversary. It is clear that a cleverly conducted negotiation in conference may increase these two relative quantities even though the absolute values concerned be reduced.

This explains the atmosphere of profound mistrust which prevails in disarmament conferences. Every delegate scrutinizes the most innocent-looking proposals with the utmost anxiety, lest his own relative position be sacrificed by his acceptance thereof. During one of the international meetings which, honestly but mistakenly, endeavored to tackle the problem of disarmament without dealing first with the preliminary condition which would make it soluble, I happened to meet one of the chief delegates on the golf course. "How are things going?" I asked. And he answered, "Do you know the story of the little Jewish boy who went changing his dollar into quarters, then in the next shop his four quarters into cents, then in the next his cents back into a dollar, and then he began again, until he was recognized by one of the shopkeepers—'Why do you keep this game up?' and the little boy answered '*Zome* day *zomebody's* going to make a mistake, and *it won't be me!*' " That is the spirit which prevails in international conferences for a premature disarmament.

In fact, in the absence of a preliminary organization of the World-Community and of its activities, all disarmament conferences are bound to degenerate into armament conferences. In all of them discussion is based on the assumption of war, and they all reveal the inevitable conflict between the ardent endeavors of the delegations present, each of which has for its main aim to secure the highest possible increase of its relative armaments in a general reduction of absolute forces, if such a reduction there must be.

Such is the true explanation of the resistance made by continental nations to divide sea from land armaments. The view that navies can be dealt with apart from armies is held exclusively by the big naval powers, who, conscious of their superiority at sea, and knowing that in any case they shall keep it, prefer to negotiate sea affairs without having to pay land favors with sea price. On the other hand, countries such as France, whose main strength is in the army, prefer to go into the market place of negotiation as a strong armed power, in order to be in a position to sell land reductions in exchange for sea positions. Technically, the French have a strong case, since there is only one armament and a nation's three services are closely intertwined in coöperation. But, though technically right, the French do not insist on the inseparability of the three forces on the ground of intellectual pedantry. Their tacit argument is far more positive: i.e., as a naval power they are in the second rank; as an armed (all-round) power they are in the first rank. But it will be seen that such an attitude rests on the assumption that so-called disarmament discussions are in fact armament discussions, and that whatever the label, the commodity bought and sold in the market is power.

Here again we meet the obvious impossibility of solving the world problem otherwise than by world methods.

The World-Community must be "run" as a World-Community. The sixty odd nations which compose it must no longer be allowed to prowl in liberty for whatever they can filch from each other—be it territories, markets, raw materials or dividends. We have advanced one step further. We do not limit our claim to the need of a World-Community which will forestall conflicts and solve them peacefully. We believe to have shown that something more is needed: a World-Community which will regulate its life from A to Z on the principle that the world is one, and that there is one common interest which should be disentangled from the knot of conflicting interests, and once disentangled, served.

Nor can we resign ourselves to be dismissed as Utopians or idealists. We claim that our view is the plain, common-sense, cool view; that, in fact, no business man would run his business as the world is run to-day.

Part II

HISTORICAL

Chapter I

THE COVENANT

VIEWED in the light of the preceding pages, and particularly, of the conclusion to which they have repeatedly led us, the Covenant is essentially a statesman-like effort to solve the problem of disarmament. It aims at organizing the World-Community in such a way that armaments may be rendered less and less useful for war, as the collective way for dealing with international events is learned and trusted by all nations, and for policy, as the ways and means devised for dealing with international life are developed in peace. Though, for historical reasons, incomplete, the Covenant carries the situation forward to a degree which we are so much used to enjoy that we can hardly realize it. Article 8, dealing with disarmament *strictu sensu*, is not of course the only article which is in actual fact devoted to it. In a sense, there is not one single article in the Covenant which directly or indirectly does not aim at disarmament. More especially, disarmament is the true end of the nucleus of the Covenant, i.e., Articles 8-20.

Let us briefly examine the economy of this admirable charter of peace:

The general principle which stands at the basis of the whole edifice is laid down in Article 11: "Any war or threat of war, whether immediately affecting any of the Members of the League or not, is hereby declared a matter of concern to the whole League, and the League shall take any action that may be deemed wise and effectual to safeguard the peace of nations."

Here the existence of the organized World-Community is asserted in unmistakable terms and its point of view declared to be paramount. The remainder of the article is the logical sequence of this most fertile of principles; it grants to all League Members rights of world citizenship: "In case any such emergency should arise the Secretary-General shall on the request of any Member of the League forthwith summon a meeting of the Council. It is also declared to be the friendly right of each Member of the League to bring to the attention of the Assembly or of the Council any circumstance whatever affecting international relations which threatens to disturb international peace or the good understanding between nations upon which peace depends."

After the rights, the obligations. Article 10 declares that "the Members of the League undertake to respect and preserve as against external aggression the territorial integrity and existing political independence of all Members of the League." Here again, the remainder of the article establishes the right of the Community to deal with any infraction of the rule thus laid down: "In case of any such aggression or in case of any threat or danger of such aggression the Council shall advise upon the means by which this obligation shall be fulfilled."

Articles 12-15 organize the peaceful settlement of international disputes:

(1) Disputes must be submitted to arbitration, judicial settlement or Council inquiry (Art. 12).

(2) Nations "agree in no case to resort to war until three months after the award by the arbitrators or the judicial decision, or the report by the Council" (Art. 12).

The second paragraph of Article 12 aims at ensuring that the dispute is not allowed to drag on in the bog of procedure. Report to the Council must be made within six months; the award of the arbitrators or the judicial decision must be made "within a reasonable time." It will be seen therefore that by the play of Article 12 nations drifting into a dispute are debarred from waging war against each other within a period which may vary between three and nine months.

(3) Disputes as to the interpretation of a treaty, as to any question of international law, as to the existence of any fact which, if established, would constitute a breach of any international obligation, or as to the extent and nature of the reparation to be made for any such breach, are declared to be amongst those which are generally suitable for submission to arbitration or judicial settlement (Art. 13). A Permanent Court to deal with such disputes (in the absence of any agreement to the contrary amongst the parties) is provided for (Art. 13, § 3; Art. 14).

Awards or decisions rendered are to be carried out in good faith, failing which the Council shall propose what steps should be taken (Art. 13, § 4).

No war is to be waged against a League Member which complies therewith (Art. 13, § 4).

(4) Other disputes must be submitted to the Council which, after enquiry, shall endeavor to effect a settlement. If successful, the Council shall make a public statement on the matter. If unsuccessful the Council (unanimous or otherwise) shall publish a report along with any minority statement that the Council Member concerned may wish to append thereto (Art 15).

If the Council is unanimous (excluding the parties) the League Members undertake not to go to war with any party to the dispute which complies with the recommendations of the Council's report (Art. 15, § 6).

Otherwise, i.e., if the Council should be unable to reach an unanimous report, the League Members retain their liberty of action (§ 7).

If a dispute is claimed by one of the parties and found by the Council to arise out of a matter which by international law is solely within the domestic jurisdiction of that party, the Council shall so report and shall make no recommendation (§ 8).

The Assembly may act as the Council. A report made by a majority of its members including all the Council Members has a value equal to that of a report of the Council concurred in by all its Members (§ 10).

(5) Action contrary to Articles 13 and 15 is considered as an act of war against all Members of the League (Art. 16). It will be noticed that this article asserts again the solidarity of the World-Community as incarnated in the League. In virtue of the first paragraph of this Article the League Members undertake

immediately to subject the Covenant-breaking State to the severance of all trade or financial relations, the prohibition of all intercourse between their nationals and the nationals of the Covenant-breaking State, and the prevention of all financial, commercial or personal intercourse between the nationals of the Covenant-breaking State and the nationals of any other State, whether a Member of the League or not.

In virtue of the second paragraph of this Article the Council shall recommend to the several Governments concerned what effective military, naval or air force the Members of the League shall severally contribute to the armed forces to be used to protect the covenants of the League. Adequate measures for carrying out such sanctions are provided for in the third paragraph of the Article and the fourth stipulates that a Member of the League which has violated any of its covenants may be declared to be no longer a Member by a vote of the Council concurred in by the Representatives of all the other Members of the League.

(6) Article 17 closes the system by stipulating that in the case of a dispute involving a State not Member of the League such a State or States shall be invited to accept the obligations of Membership for the purposes of the dispute. Should the invitation be accepted the League system as outlined above applies. Should it be refused and should the State in question resort to war against a Member of the League the provisions of Article 16 shall be applicable as against it.

(7) The system thus closed, steps must be taken to ensure that the framework of contracts out of which

disputes might arise is not in itself inconsistent with the spirit of the Covenant. Such is the aim of Articles 18, 19 and 20. Article 18 enacts that treaties must be registered and published by the League, without which condition they shall not be binding; Article 20 abrogates all existing obligations inconsistent with the Covenant and forbids all such engagements in the future. Finally, in order to adjust the framework of treaties to the changing conditions of life, Article 19 stipulates that treaties which have become inapplicable as well as international conditions whose continuance might endanger the peace of the world may be reconsidered from time to time on the advice of the Assembly.

As an appendix to this group of Articles and particularly to Article 20, Article 21 provides that "nothing in the Covenant shall be deemed to affect the validity of international engagements such as treaties of arbitration or regional understandings like the Monroe Doctrine for securing the maintenance of peace." In so far as this Article mentions the Monroe Doctrine, which is neither a treaty of arbitration nor a regional understanding, this text is incomprehensible. But the discussion of the issues it raises had better be left for special treatment.

What is the accumulative effect of this system of rights and obligations?

The rights surrendered by League Members in relation to war are the following:

A. (1). Right to go to war in order to settle a difference without first submitting the difference to a peaceful settlement (Art. 12).

A. (2). Right to go to war *in any case* within three months of the announcement of the award, judicial decision or Council report on the dispute (Art. 12).

A. (3). Right to go to war against a State which complies with the World-Community decision under dispute (Arts. 13; 15, § 6).

The rights retained are the following:

B. (1). Right to go to war against a State which does not comply with a World-Community decision on a dispute, but only after three months have elapsed since the decision stands (Art. 12; Art. 13, § 4 [by implication], and Art. 15, § 6 [by implication]).

B. (2). Right to go to war against a State party to a dispute if the Council fails to reach a unanimous report, but only three months after such a failure stands (Art. 15, § 7).

B. (3). Presumably, right to go to war (three months after?) if the Council admits that a dispute arises out of a matter on which the plea of domestic jurisdiction is plausible.

League Members moreover undertake certain obligations which may involve them in war. They are the following:

C. (1). They must not only respect but preserve as against external aggression the territorial integrity and existing political independence of all the Members of the League (Art. 10).

C. (2). They must take measures of an economic and financial character and even of a military nature against Covenant-breaking States.

As will be seen, the free scope left to war tendencies before the Great War has been reduced by the Covenant to a minimum, i.e., cases B. (1), (2) and (3). This minimum, theoretically small, is practically much smaller still, indeed almost negligible. Leaving aside case B. (3) which is purely specific and in fact, in spite of its general wording, in the nature of a reserve in favor of the domestic jurisdiction for immigration conflicts, the cases in question presuppose that the dispute has been submitted to a long public procedure of either arbitration, judicial settlement or conciliation; that this procedure has failed; that the nations concerned have waited three months, and that after all this time has elapsed they leap at each other's throats. No person in his senses can claim that such an event is likely to occur easily. On the mere law of probabilities, the cases must be very few. On psychological laws they are bound to lead more often than not to a kind of boredom with the subject of the dispute unless the press and government organizations on either side are determined to keep the fires burning which in these days of international news and views it would be difficult to do. Moreover, even at this eleventh hour, that most admirably numbered of Covenant Articles, Article 11, would come into operation and the Council having failed in its endeavors as a conciliatory body on Article 15 would still have the right and the duty to try its powers as a negotiator under Article 11. The difference between the two procedures is that while under Article 15 the Council would sit between the parties and the parties on each side of it and so to say outside it, under Article 11 the parties would be an integral part of the Council and the adjustment of the difference would have to be weighed by political methods and by appealing to the direct responsibility of the parties concerned as full members of the Governing Body of the World-Community. Moreover according to Article 11 the League in case of war or threat of war may take any action that may be deemed wise and effectual to safeguard the peace of nations. This is a wide and statesmanlike provision which, wielded by a Council worthy of it, could effectually stop any possible war.

The Covenant provides therefore a system admirably devised both theoretically and practically to reduce chances of war to an almost negligible minimum. And yet Article 8, which provides for a reduction of the armaments of all League Members, is still unfulfilled. We know of course the ultimate reason why this is so. We know that armaments are not merely instruments of war but instruments of policy, i.e., means whereby nations get their ends by inducing prudence into would-be recalcitrants. But the argument cannot rest there. It is evident that though a strong nation need not shoot in order to use its guns effectively, guns would lose much of their moral effect were it known that the League Covenant would prevent their being fired.

Ultimately the power of armaments as instruments of policy is of course but an extension of their power as instruments of war. Why is it then that, though the Covenant is an effective measure for reducing wars to an almost negligible minimum, the work of Disarmament does not show any tangible progress?

Chapter II

THE WAVE OF REACTION

THE fact may be explained at least in part by the wave of political reaction which set in as the War tension relaxed. The numerous political after-effects of this wave cannot be appraised in their true import unless they are placed in their proper relation with regard to the events that followed the Armistice. When peace broke out the world had been tuned up to international coöperation and self-sacrifice. These feelings, due in part to the store of noble ideas kept in excellent repair by the French Nation ever since the French Revolution, in part to the moral emotion which the Anglo-Saxon world required in order to follow its leaders into the War and which it found in the invasion of Belgium, determined the direction of the intellectual and moral movement which made so protracted a war possible. Democracy and nationality, the liberation of man and that of nations were the banners of the Allies. Towards the end of the War the movement found an eloquent exponent in President Wilson and later an admirable charter in the Covenant.

Yet it was obvious to any one living in Paris during the Peace Conference or even reading the newspapers at home with wits a shade sharper than the average, that the drafts on the bank of idealism which the Allies had signed for four years were beginning to loom too large in the eyes of the statesmen in charge of the bank. Events were to show that the assets of the bank were notoriously below its liabilities. Troubles poured in from all quarters. We may classify rather than summarize them:

New-born or resuscitated nations showed themselves unable to grant the conquered nations the benefits of racial nationalism to which they themselves owed their own existence;

France represented by an admirable war-man, as incompetent for peace work as a tiger for making honey, was unable to put any faith in the principles which she had freely chosen as her banner and led the Conference debates on the rule that force and nothing else counts;

The British Dominions—all except Canada—demanded their pound of flesh and forced the British representatives to give up principles which might have prevented them from acquiring territories;

The reactionary wing of American public opinion grew restive and began to shoot at President Wilson in the back.

President Wilson held the fort with admirable vigor. He insisted that the Covenant was to be an integral part of the Treaty. Had he yielded on that point the League of Nations would not exist to-day. For, when all is said in reproach of America's defection, the fact remains that not one single Big Power—and hardly any Small—would sign the Covenant in cold blood to-day had they not signed and ratified it when it was presented to them covered with a heavy coating of advantages.

The Covenant had then to compromise not merely to live but even to be born. It was in fact born in original sin. Its very text is a compromise of creative idealism and hardbaked realities. President Wilson's greatest title to fame is that even at that price he insisted that the "living thing" was to be. But ever since, the Covenant has been battered by adversity after adversity.

The first and most formidable adversity with which it met was the American Senate. The defection of America was a disaster the ultimate responsibility for which must be borne by the American nation. A free, honest, impartial opinion is rarely heard on the matter. Political prudence, obsequiousness, politeness, a certain sense of public responsibility, noble national or ignoble personal interest too often veil or attenuate what in plain honest words should be said as often as possible. The United States of America gave mankind in President Wilson its first world statesman and in the Covenant its first immortal charter. Then the same United States drew back and lost her glorious advantage in an inglorious retreat from the position of leadership and sacrifice which her great President had conquered for her. On the day America withdrew, the wave of reaction which President Wilson had bravely faced in Paris and in Washington leaped forward. We are still struggling with it. May we live to forgive America.

There were explanations by the dozen; some bad,

others worse. There were all kinds of reasons. But every skeptic winked and every reactionary exulted and every nationalist beflagged the balconies of his heart. America had backed out. Of course she would. No fools, Americans! If only we had a Senate! Now they can do what they wish in their Mexicos and Nicaraguas, while we in our—

President Wilson had dreamed the Covenant as the palace of the World-Community. America taught the World to think of it as its prison.

And then, think of the pretext. America is not with us. What can we do? Pretexts blossom best when grafted on a stem of reason, and here the stem of reason was well rooted. The first result of America's defection was that France lost the prop of the British-American guarantee which President Wilson and Mr. Lloyd George had offered her as an inducement to conciliatory dispositions towards Germany. France knew the Treaty was top-heavy and that she could not keep it standing with her unaided strength. The position led to the obsession with "security-guarantee-sanctions" which dominates the mind and soul of France since 1919. This kind of psychosis which afflicts France is one of the determining factors in the evolution of what is called disarmament.

While France sought to transform the sanctions of the Covenant into a World Army at her service and Article 10 of the Covenant into a line of fortifications along the frontiers set by the Peace Treaties, England and the Dominions were beginning to cool down and to ponder on the consequences of Articles 10 and 16.

They had by then digested the vast territories which under one form or another had been attributed to them as the spoils of the battle—those territories which the *Manchester Guardian*, with a phrase in which puritanical prudishness reaches an unexpected degree of elegance, described as "spacious responsibilities." Colonies and Mandates were already part and parcel of the Empire. But what about the price which had been paid for them?

Here again the absence of America provided a pretext admirably grafted in reason. No one could expect Articles 10 and 16 to be applied while the most powerful nation in the world remained free to behave as she wished and could take up the position either of the aggressor against whom the Members of the League undertook to guarantee the political independence and territorial integrity of their co-Members, or of the neutral as between a Covenant-breaking State and the League Members intent on upholding the Charter of the League. The argument could not be more reasonable. And that is why it weighs in League discussions with so much force. But if the hand on the lever is that of the British Empire, the fulcrum is in America.

Two consequences follow: France feels the gradual weakening of the system of legal fortresses and forces set up by Articles 10-16; she therefore proceeds to replace it by a network of treaties with her European friends; England endeavors to whittle down the system of definite obligations implied or expressed in the same group of articles and thereby stimulates France to persevere in the path which she has been led to choose.

Two diverging policies but the same spirit. In fact both France and England move away from the hearth of the Covenant. Both seek power: France in a system of treaties which may enable her to keep her strength yet not lose the possible advantages of the Covenant; England in freedom, for she wishes to be able to say whom and when she will help; she endeavors to regain the full use of her fleet as an instrument of policy in time of peace.

Such was the political background in which the League endeavored to carry out her disarmament program.

Chapter III

THE LEGAL MACHINE

IN its narrowest and technical sense the disarmament program of the League is defined in Article 8 of the Covenant. Article 1, § 2 must also be considered. Procedure and organization are barely outlined in Article 9. Article 23, § d, though perhaps not connected with disarmament in a direct way, is indirectly linked up with the question.

Article 8. Even if the fact that it deals with disarmament were left aside, Article 8 is one of the most significant provisions of the Covenant, for it may be considered as a kind of sample box or exhibition window of the conflicting principles and tendencies which go to the building of the League. Its first paragraph is a compromise between the two schools which have been described in the first part of this book as the "pacifist" and the "realistic" points of view. It begins on a pacifist tone asserting that arms are the cause of war: "The Members of the League recognize that the maintenance of peace requires the reduction of national armaments to the lowest point . . ."; and it ends as a realist admitting that wars may well be after all the cause of arms: ". . . . consistent with national safety and the enforcement by common action of international obligations." It is on the whole a fine effort of constructive idealism, since, in its realistic second part it limits independent national criteria to strictly national safety, leaving no doubt as to the "common" character of all other obligations.

Having thus defined a general principle in its first paragraph on the implicit basis of the World-Community, the Article lays on the Council the burden of its application: "The Council, taking account of the geographical situation and circumstances of each State, shall formulate plans for such reduction for the consideration and action of the several Governments. Such plans shall be subject to reconsideration and revision at least every ten years. After these plans shall have been adopted by the several Governments, the limits of armaments therein fixed shall not be exceeded without the concurrence of the Council." We are again in the presence of compromise. The Council as an organ of the World-Community formulates plans, but the consideration and above all the action to be taken remains under the sovereign jurisdiction of each and every Member. Yet paragraphs 2, 3 and 4 of this Article constitute a bold step forward in the matter of armaments and one which deserves special notice. For what is the effect of these stipulations? The Members of the League may take a longer or a shorter period in acquiescing to the plans formulated by the Council, but once they have accepted them they cannot get out of them except with the Council's concurrence. Thus you have a say in the shaping of the house while it is being built but you cannot get out of it once it is finished. True, paragraph 3 stipulates that plans shall be subject to reconsideration and revision at least every ten years and it may be fairly argued that the procedure for such a reconsideration and revision must be the same as that under which the plans were first formulated. Every State remains therefore free to accept or reject the revised plans. Whether this right implies that of rejecting the plan if, after revision, the armaments of the State concerned remain unaltered is a purely academic question for, since armaments are essentially a relative notion, the negative conclusion could only be defended on the ground that all armaments of all signatories remained unaltered—a most unlikely event. But even if through the operation of the third paragraph, nations may automatically release themselves every ten years, the point is that the combination of these three provisions reduces the possible situations of the League and its Members with regard to armaments to only three possibilities. They must be:

(1) either in the initial stage, i.e., preparing plans for the Council to formulate with a view to a convention (the present stage);

(2) or under a convention, bound by limits which cannot be exceeded without the concurrence of the Council;

(3) or reconsidering and revising the convention for a new lease of situation number 2.

The convention of disarmament to be concluded under Article 8 is therefore perpetual. It can be revised but it cannot be abrogated. This conclusion is of the highest importance from the point of view of the

World-Community. We may have to refer to it when dealing with the draft conventions actually discussed in Geneva.

A point may here be mentioned which completes the set of legal texts bearing on the matter. The "neutral" Members of the League signed and ratified the Covenant as an isolated document. The belligerent States of the Great War signed and ratified it as an integral part of the Peace Treaties. Now, in the four Treaties of Peace, the part dealing with the military, naval and air clauses in virtue of which the defeated party is disarmed, is preceded by a preamble couched in the following terms: "In order to render possible the initiation of a general limitation of the armaments of all nations, Germany undertakes strictly to observe the military, naval and air clauses which follow." It is doubtful whether this sentence can be interpreted as a legal obligation, in view of the natural tendency of jurists to put a minimum value on their own words—one of the most attractive features of this much maligned class of experts. But, whatever the legal value of the phrase, its worth as a moral obligation cannot be gainsaid, and moreover M. Paul Boncour, speaking in Geneva with the political authority of a French Official Delegate and with the technical authority of an eminent lawyer has asserted more than once in unhesitating terms his belief in the value both legal and moral of this contractual engagement—a noble attitude which must stand to his credit and to that of his country. Thus the disarmament of Germany and of Hungary becomes an obligation dependent on the disarmament of their ex-enemies. When could it be fairly argued in Berlin and Budapest that the failure of their co-signatories to disarm released Germany and Hungary from their treaty obligations? Nothing but a non-possumus of the Council could in my opinion provide a sufficient ground for so grave a decision. But the non-possumus need not be formal and explicit. On the day the Council tacitly allowed the work of disarmament to stop or even to slacken its pace, Germany and Hungary would be entitled to provoke a formal pronouncement from the Council. Thus the work of disarmament of the League must proceed uninterruptedly. The Covenant lays it down as a duty. The preamble to Part V of the Treaty of Versailles provides a political sanction against any tendency that might arise to shirk it.

Article 8 pure and simple applies to the original members of the League including those invited to accede to it from its inception. As for newcomers, Article 1, § 2 stipulates that "any fully self-governing State, Dominion or Colony not named in the Annex may become a Member of the League if its admission is agreed to by two-thirds of the Assembly, provided that it shall give effective guarantees of its sincere intention to observe its international obligations, and shall accept such regulations as may be prescribed by the League in regard to its military, naval and air forces and armaments." We are concerned here with the concluding words of this provision. They mean that the League reserves for itself the right to prescribe what armaments its new members shall have. This provision is perhaps the most drastic inroad on sovereignty in the whole Covenant. In actual practice it only works inasmuch as the balance of power in the case permits. It would not be strictly applied nor indeed applied at all to a great country such as Russia or even to Turkey. If Mexico came in before the United States of America it would not be applied at all to her; if after, an attempt might be made to take the provision in earnest should the United States of America wish it so. The result of the attempt would depend on whether the League was more anxious to admit Mexico than Mexico to get in or vice versa.

The remaining provisions of Article 8 as well as § d of Article 23 may be considered as complementary to the stipulations of the Covenant analyzed above. Though at first sight they may appear somewhat disconnected, experience has shown their close relationship to the central problem. For in effect § 5 of Article 8 seeks to regulate the manufacture of arms while § d of Article 23 aims at supervising the international trade in arms—two objects which six years of discussions at Geneva have shown to be:

(a) Inseparably connected;

(b) Closely allied to the limitation or reduction of war material affected by international convention;

(c) Only attainable in practice by means of systematic publicity.

It will be seen that this last feature connects the two provisions concerned no less closely than § 6 of Article 8 which provides that the members of the League "undertake to interchange full and frank information as to the scale of their armaments, their military, naval and air programmes and the condition of such of their industries as are adaptable to war-like purposes."

Finally Article 9 of the Covenant is devoted to the machinery whereby the disarmament tasks of the Council may be carried out by the Covenant. The Article is as vague as any statesman should wish: "A permanent Commission shall be constituted to advise the Council on the execution of the provisions of Articles 1 and 8 and on military, naval and air questions generally."

Chapter IV

THE HANDS AT THE LEVERS

SO much for the machinery. What about the hands which were to move it? The first hint of their intentions appears in May, 1920, when the Council, sitting in Rome, adopted a report submitted by the French Representative M. Léon Bourgeois, organizing the Commission provided for in Article 9. The choice of rapporteur was in itself significant. Disarmament questions were to pass through the mill of French ideas and tendencies before they were discussed by the Council. Every one conversant with the methods of work adopted by the League, particularly in those early days, will realize the importance of a step which gave the French War Office such an advantage over the other nations represented in the Council.

The report was all that could be expected. The Commission was to be entirely composed of military, naval and air men. Each of the nations represented in the Council was to send a delegation of three experts, one for each of the three Services. The secretariat was also to be composed of a group of three experts, one for each Service. The Commission would be divided into three sub-committees, Military, Naval and Air, for each of which one of the three members of the secretariat would act as secretary. As if further to emphasize what it all meant, it was verbally agreed that the secretaries would be selected as follows: the Military Secretary from the French Army; the Naval Secretary from the British Navy; the Air Secretary from the Italian Air Service. Business first, pleasure afterwards, as Sam Weller used to say.

It was as foolish to expect a disarmament convention from such a commission as a declaration of atheism from a commission of clergymen. But this opinion must be clearly defined. Much offensive and inoffensive scorn has been poured on the several military commissions which have dealt with disarmament matters in the League. "Soldiers cannot agree as to the means to abolish their jobs" and "dog does not eat dog" have been for years favorite taunts of the cynic and the pacifist in this respect. In my opinion such an attitude is grossly unfair to the military profession. The incapacity to reach conclusions and the peculiar inefficiency in debate which have been observed in military commissions are due to deeper causes and call for graver comment. The military profession cannot recognize any duty above that which constitutes its very essence: the ensuring the safety of its country. A military delegation sent to discuss disarmament problems cannot and should not envisage them—as it is implicitly requested to do—in a somewhat general and abstract light. It can only view them as it should only view them, with an eye on the home forces. "Which of the possible answers to the question will increase my strength or weaken that of my potential adversaries?" Such is the only possible criterion which a military delegation can and should adopt, and any one who expects military men in Geneva to think in the abstract ways of the intellectual or in the give-and-take ways of the politician misses the main point. But if that is so, it will be easily seen that a commission composed of military delegates can seldom find unanimity outside general negative propositions. To this objective limitation a subjective obstacle should be added. By temperament the soldier is not a good negotiator. His tactics are those of war: surprise, stratagem, deep laid plans, concealment and rush—while his aim and glory is complete victory.

When the first Assembly of the League of Nations met in November, 1920, it found that the Commission had reported negatively on practically every point of the program submitted to it by the Council. What else could be expected? The Assembly, led by Lord Cecil, took a bold and statesmanlike course. The Council had chosen to stultify the effect of Article 9 by creating a commission of military men; the Assembly decided to set up another commission which would differ from the first on two all-important points:

(1) It would be predominantly civilian though containing a certain number of military experts chosen in the other commission.

(2) Its members would not be government representatives nor government nominees. They would be chosen by the Council on their own merits. The pattern of competencies included:

A number of representative political men, at first six, but gradually increased to twice their original number,

Six experts (two land, two sea, two air) chosen in the Permanent Advisory Commission,

Four experts (two economists and two financial experts) chosen from amongst the members of the Economic and Financial Committee of the League,

Three Labor and three Employer members chosen by the governing body of the International Labor Office.

The secretariat of this Commission was to constitute a section of the League of Nations Secretariat under the authority of the Director of Disarmament to be responsible also for the secretariat of the Permanent Advisory Commission.

The Council, however, in carrying out these suggestions, saw that the hands at the levers remained of course the same. It was carefully stipulated that the new Commission would be temporary and so that there was no mistake about it the word was actually branded on its name: *Temporary Mixed Commission.* The President of the Commission was to be a Frenchman, no less a man than M. Viviani, the Prime Minister who was in office when war broke out. As for the secretariat, its organization—or rather lack thereof—was designed so as to leave the work in the hands of the fighting departments of the three most effectively armed nations: England, France and Italy.

When I was appointed as Chief of Service on the promotion of the Director of Disarmament (who remained nominally the Director of the Section) to succeed Judge Anzilotti as Italian Under-Secretary-General, I found the Section frankly split into two independent units: the secretariat of the Temporary Mixed

Commission was a part of the general Secretariat; the secretariat of the Permanent Advisory Commission was an autonomous unit; each of the three officers had his own self-governing establishment; each came and went as he wished; the files of the military department were not kept in the general registry of the Secretariat of the League. And as truth will blurt out of the mouth of the innocent, the League staff list gave the two secretariats as separate units: that of the Temporary Mixed Commission under the name of *Disarmament Section* and that of the Military Commission under the name of *Armaments Section.* When the Permanent Advisory Commission met for the first time after my appointment, it was tactfully conveyed to me that my right to be present at its meetings was not evident nor even clear. I solved the difficulty by being present.

Let not the reader dismiss the subject as unimportant. The future of the world is being shaped up in the mill of Geneva and nothing in the complicated machinery of that mill should be indifferent to a true world citizen. Deeply convinced of this, I proposed to the Secretary-General that the Council should be asked to alter its own Rome Report in two ways, to both of which I attached some importance:

(1) The Secretary of the Permanent Advisory Commission to be the head of the Section assisted by the three experts.

(2) The experts to be given long-term contracts similar to those of the remaining members of the Secretariat of the League.

My aim was two-fold: first to achieve complete unity

of purpose and inspiration between the work of the two commissions; then to make certain that the actual authority over the three military experts was that of the Secretary-General and not that of the fighting departments of the three Great Powers. This objective ran, of course, contrary to the wishes of the fighting departments in question, and particularly of the British Admiralty and of the French War Office; and as ill-luck would have it the Military Commission to which the Council referred my proposals for consideration happened then to be presided over by the French War Office expert, Colonel Requin, one of the clearest brains, most determined wills and most commanding personalities which the peculiar world of Geneva experts has known. Colonel Requin argued that the work of the secretariat of his Commission was of a strictly technical character which required that the three men in charge should be highly specialized, indeed so highly specialized that they were to be on active service and to return to their regiments, battleships and air formations at the end of their three-year term in Geneva, to be replaced by new men fresh from the schools of Mars. The argument was of course stretched to suit the particular tall story which it had to fit. The point was that active service men lent on short-term contracts to Geneva were expected to remain first and foremost members of their own fighting services, even though serving in Geneva as international officials. A compromise had to be patched up. The secretariat of the Military Commission remained in military hands but the men were definitely put under the administrative authority of the civil head, who was to receive all papers. The story had a curious and significant epilogue. The Spanish Delegation in the Military Commission moved that at the expiration of the term of office of the three secretaries in service their successors should be chosen from other nationalities. The French Delegation, with its usual mastery in procedure, moved that the Commission was not competent to discuss the point; the motion of incompetence was carried and the tacit arrangement whereby the three international posts, paid by fifty-five nations for international service, became the advanced posts of the three fighting departments of Great Britain, France and Italy, remained in force.[1]

[1] That, after some initial difficulties, I was fortunate enough to secure men whose behavior in this most delicate of situations was unimpeachable, men indeed with whom it was a pleasure and a privilege to work, does not in the least detract from the utter incompatibility between the spirit of the Covenant and the exceptional privilege granted not so much to the three Great Powers as to their three fighting departments.

Chapter V

THE DIRECT METHOD

WITH its two Commissions, its Secretariat, the Council at the helm and the Assembly providing the gentle gales of inspiration, the ship of disarmament sailed forth into the seas of time. Its course was somewhat wayward at first. Disarmament, we know, is a tendency prompted by two different lines of thought: arms cause wars; wars cause arms. And just as the two schools are blended in the first part of Article 8 of the Covenant, so we find the methods followed by the disarmament organization of the League influenced now by one now by the other of these two ways of thinking.

For it is obvious that if arms are the cause of wars the proper way to set about is to disarm, and so the school here called "pacifist" leads to what might be described as the direct or technical method, a method whereby a direct solution is sought in the examination of the technical means for reducing and limiting armaments at once; while if wars are the cause of arms the right thing to do is to study the cause and cure of war, and therefore the school here known as "realist" leads to what might be described as the indirect or political method whereby the solution of the problem is sought in the creation of the political circumstances required for disarmament to take place, so to say, of itself. The evolution of the work of disarmament is determined by the interplay between these two methods and schools, in its turn dependent on the evolutions which take place in the public opinion and policy of the two protagonistic nations: France and England. For reasons of national psychology, on which I need not dwell here, England evolved from the "pacifist" to the "realist" point of view while France evolved from the "realist" to the "pacifist." Such is the pattern of tendencies and policies which determines the pattern of events.

It is in the nature of things that the "realist" should wait for things to move when the move in question leads away from realism. Disarmament is not in itself an idea appealing to the realist. Hence the true explanation of the fact that leadership in the first phase of the work should have been in British hands. There had been of course a preliminary phase—that in which the Permanent Advisory Commission worked alone—during which the realist had led towards still harder realism. During this first period, the French delegation in the Commission is predominantly interested in how to utilize the disarmament machine of the League to secure a complete hold over the situations brought about by the Treaties of Peace. The direct method still prevails during the first years of the work of the Temporary Mixed Commission, between November, 1920, when it is created, and September, 1922, when Lord Cecil takes over the leadership of the work. During this period the Temporary Mixed Commission as the initiating body and the Permanent Advisory Commission as the technical body are engaged in investigating the possibilities of a technical solution for the problem of disarmament. Two attempts are made in this direction: the plan known as Lord Esher's scheme, and the Anglo-Franco-Italian proposals for extending the principles of the Washington Treaty to the non-signatory powers.

In a sense, both these plans emanate from the Washington Conference. This Conference may be said to be the only endeavor to reduce and limit armaments which has led to any tangible results. The American Government is entitled to all the merit which it has claimed now and then for this success. If in the remarks that follow the achievement is not put quite so high, allowances must be made for a difference in perspective and for the natural effects of distance. It is no disparagement of the Woolworth Building to say that it looks less tall from Geneva than it does from the opposite side of the street on which it stands in all its proud yet unassuming height.

At the time of the Washington Conference there was in Geneva an international worker who now and then sought relief for his none too easy life of toil by indulging in good-humored cynicism. I thought that his opinion on the event might be valuable to me and I knocked at his door in search of illumination. The wise though youthful observer smiled and said: "The choicest things in life—and the Washington Conference is one of them—can best be understood in terms of parables. In the old days when Florence led the world both in the arts of the spirit and in those of trade there were five bankers in the city well known for their friendly rivalry. They all were solid and sound men, fearful of God, loving their good wives and enjoying their still better mistresses. Of these, Signor Jonathani and Signor Giovanni Toro had so many that neither the curious town nor the fortunate bankers themselves knew the exact number thereof; Signor Nipponi, Signor Gallo and Signor Savoia had a lesser though still comfortable number. But winds cannot always blow fair, and a foul weather having set in on the seas of business, the five rivals and friends bethought themselves of the necessity of reducing their costly establishments. So, Signor Jonathani, the wealthiest of the group and therefore its leader—for you must know that amongst bankers the wealthiest leads as amongst holy men the holiest—called a conference of the five and it was decided, not without difficulty, for the five men were healthy and loved their flesh and the ladies were fair and brought them much pleasure and prestige, it was decided, I say, that Signor Jonathani and Signor Giovanni Toro should limit the number of their fair friends to five apiece; Signor Nipponi to three, while Signori Gallo and Savoia should be reduced to one each with occasional visits to one other, which visits they would carefully keep equal in number—and, in order that their credit, I mean their financial prestige, should not suffer thereby, the five friendly rivals agreed to make it quite clear to the curious city that their sacrifices were made in deference to the sanctity of marriage."

My skeptic friend's parable does not of course exhaust the aspects under which the Washington Conference can be envisaged, yet I confess to some inclination to agree with his views in so far as they represent the Conference and its results as inspired mainly in financial considerations. There is no question that the five Washington Powers refrained then from doing a very foolish thing, i.e., starting a race which would have brought some of them to the verge of ruin. The world has become so modest that the abstention from folly is nowadays trumpeted forth as wisdom. Let us grant the claim for the sake of modesty. But can it be said in all honesty that the Washington Conference was as rich in true international wealth as it was in five national savings? The reader may recollect the observations on premature disarmament conferences made in the last chapter of Part I. The Washington Conference was a typical illustration of them. While much Christian feeling was aired—indeed a trifle too much for the French delegation, in whose country Christianity has gone out of fashion, politically at least—the undercurrents of mistrust, resentment and ill-feeling were strong and intense. Any one who cared to hear candid comment could get an earful of it per second at the time in Washington. Every delegation was convinced that every other delegation had "done it in." The Machiavellism of a prominent Englishman in charge of the Press was the object of delighted or indignant comment according to taste and nationality, while the French delegation so fiercely attacked both in Washington and in London came home in a state of utter discontent and irritation. The aftermath was hardly better. Distrust continued. The fulfillment of the clauses was jealously watched and alleged violations denounced. The construction of the Singapore Base, strictly within the letter of the Treaty yet less strictly within its professed spirit, was an admirable illustration of the ultimate inanity of these half-measures for premature disarmament. The Washington Conference proved once more that, in the absence of a constructive effort to organize the World-Community, disarmament conferences turn into armament conferences.

The Washington Conference in other words was a typical example of the inadequacy of the direct method. Similar though quicker effects were experienced by the League in its two attempts along this line. Lord Esher's plan sought to reduce armaments by setting up a unit of armament, say 30,000 men, and attributing to each nation a figure or co-efficient which multiplied by the unit of armament would represent the army allowed to the nation concerned. Thus, France would have a co-efficient of 6, Italy of 4, England of 3, and therefore their respective armies would be 180,000, 120,000 and 90,000. The Permanent Advisory Commission to which the scheme was referred for technical advice rejected it on the ground that no practical criterion existed to determine a unit of armament having a reasonable degree of comparative value. The reader knows by now that no comparison is possible between identical numbers of soldiers in different armies. If the difficulty arising out of the remaining military factors (material, credit, geographical position, etc.) be added, it will be seen that the proposal put forward by Lord Esher was not acceptable. But, though the technical reasons against it were numerous and substantial, the strength behind the reasons, the impulse that brushed it aside—somewhat curtly—was political. Lord Esher's plans were too exclusively directed towards the limitation of land forces to the neglect of sea armaments. Now, we know that for France as well as for Italy and for almost every other continental power, the question of naval disarmament cannot be separated from that of land disarmament. Hence the short-lived course of Lord Esher's scheme.

The second effort of the League on the path of direct disarmament was not more fortunate. The Members of the League signatories of the Washington Treaty were anxious to make other naval nations benefit by the blessings which they were experiencing under their enlightened régime. In other words, having voluntarily limited their fleets, they sought to induce Spain, Brazil, Holland, Sweden, the Argentine Republic, Chile, Greece, Turkey and other naval nations of lesser importance to reduce their own. We are now in a position to estimate the true intention of this move. We know that a disarmament conference in the present state of development of the World-Community is bound to turn out as an armament conference. England, France, Italy and Japan aimed therefore at improving their relative armaments by limiting the tonnage of the remaining naval nations. And as most of these nations were European, the initiative was taken by England, France and Italy, whose nationals in the Temporary Mixed Commission put forward definite proposals to that effect. A technical conference took place in Rome in 1924. The Soviet Government was represented. After long and arduous debates the conference failed to discover a ground for agreement. How could it? The position was almost naïve. What were the British, French, Italian and Japanese delegates doing in that conference? Their navies were not being discussed. Why were they there? As advisors and experts in the mysteries of the Washington Treaty? But that would not have given them the right to a vote which they took as a matter of course. Please note that when the navies of Holland or Brazil were being discussed these four nations had a vote, though presumably when the treaty was ready they would not be entitled to sign it. The explanation is of course that under the guise of disarmament we were discussing armaments, and that since the objects in debate were not so much the naval armaments of Holland and Brazil and the others but the differences in armaments between these second-rank Nations and the Washington Powers, Britain, France, Italy and Japan were primarily interested in whatever subject happened to be debated or voted upon.

That did not make their position any easier. "See," they said, "we limited our fleets in Washington. We sacrificed ourselves for the common good. Do as much." To which the other nations answered: "We did not build during the War. You over-built heavily. We do not feel any financial pressure against our naval growth. You do. You had to readjust your navies to your normal needs by reducing them. We, prevented from building by the War, have to readjust our navies to our needs by building up." The argument offered no hope of conciliation. Conciliation however was tried and in a few cases with success. But the conference broke down mostly on Russia and Spain. Russia put forward her three sea fronts, at such colossal distances that she could reasonably claim to need three separate fleets: Baltic, Black, Pacific. One day some one put forward the suggestion that regional limitation might be tried and gave as an example the Baltic in which the riparian States might limit their tonnage to a given figure. The Russian representative, a clear-minded quiet commander of the old régime who had rallied to the Bolsheviks retorted: "When the straits are open there is but one sea." His answer was obviously right. How limit the fleets of all the riparian States as long as the non-riparian States can rush in and alter the balance of power? I whispered to the parties that they might innovate. Without closing the Baltic and the Black Seas altogether they might limit the tonnage of non-riparian navies to a figure to be negotiated. We might even innovate in names and call such straits, neither closed nor open, "straits ajar." But the proposal was not liked by the Big Power delegations nor did the Russian expert seem very pleased. And the dead-lock remained unsolved.

As for Spain, she refused to remain within the bounds of her, then, much depleted status quo. She argued that though she was in no need of limiting her fleet she would do so out of deference for others but at a higher figure than the status quo, if lower than her contemplated program had determined it. This decision did not suit any of the Washington Powers. One day the Spanish Admiral accosted the British Admiral at the end of the sitting and declared himself ready to accept the status quo. His British colleague was very much elated. Then the Spaniard added: "But we must discuss one point, the year to be chosen to define the status quo." "Why," said the Englishman, "1921." "Oh, no," said the Spaniard: "I suggest 1588."

Chapter VI

THE INDIRECT METHOD

IN 1922 Lord Cecil, who had created the Temporary Mixed Commission, joined it. From that moment the Commission fell under the leadership of this most attractive of international figures yet most representative of Englishmen. He has often been described in his country and out of it as a dangerous idealist. Public opinion in the United States and in other quarters has been apt at times to judge with much severity and even now and then with scant courtesy the line of action which he had either taken or been forced to take. These two opinions, while in apparent conflict, explain each other. A true view of the eminent statesman to whom the League owes more than to any living man would bring him down from the cloudy heights of "dangerous" idealism to the solid ground of clear-sighted statesmanship, and in so doing would discard the foolishly "idealistic" standards on which some of his political actions or omissions have been condemned. Lord Cecil is a supremely intelligent Conservative British statesman—a rara avis, I grant, in English Conservatism. And if he finds himself somewhat isolated in his own country, it is not at all owing to his "radicalism" of which he has no trace, but to his intelligent vision, of which he has perhaps more than his British Conservative friends can bear without feeling uncomfortable. Lord Cecil was therefore admirably placed to act as the leader of the League in its first years. For the strongest claim which the League would make to a world just out of an orgy of destruction was not that it brought still more turmoil with it but that it came to heal, purify and maintain. Now, that message Lord Cecil was admirably fitted to deliver, being in his heart and soul a British Conservative aristocrat.

But a message cannot carry in international life if it is not delivered in an international idiom. I do not refer here to the language. Those poor well-meaning folks who still preach Esperanto (with that silly sentimental name too) seem unable to realize that the true obstacle for international understanding is not the language but the idiom, the mental attitude. Men in discordant mental attitudes shall never understand each other even though they may speak the same language, natural or artificial; men in similar or harmoniously different mental attitudes even if speaking different languages shall understand each other the moment they strike contact through an interpreter. What Lord Cecil brought to Geneva was a marvelous capacity for putting things in an international idiom—a gift of the mind in him, for it is but fair to add that as a Briton and as an aristocrat his instincts could hardly help him in this apostolate.

By training and nationality Lord Cecil belongs to the "pacifist" school. I mean that his heart is with disarmament. By intellectual adaptation however he rises above his national limitations and realizes that the direct method is premature. Yet he does not altogether espouse the indirect method pure and simple. He strives at a middle course. Such is the origin of his famous proposals in which for the first time the technical or direct and the political or indirect aspects of the problem appear firmly bracketed together under the respective names of *disarmament* and *guarantee*.

Lord Cecil realized the fact that disarmament has no separate existence and that it is not so much intimately connected with the general political problem as in fact one of the aspects of this problem itself. Now, at the time, the predominant feature in the situation was the sense of insecurity which prevailed in certain European quarters. Curiously enough, these regions apt to suffer from nervousness were not the defeated and disarmed, but some of the victorious and still armed, nations. The paradox is easily solved once it is realized that victory had transferred territories and privileges from the former to the latter. Lord Cecil realized that the problem of disarmament could not be solved unless this all-important psychological situation was taken into account. He sought to meet the position by means of a general treaty of guarantee which would act as a rider to the Covenant.[1]

[1] His initial proposals as they emerged from the debates which took place during the Assembly in September, 1922, summed up the position in the following terms:

"(a) The Assembly, having considered the report of the Temporary Mixed Commission on the question of a general Treaty of Mutual Guarantee, being of opinion that this report can in no way affect the complete validity of all the Treaties of Peace or other agreements which are known to exist between States; and considering that this report contains valuable suggestions as to the methods

The Commission was divided as to the respective stress to be given to disarmament and to guarantee and also as to whether the most adequate instrument for securing the aim in view would be a general treaty of guarantee or special treaties between states closely united by the same feeling of insecurity. The inner meaning of these differences lies deeper than one of mere method. It flows from a difference in spirit and in faith. On the one hand the ex-victorious nations, except England, were at the time convinced that the maintenance of a military superiority over the defeated countries was indispensable to the stability of Europe. Their efforts were thus directed towards setting up a system of treaties enabling them to extract the utmost service from both the provisions and the gaps of the Covenant. By reason of its military and also of its mental power, France took the leadership of this move-

by which a Treaty of Mutual Guarantee could be made effective, is of the opinion that:

"1. No scheme for the reduction of armaments, within the meaning of Article 8 of the Covenant, can be fully successful unless it is general.

"2. In the present state of the world many Governments would be unable to accept the responsibility for a serious reduction of armaments unless they received in exchange a satisfactory guarantee of the safety of their country.

"3. Such a guarantee can be found in a defensive agreement which should be open to all countries, binding them to provide immediate and effective assistance in accordance with a prearranged plan in the event of one of them being attacked, provided that the obligation to render assistance to a country attacked shall be limited in principle to those countries situated in the same part of the globe. In cases, however, where, for historical, geographical, or other reasons, a country is in special danger of attack, detailed arrangements should be made for its defence in accordance with the above-mentioned plan.

"4. As a general reduction of armaments is the object of the three preceding statements, and the Treaty of Mutual Guarantee the ment. M. de Jouvenel on the political side and Colonel Requin on the technical side presented the case with the mastery which we are used to acknowledge in their gifted race. What was to be their plan of campaign? (For, though the subject was disarmament itself, there is a bellicoseness in the mental vitality of France which gives French method and vigor a truly military dash.) It may be divided into two objectives:

(1) To exploit to the full the military possibilities of Article 16 with a view to strengthening international action.

(2) To obtain the maximum military efficiency in the application of the rights to private war left over by the so-called gaps in the Covenant.[1]

The first objective comprised:

(a) The strict recognition of the obligation some-

means of achieving that object, previous consent to this reduction is therefore the first condition for the Treaty.

"This reduction could be carried out either by means of a general Treaty, which is the most desirable plan, or by means of partial treaties designed to be extended and open to all countries.

"In the former case, the Treaty will carry with it a general reduction of armaments. In the latter case, the reduction should be proportionate to the guarantees afforded by the Treaty.

"The Council of the League, after having taken the advice of the Temporary Mixed Commission, which will examine how each of these two systems could be carried out, should further formulate and submit to the Governments for their consideration and sovereign decision the plan of the machinery, both political and military, necessary to bring them clearly into effect.

"(b) The Assembly requests the Council to submit to the various Governments the above proposals for their observations, and requests the Temporary Mixed Commission to continue its investigations, and, in order to give precision to the above statements, to prepare a Draft Treaty embodying the principles contained therein."

Such was the famous Resolution XIV which stands at the basis of all the subsequent work of the Commission and even of all the work done in disarmament under the League auspices ever since.

[1] See p. 72.

what vaguely defined by the Covenant in Article 16.

(b) The drawing-out of preëstablished plans for the financial, economic and military coöperation towards the defeat of the outlaw State.

(c) The taking of whatever definite measures might be necessary in order to ensure the success of the preestablished plans.

The second objective comprised:

(a) The conclusion of special treaties with nations politically interested in the European status quo;

(b) The recognition of these treaties as compatible with the Covenant so as to ensure international cooperation in their favor if and when necessary;

(c) The recognition of such rights of intermediate application of the special treaties as would guarantee an effective military action unhindered by Covenant obstacles in case of need.[1]

On the other side Lord Cecil and the Northern Neutrals held different views. They were particularly anxious to reduce the burden of armaments everywhere and in order to attain their end they were ready to discuss a treaty granting "nervous States" certain guarantees of security in case of unprovoked attack. On the other hand, they demanded that the question should be put on a general footing; that no use should be made of the proposed treaty in order to re-introduce in Europe the system of private groups which had led

[1] This analysis is of course entirely personal and deduced from a study of French argument and from the observation of French activity in Geneva. It does in no way purport to represent an authoritative or even an acceptable summary of official views.

to such disastrous results; and that disarmament should be simultaneous with the guarantee. Yet the picture would not be complete without certain re-touches which though they make it truer may not make it clearer.

To begin with the Scandinavians were not particularly enthusiastic about the guarantee part of the scheme. The idea to go and set up on its feet any tottering nation attacked by a powerful adversary was not palatable to them, nor was the case of Finland, one of the "nervous States" owing to the vicinity of the Soviets, a circumstance particularly favorable for their conversion. Italy was mostly preoccupied with the possibility of making good in law as well as in fact her claim to armament equality with France. Spain wavered mostly according to the particular representative in charge of her affairs, though on the whole inclined to Lord Cecil's views. As for England, no one knew what England thought on the matter, Lord Cecil least of all. It was obvious that the British military, naval and air experts felt no enthusiasm for Lord Cecil's ideas, but that was to be expected as a mere matter of technical limitation. The point, and one which if more adequately felt at the time would have saved many a disappointment, is that Lord Cecil was an international personality out of touch with his own country and perhaps particularly with his own party.

Such was the atmosphere in which the Draft Treaty of Guarantee was prepared. Nothing can be gained for our purpose from a detailed account and analysis of an instrument still-born, the interest of which remains purely historical. The Draft Treaty and even the Protocol, which was the reincarnation of the same spirit one year later, must be for us as milestones on the road of our evolution towards the full realization of the World-Community. That politicians rejected them and newspaper editors condemned them need not alter the fact. They came and went in their time as milestones do in the eyes of the traveler. All we need retain of the Treaty are its essentials. They may be studied under three heads:

Guarantee: The Treaty stipulates a double guarantee: one of all to all—limited only by a proviso that nations need not coöperate in military operations outside their own continent—the other, by means of special treaties linking together States which may wish to prepare more definitely the plans they would eventually carry out in case they were attacked. These treaties to be examined by the Council with a view to ascertaining that they do not conflict with the Covenant nor with the general treaty and to be open to all other signatories of the general treaty. In exchange for these concessions to the Cecilian school the French school obtained the right to put into operation the prearranged plans provided for in their special treaties without necessarily waiting for the Council to declare the aggressor, yet with the proviso that the Council would immediately be informed and that even after hostilities had begun the parties would submit to its decision.

Disarmament: The Treaty stipulates that the Signatory Powers must communicate to the Council the reductions or limitations which they may be ready to adopt in view of the additional security gained by the Treaty itself. The guarantee clauses of the Treaty are not to come into force until the Signatory Power concerned has reduced its armaments according to the plans prepared by the Council.

Aggression: Article 1 of the Treaty declares aggression to be an international crime, and the Signatory Powers solemnly declare that they will not be guilty of it. The Treaty provides for specific measures to be taken by the Council not merely in case of aggression but even in case of threat of aggression or even of aggressive policy. The list of measures typifies the strong military direction impressed on the work by the brilliant and forceful mind of Colonel Requin:

In particular, the Council may:

(a) Decide to apply immediately to the aggressor State the economic sanctions contemplated by Article 16 of the Covenant, the Members of the League not signatory to the Treaty not being, however, bound by this decision, except in the case where the State attacked is entitled to avail itself of the Articles of the Covenant;

(b) Call on the High Contracting Parties whose assistance it requires to provide such assistance. No High Contracting Party situated in a continent other than that in which operations will take place shall, in principle, be required to coöperate in military, naval or air operations;

(c) Determine the forces which each State furnishing assistance shall place at its disposal;

(d) Prescribe all necessary measures for securing

priority for the communications and transport connected with the operations;

(e) Prepare a plan for financial coöperation among the High Contracting Parties with a view to providing for the State attacked and for the States furnishing assistance the funds which they require for the operations;

(f) Appoint the Higher Command and establish the object and the nature of his duty.

But what is an aggression? The Council was to find out within four days who had been the aggressor. The military experts gave no help. The obvious solution was to remove the difficulty from the war to the pre-war period. The two Spanish members of the Commission submitted a proposal to that effect.[1]

[1] In the event of one of the High Contracting Parties considering that the policy of any other High Contracting Party in regard to third Powers is likely to endanger peace, the former may in conformity with Paragraph 2 of Article 11 of the Covenant draw the attention of the Council to that fact.

The Council shall consider the question and shall hear the statements of the High Contracting Party which has made the appeal, that of the High Contracting Party which has been accused, and, if necessary, that of any third Powers which may be menaced. If necessary, the Council may exclude the High Contracting Party accused from the benefits of the guarantee.

Article 10. At the request of any Member of the League of Nations, the Council of the League which, on receipt of that request, must be immediately convened by the Secretary-General, may declare that the political situation between the two States Members is such that precautions with a view to preserving peace are indispensable. The following precautionary measures may be applied:

(a) Both Parties may be asked to withdraw their troops to a certain distance, to be determined by the Council, on both sides of the frontier,

—To abstain from flying over a certain neutral zone between the two countries;

—To abstain from allowing their navies to enter the territorial waters of the other State.

This proposal was of course lost in commission but its disembodied spirit survived in the commentary on the definition of aggression which was sent to the governments along with the draft. In this interesting document the question of aggression is discussed in all its bearings and the Assembly having come to the conclusion that no simple definition of aggression can be drawn up and "that no simple test of when an act of aggression has actually taken place can be devised" went on to suggest that complete discretion should be

(b) The Council may invite the High Contracting Parties to apply to the State which is endangering peace penalties similar to those provided in Article 16 of the Covenant against a Covenant-breaking State;

(c) It may address a request to each of the High Contracting Parties to prepare such military forces as they think necessary for the purpose of averting the menace of war;

(d) It may further choose, in agreement with the State threatened, the State which shall nominate the Commander-in-Chief of these forces and define the character and purpose of his command.

(e) It may make every provision for the necessary priority of communications.

Article 11. In the event of any of the High Contracting Parties becoming engaged in hostilities with any other State, whether a party to this Treaty or not,

(a) It shall so inform the Secretary-General of the League of Nations who shall summon a meeting of the Council of the League without delay;

(b) It shall be the duty of the Council of the League of Nations, acting by at least a three-quarters majority, to decide within four days from the date on which the Secretary-General receives such information, which of the States so engaged in hostilities has been the aggressor. If the Council is unanimously of the opinion that its decision cannot be taken within this period of four days, it may decide to postpone it for a further period. For the purposes of this Article, the Powers engaged in hostilities shall not take part in the vote.

(c) Shall be presumed to be the aggressor:

—Any State which has refused to submit to the Permanent Court of International Justice or to the Council of the League of Nations the dispute which is the cause of the threat of war;

—Or any State which has refused to take the precautionary measures indicated in Article 10 when the Council has recommended their application.

left to the Council in the matter while indicating various factors as providing "elements of a just decision" amongst which the Assembly suggested the following: "refusal of either of the parties to withdraw their armed forces behind a line or lines indicated by the Council" and "a definitely aggressive policy by one of the parties towards the other, and the consequent refusal of that party to submit the subject in dispute to the recommendation of the Council or to the decision of the Permanent Court of International Justice and to accept the recommendation or decision when given."

The British Government rejected the Treaty in a letter dated July 5th, 1924, and signed "J. Ramsay MacDonald, P.M." The only plausible argument in the letter is its signature. Mr. Ramsay MacDonald was then engaged in the superhuman task of carrying on two ministerial departments, any one of which suffices to exhaust a stronger man and a man more able than he seems to be to delegate part of his work to collaborators. His departments moreover were no exception to the rule which every well-informed observer soon detected in English public life when the Labor Government was in office, i.e., that the permanent officials were never more powerful than under Labor chiefs. I had often heard this remark from my British friends but I was able to observe it myself at close quarters in Geneva. It is my personal experience that the military, naval and air "advisors" of the British Government were never more powerful than during the brief Labor spell. While waiting one day in the Council room a few minutes before the sitting in which the Council was to decide whether the Permanent Advisory Commission should or should not deal with a specific point (which the French experts therein wanted to discuss and the British did not) one of my British naval friends said to me: "I warn you that no matter what the Council decides *we* shall not discuss the point for we have no instructions." And I, pointing to Lord Parmoor, who being the representative of Mr. Ramsay MacDonald and of the British Government on the Council was in my innocent opinion the head and chief of the whole British Delegation to the Council in Geneva, said: "Why, just ask him." And my naval friend: "He won't do. My instructions come from the Admiralty." Mr. Ramsay MacDonald's instructions came also from the Admiralty and from the War Office when he signed that extraordinary letter of July 5th in which the first question he raised in connection with the Draft Treaty was: "Are the guarantees contained therein sufficient to justify a State in reducing its armaments?" This sentence must have thrilled Colonel Requin of the French General Staff (Geneva Division). Mr. Ramsay MacDonald is made to conclude that the Treaty is not effective from the military point of view, but, though that is bad enough, worse is still to come. "His Majesty's Government," he says, "are persuaded after careful examination of the Draft Scheme, that if the obligations created by the Treaty be scrupulously carried out, they will involve an increase rather than a decrease in British armaments." Now, this is . . . Well, let us not say what it is, but it is not cricket.

The Treaty is summed up by its drafters in the following terms:

"(1) The general guarantee is established in principle and defined by the Treaty—first stage;

(2) In the case of certain States the guarantee is supplemented by special Treaties;

(3) Each State establishes an estimate of the reduction which it can effect in armaments in virtue of the operation of this single or double guarantee—second stage;

(4) On the basis of these estimates, the Council draws up the plan of reduction as provided in Article 8 of the Covenant—third stage;

(5) After having adhered to the plan, the several States undertake to put this plan of reduction, in so far as it affects them, into operation within a period laid down in the Treaty—fourth stage;

(6) When this undertaking has been given, the guarantee comes into force, and the provisions of Article 8 of the Covenant regarding disarmament are in a fair way to fulfilment."

It is obvious that points 3 and 4 in this analysis would have enabled the British Government, a permanent Member of the Council, to subordinate the whole Treaty to so drastic a reduction of armaments that the new scale of the British fleet (including the "increase" necessitated by new obligations, granting that there are any) would have been altogether sensationally small. The argument is obvious. But the British Prime Minister did not like the Draft Treaty and he was perhaps too busy to weigh his arguments.

The situation was indeed paradoxical and revealed how complex the life of the League is apt to be owing to the changes which take place in the internal politics of its several members. The French delegation had endeavored to instil into Lord Cecil's scheme of disarmament as much *military* guarantee as possible, only to find the result defeated by a Labor pacifist Government on the ground that as a military instrument the Draft Treaty was not effective enough. And this surprising declaration, with the implied assumption that more guarantees are necessary before any disarmament can take place (an assumption dear to the French but abhorrent to the English and particularly to the Laborite English) sees the light as an official English Labor opinion when France, having veered to the left, is ready to launch forth a bolder disarmament policy more genuinely in line with the Covenant of the League and with the Cecilian and even Labor tendencies in the matter.

Nothing better shows the superficial and immature character of the reasons brought forward by Mr. Ramsay MacDonald to reject the Draft Treaty than his splendid attitude in Geneva when hand-in-hand with M. Herriot he laid down the basis of the Protocol (1924). In its components the Protocol does not differ from the Draft Treaty; but it does in the emphasis laid on each of them. The Draft Treaty was mostly guarantee and disarmament; arbitration was relegated to an annex as one of the criteria whereby the Council might well detect the aggressor. In the Protocol arbitration is brought to the foreground. In one year, at most in two, the idea had made great strides in the conscience of the world. It is to the honor of Mr. Ramsay MacDonald that he brought it boldly to the fore in the League Assembly and that he made of it the very basis of the work of disarmament in Geneva.

Chapter VII

THE INDIRECT METHOD (*Continued*)

THE GENEVA PROTOCOL

IN the depths of the human mind there lives a three-beat rhythm which makes it think in trinities. The process of disarmament illustrates this curious law of human psychology in a striking manner. It began with a one-beat time: Disarmament. It was improved upon by Lord Cecil who discovered the second beat: Disarmament-Guarantee. But it was due to Mr. Ramsay MacDonald and to M. Herriot in a powerful duet to vociferate the final three-beat rhythm which has since then filled the world with its whole round sonority: Arbitration-Security-Disarmament. The work found then its beat, the progress its pace.

In the process, a readjustment had taken place which was not without significance. Disarmament began all by itself, not only first but unique. When Guarantee (the first form which Security took) made its appearance, it took the second beat, at any rate in England, though it was apt to pass first when the phrase was put into French, so that Disarmament-Guarantee was often translated into Garantie-Désarmement. Finally when the rhythm attained its plenitude we saw the last term arrived take precedence over the other two, so that the final leit-motif became Arbitration-Security-Disarmament.

The Protocol thus means the triumph of the indirect method, or at least, the nearest approach to triumph which the indirect method has been allowed to make in the history of the League. Let us examine the broad principles on which it is built:

I. Arbitration. This word is used in the Protocol in a wider sense than the customary. It is no mere "settlement of disputes between States by judges of their own choice and on the basis of respect for law" but a specially defined system having for its main features:

(a) to be the machinery for the pacific settlement of disputes set under the direction of the Council of the League of Nations;

(b) to seek, not merely justice, but peace, and therefore, while relying on the rules and principles of international law, whenever available, to judge on equity if necessary;

(c) to be automatically put into operation by intervention of the Council independently of the ill-will of any one of the parties.

The machinery comprises the following stages:

(1) The parties recognize as compulsory the jurisdiction of the Permanent Court of International Justice for all judiciable cases.

(2) The parties apply the procedure of the Covenant to the other cases.

(3) Should this procedure fail, as foreseen in Ar-

ticle 15, § 3, instead of remaining free to take any action they wish, as the Covenant allows, they must submit the dispute to judicial settlement or arbitration.

(4) Should they fail to agree to do so, the wish of one of the parties suffices to render compulsory the appointment of a Committee of Arbitrators, the details of which are to be settled by the Council if, within a time limit defined by the Council, the parties have not been able to settle with themselves.

(5) If none of the parties ask for arbitration the Council takes up the matter again and, if unanimous, settles it.

(6) If not unanimous, the Council sets up a Committee of Arbitration, this time with complete independence from the parties concerned, and the Committee of Arbitration is empowered to settle the matter.

The system is therefore automatic and provides a method whereby all disputes must be settled by peaceful means. There remain a few categories of disputes however which the system leaves out of account:

(a) Those previously settled unanimously by the Council when the Council's award has been accepted by one of the parties.

(b) Those resulting from measures of war taken by one or more Signatory States in agreement with the Council or Assembly of the League.

(c) Those which aim at revising treaties or international acts in force or seek to jeopardize the existing territorial integrity of Signatory States.

(d) Those which a decision of the Permanent Court of International Justice declare to fall within the domestic jurisdiction of one of the parties.

II. SECURITY. This part of the Protocol must be analyzed under two headings: Aggression and its definition; and Sanctions.

(a) *Aggression.* We know that military opinion is against defining aggression by invasion. It is therefore necessary to seek a definition in some action previous to actual hostilities, i.e., in a violation of a collateral or international engagement. Yet such a violation does not become an aggression until there are hostilities, and even then the possibility is not excluded that the State whose policy has been aggressive may have in actual fact been the victim of the physical attack. Moreover were the Council to define the aggressor, its procedure might be a serious hindrance to its efficiency: if deciding under the rule of unanimity, because it might lead to a deadlock; if under the majority rule, because States placed in the minority might have to take action against their own judgment.

The Protocol sought to turn all these difficulties by devising a system whereby a State on its own action puts itself in the position of the aggressor, which it shall then be presumed to be unless the Council unanimously clears it from such a presumption. In this way the procedure of the Council is put in operation not to define aggression but to wash a State clean from the accusation if exceptional circumstances should arise to render it necessary. The presumption of aggression would arise in the three following cases:

—By refusal to accept the procedure of pacific settlement or to submit to the decision resulting therefrom.

—By taking any measures likely to alter the relative military power of the parties to a dispute or refusing to comply with the Council's summons in case any complaint should be made on this account.

—By disregard of a decision declaring the dispute to refer to matters lying within the exclusive domestic jurisdiction of a party and going to war without first appealing for conciliation to the Council or the Assembly.

If none of these criteria applies the Council must declare the aggressor directly by an unanimous vote. If the Council cannot reach unanimity, it must enjoin an armistice by a two-thirds majority, and the party which rejects or violates the armistice is declared to be the aggressor. The declaration of aggression must therefore always take place:

either automatically, by the State's own action;

or by the Council on an unanimous vote;

or by the fact that the State violates or rejects the armistice.

(b) *Sanctions.* The sanctions provided for in the Protocol are the same as those in the Covenant, but the system has been screwed up to a higher pitch. Briefly put, the differences are the following:

In the Covenant, the sanctions arising out of Article 16, § 1, i.e., the economic and financial sanctions, are compulsory, but the Covenant does not specify when. "Should any Member of the League resort to war in disregard of its covenants under Article 12, 13, or 15, it shall ipso facto be deemed to have committed an act of war against all other Members of the League, which hereby undertake . . ." But who says that the League Member has resorted to war? Experience shows how difficult this problem is. Nicaragua is a Member of the League. American Marines are fighting there. Is that a war? So much for economic and financial sanctions. As to military sanctions the Council "recommends to the several governments concerned what effective military, naval, or air force the Members of the League shall severally contribute to the armed forces to be used to protect the covenants of the League," but the Members of the League need not follow the Council's recommendation. Finally under the Covenant the Council may fail to agree as to who is the aggressor and then the League action is nullified.

The Protocol shows none of these gaps. The automatic machinery described above is bound to lead to the designation of an aggressor and, this done, Article 11 of the Protocol places on every Signatory State the obligation to apply the sanctions of both paragraphs of Article 16 of the Protocol (the economic and financial as well as the military paragraphs). Article 11 moreover provides an interpretation of these two paragraphs: "Those obligations shall be interpreted as obliging each of the Signatory States to coöperate loyally and effectively in support of the Covenant of the League of Nations and in resistance to any act of aggression in the degree which its geographical position and its particular situation as regards armaments allow." These words should not be read as in any way limiting the sovereignty of States. As M. Beneŝ put it in his explanatory report, *the States remained the judges of what they will do but no longer the judges of what they should do.*

The Protocol moreover goes further than that. Its Article 12 stipulates that economic and financial plans for common action in sanctions shall be prepared forthwith and its Article 13 provides that "The Council shall be entitled to receive undertakings from States determining in advance the military, naval and air forces which they would be able to bring into action immediately to ensure the fulfillment of the obligations in regard to sanctions which result from the Covenant and the present Protocol." Not content with this, the French General Staff obtained further that the second paragraph of the Article should read: "Furthermore, as soon as the Council has called upon the Signatory States to apply sanctions . . . the said States may, in accordance with any previous agreements which they may previously have concluded, bring to the assistance of a particular State which is the victim of aggression, their military, naval and air forces."

III. Disarmament. The Protocol was made dependent on a Disarmament Conference to take place on June 15th, 1925: "If within such a period after the adoption of the plan for the reduction of armaments as shall be fixed by the said Conference, the plan has not been carried out the Council shall make a declaration to that effect; this declaration shall make the present Protocol null and void" (Article 21).

The Protocol is thus the masterpiece whereby the patient constructive genius of France obtains security for her Europe in exchange for disarmament to satisfy British Liberal opinion. The whole instrument is inspired with that deep sense of prevision and distrust of unforeseen events which is an inherent feature of the French character, worked up to an exceptionally high pitch by the peculiar circumstances created by the Peace. By a curious law of psychological reaction, this very fact, obscurely but definitely felt by British instinct, killed the Protocol in England. For England objected both to foresight in itself and to the status quo which such a foresight was destined to protect. British public opinion was loud—is still loud—in its condemnation of the Protocol on the ground that it is an instrument devised for the preservation of the status quo. In the eyes of a detached, but, I hope, friendly observer, such an attitude is somewhat disconcerting, on at least three heads:

The first is that this status quo which revolts the Englishman is his own handiwork. He was not absent while the world was being shaped up in Paris. He was represented. In fact, he was typically represented, for the delegation of what is known in the world as "England" was made up of a Welshman (Mr. Lloyd George), a Scotchman (Lord Balfour), a Scotch-Canadian (Mr. Bonar Law) and a Jew (Lord Reading). The Englishman therefore had his say in Paris, very much of a say. So much of a say that the British Empire came out of the most disinterested war of all enlarged by hundreds of thousands of square miles of what the Manchester Guardian calls "responsibilities" —some of them, in fact most of them, not only "spacious" but rich with a wonderful economic future. Now the Treaty was hammered out in conference and it is obvious that its various parts cannot be judged on their separate merits with no connection whatsoever with the remaining stipulations. In a round table negotiation, all is one and the same, all is inter-related, inter-explained. A concession here bears fruit in an acquisition there; a corridor allowed in the East of Europe blossoms out into a mandate obtained in the West of Africa; and a few well-chosen but tiny provinces bartered away in the center of Europe may be worth a strategic "responsibility" in Asia Minor. But then, why this fuss about the status quo? Is not the status quo one only thing begotten in one only conference? And, if its nose is not worth keeping, can its toes and knees, its belly and its heart itself be more entitled to our respect and affection?

Furthermore, is Great Britain the nation best qualified to throw stones at "status quo's"? Many an honest Briton, usually cool even in the worst period of Anglo-Irish relations, waxes hot at the sight of the Polish corridor. But is it wise that the campaign against corridors should be led by the British, the most ingenious corridor-builders in the world? Is not the British Empire a net-work of corridors, and mighty draughty some of them too? If the liquidation of queer cases of status quo was to begin some day, and if it was to begin by the queerest case of all, would the Polish corridor be the first to be considered? These are questions which Great Britain would do well to ponder on, capitally interested as she is in an international policy truly deserving the name of conservative.

And finally, it is all very well to attack the Protocol because it tends to preserve the status quo. But what lies behind this strange argument? Are we to understand that the enemies of the Protocol would favor a war as a means to do away with the particular Danzig, Saar or Upper Silesia which offends their fastidious eye? The idea would appeal to us as on a par with suggesting a fire in order to improve the architectural features of a defective villa. In point of fact, the present peace settlement is defective because it is the outcome of a war. Would the outcome of another war be any better? And are the strange advocates of the method ready to guarantee that a war to right the wrongs of Eastern Europe would not destroy Western Europe in the process?

The fact is that this often heard argument against the Protocol was not the determining factor in the situation though it added force to Britain's rejection of the scheme. The two main factors which explain this rejection are the position of the United States of America and the psychological attitude of Great Britain herself towards the scheme.

The position of the United States of America was bound to be of the first importance for British statesmen. It is obvious that no nation can lightly assume obligations which may eventually bring her into armed opposition with the United States. Now, the Protocol might have worked automatically in this highly dangerous way. The lonely path followed by the American nation might lead her to take action which the more elastic Covenant would in all likelihood stare blankly at while the more rigid Protocol would have to register as contrary to its tenets. In such a case, the position of Great Britain would not be theoretically worse than that of the remaining members of the League but practically she would have to bear the brunt of the difficulty both in actual responsibilities and in the psychological consequences of the conflict. Now, there is little doubt that the United States of America could not be expected to be friendly to the Protocol. Since their public opinion was not sufficiently educated in its international duties to accept the Covenant, how could it be expected to accept an i-dotted and t-crossed Covenant such as the Protocol was? The attitude of American public opinion was well illustrated by the reactions called forth when the Japanese amendment was discussed. The purport of this amendment could not be more inoffensive. It merely removes the *presumption* of aggression in the case of a State which happens to be at war after the Court has declared the dispute to be reserved under domestic jurisdiction if the State in question has first submitted the case to the Council or to the Assembly under Article 11 of the Covenant, i.e., on a procedure of conciliation. The position may be summed up as follows (names of nations blurted out for the sake of plain speaking):

(a) Japan is involved in a conflict with the United States of America. In virtue of Article 17 of the Covenant and of Article 16 of the Protocol, she refers the matter to arbitration under the Protocol and invites the United States of America to adopt the same procedure.

(b) U. S. A. accepts.

(c) If U. S. A. claims the dispute to arise out of a matter which by international law is solely within her domestic jurisdiction, the arbitrators are bound by Article 5 of the Protocol to take the advice of the World Court on this point and to abide by it. Should the Court agree with U. S. A. the matter rests there.

(d) *If then a war arises* between U. S. A. and Japan, Japan may not be *presumed* to be the aggressor if she has previously requested the Council or the Assembly to take up the matter again with a view to conciliation, according to Article 11 in the procedure of which no decision can be binding on the parties unless they have concurred in it. Japan may be found out to be the aggressor even in such a case but she may not be presumed to be so.

Now, in spite of this, and in spite also of the fact that Japan is, from fear of Chinese labor, at least as anxious as the United States to keep immigration matters reserved under the plea of domestic jurisdiction, the Japanese amendment was first-class "news" to American correspondents in Geneva in 1924. There is no question that the dramatic element which constitutes ninety per cent. of the news value of events was more abundant in it than in the truly substantial parts of the Protocol. But while the masses were caught by the Japanese episode, the more conscious leaders of politics in Washington reaped the harvest of sovereignty which was at hand. The United States remained disentangled.

Which of course made it easier and more reasonable that England should remain disentangled also. For the fact is that neither of the ingenious and at times amusing reasons given in the British official answer are any more than intellectual "superstructures" sincerely and honestly held, yet superstructures explaining a posteriori an opposition springing from the subconscious being of England. England turned down the Protocol because she is not yet ready to give up or even to qualify or in any way to hinder her freedom of action. While France intellectualistic, foreseeing and relatively weak, saw in the Protocol a juridical prop to her power, England, empirical, strong, felt in it a shackle for her liberty. The outcry in England about putting the British fleet at the beck and call of a council of foreigners (it is one of the worst drawbacks of international life that it cannot be carried on without foreigners) is characteristic in this respect. The argument is of course valueless. Sanctions can only be applied by an unanimous vote of the Council and Great Britain as a Permanent Member of the Council need not vote herself to participate in sanctions unless she wishes to do so. But though hopelessly wrong the argument is significant of the way thought was moved by instinct at the time. In the last analysis, though the words were *peace* and *coöperation* the thoughts and still more so the instincts were *power* and *rivalry*.

Hence France's insistence on sanctions and England's dodging of arbitration. For France, sanctions meant more soldiers at her disposal in case of need. For England, compulsory arbitration meant less freedom in the use of her fleet as an instrument of policy. The claims could not be reconciled and the Protocol was born dead.

Chapter VIII

THE INDIRECT METHOD (*Continued*)

LOCARNO

DEATH however is not an idea on which the British mind cares to rest. There is a deep-lying healthy instinct in Britain which bids her go forward and seek a positive expression. Just as Mr. Ramsay MacDonald put forward the Protocol a few months after he had killed the Treaty of Guarantee, Sir Austen Chamberlain adumbrated Locarno in the very peroration of the Balfourian elegy which he sang melodiously over the tomb of the Protocol. "Since the general provisions of the Covenant cannot be stiffened with advantage, and since the 'extreme cases' with which the League may have to deal will probably affect certain nations or groups of nations more nearly than others, His Majesty's Government conclude that the best way of dealing with the situation is, with the coöperation of the League, to supplement the Covenant by making special arrangements in order to meet special needs. That these arrangements should be purely defensive in character, that they should be framed in the spirit of the Covenant, working in close harmony with the League and under its guidance, is manifest. And, in the opinion of His Majesty's Government, these objects can be best attained by knitting together the nations most immediately concerned and whose differences might lead to a renewal of strife, by means of treaties framed with the sole object of maintaining, as between themselves, an unbroken peace."

Thus the wheel had turned and English thought was now putting forward the advantages of "special treaties" once dear to France, while French thought advocated an universal treaty, once dear to England. The chorus of other nations, patiently waiting to see what the hero and the prima donna were to do before deciding whether they were to weep or laugh, kept cautiously grinning, wondering how the two protagonists would agree when they could so easily exchange their rôles. Yet there was of course a distinct progress both in the central idea put forward and in the entity on behalf of which it was advanced. We were no longer listening to a dialogue between two free-lances, M. de Jouvenel and Lord Robert Cecil. France was speaking through M. Briand and England through Sir Austen Chamberlain, both Foreign Secretaries. And moreover, the "special treaties" suggested by Sir Austen Chamberlain were no longer treaties between friends to guarantee each other against aggression (otherwise alliances) but treaties between would-be adversaries entering into a mutual pledge not to resort to war. Such are the reasons which justify the view often heard in Geneva that the Locarno Treaties are in fact the direct result of the Protocol. A comprehensive view of world politics from 1925 onwards would consider Locarno as one of the elements in a kind of post-Protocol which would be to the Protocol itself what the spectrum of the seven lights is to the light of the sun. Split by circumstances as crystallized in the British opposition, the Protocol remains coloring world politics with its separate components: the period thus gives rise to the following lines of activity:

(1) The Locarno Treaties and Conventions, which amounted to the local application of the Protocol minus disarmament.

(2) A study of the measures which might be immediately acceptable towards an extension of arbitration and conciliation methods in special cases and between small groups of nations—which amounts to the application of as much of the arbitration part of the Protocol as the world is ready to assimilate.

(3) A study of the measures which might be immediately acceptable towards increasing the faith in and value of the Articles of the Covenant more directly connected with peace—also an effort towards applying the security and sanctions part of the Protocol.

(4) A study of the measures of disarmament which might be immediately acceptable in view of the added security created by the Treaties of Locarno—which of course corresponds to the disarmament part of the Protocol.

We are to see points 2, 3 and 4 above taken up by a special Commission and its ancillary organizations. Point 1 was dealt with direct by the governments which, on the statesmanlike initiative of the German Foreign Secretary Dr. Stresemann, met in Locarno towards the end of the year 1925.

THE LOCARNO TREATIES AND CONVENTIONS

Much as the detached observer may regret that the Protocol should have been branded by its enemies as a scheme in the clouds and insulted with the scathing criticism that it was the work of idealists, it is but fair to acknowledge the great service rendered the world by Dr. Stresemann, M. Briand and Sir Austen Chamberlain when they showed in Locarno that disarmament is but one of the aspects of politics and that, even if good principles must wait, a political good job is a good job for all that. It would be foolish to imagine that all will be well with the world when a bridge of mutual faith and amity has been built and consolidated across the Rhine, but still more foolish to minimize the importance of the Franco-German difficulty as one of the main lines of stress in the world's net of difficulties.

The system of treaties and conventions known as Locarno aims at something more than the solution of the Rhine question. In its essentials it may be described as the application of the ideas and tendencies which shaped the Protocol to the area of possible conflicts lying west, south and east of Germany. Locarno comprises under the general "roof" of its final protocol (acte final) the following instruments:

I.—1. Treaty between Germany, Belgium and France, Great Britain and Italy.

—2. (a) Arbitration Convention between Germany and Belgium.

(b) Arbitration Convention between Germany and France.

—3. (a) Arbitration Convention between Germany and Poland.

(b) Arbitration Convention between Germany and Czechoslovakia.

II.—1. Treaty between France and Poland.

—2. Treaty between France and Czechoslovakia.

III.—Letter to the German Government on Article 16.

The full understanding of the system and its value requires a brief analysis of each of these groups of instruments.

I. This group comprises the five instruments which in a strict and narrow sense constitute the Locarno system: i.e., those which all the parties approve and declare to be mutually interdependent. They comprise:

—1. The Treaty between Germany, Belgium, France, Great Britain and Italy. This treaty provides that:

Germany, France and Belgium undertake to respect their present frontiers.

Germany, France and Belgium undertake not to attack or invade each other nor resort to war against each other.

The following cases are excepted from this general denunciation of war:

Legitimate defense as resistance to violation of frontiers or of the articles of the Treaty of Versailles (42 and 43) which demilitarize the Rhine zone.

Action in pursuance of Article 16 of the Covenant, i.e., League action against a Covenant-breaking State.

Action in pursuance of Article 15, paragraph 7 of the Covenant, i.e., failure of the Council to reach agreement on a conflict provided it is taken against a State which was the first to attack.

Germany, France and Belgium undertake to settle all their conflicts without exception by peaceful means.

England and Italy guarantee the execution of the above undertakings and pledge themselves to come to the assistance of the victims of the breach upon being notified of the breach by the League Council or in case of flagrant breach on being satisfied that it constitutes an unprovoked act of aggression.

The rights and obligations of the Covenant remain intact.

—2. Arbitration Convention between Germany and Belgium and between Germany and France. These Conventions provide the principles and machinery whereby the disputes between the contracting parties are to be settled. Their essential features are the following:

No disputes of any kind are excepted.

The usual distinction is made between questions as to rights (for which some positive, general textual basis exists) and conflicts of a political nature. Those of the first category must be submitted to the World Court or to an arbitral tribunal. The parties may also agree to submit the matter to the Permanent Conciliation Commission hereafter described with a view to an amicable settlement failing which the World Court's jurisdiction is compulsory.

Conflicts of the second category, i.e., political conflicts, must be submitted to the Permanent Conciliation Commission created in virtue of the Treaty. This Commission comprises one member from each of the two parties and three other members (of which the president) chosen by the parties in three other different nationalities; should this Commission fail, any of the parties may bring the question at issue before the Council which will settle it under Article 15 of the Covenant.

The Conventions stipulate that the Arbitration Court, the League Council, the Permanent Court or the Permanent Conciliation Commission as the case may be shall lay down within the shortest possible time the provisional measures to be adopted should the question arise out of acts already committed or on the point of being committed. The parties undertake to accept such measures and to abstain from actions likely to influence adversely the peaceful settlement of the dispute.

—3. Conventions between Germany and Poland and between Germany and Czechoslovakia. In their actual clauses these Conventions are identical with the Belgian and French Conventions. They differ however in their preamble. Instead of the short and bald statement which precedes the Conventions with Belgium and France, the Polish and Czechoslovakian Conventions are introduced by a more elaborate declaration destined to cover with a plank of pious principles the gap left by the absence of a treaty of non-aggression and guarantee similar to that which Great Britain and Italy agreed to sign in the case of France and Belgium.

II. Treaties between France and Poland and between France and Czechoslovakia. In virtue of these treaties, France pledges herself to come to the help of Poland and Czechoslovakia if and when

(a) Article 16 of the Covenant is to be applied owing to a breach of the above Treaty and Conventions.

(b) In the event of an unprovoked attack under Article 15, paragraph 7 when the Council has failed to reach an unanimous decision on the dispute and the matter remains open.

III. Letter to the German Government. This letter is an interpretation of Article 16 of the Covenant to meet the case of a disarmed power such as Germany. It merely explains that the duties and obligations of the League Members under Article 16 must be understood in relation to the geographical situation and armed forces of the nation concerned.

Such is the economy of Locarno. It is worth noticing how much it owes to the Protocol. First and foremost, it adopts the principle of peaceful settlement, providing definite machinery in order to ensure a concrete result. Unlike the Protocol, the Locarno system does not exclude the possibility of a deadlock, but it must be noticed that all possibility of war is excluded in the west under threat of armed intervention by Great Britain and Italy as guarantors. Moreover, owing to the provisions of Article 19, that most important of Protocol ideas, the preventive or "conservatory" measures to be taken in order to limit the conflict while the dispute is argued out, is introduced into the Locarno system, not only in the west but in the south and east also. These provisions are of the utmost importance because they contribute in a large measure to force the parties to declare their attitude in the period preceding hostilities so that the would-be aggressor designates itself, so to say, by its own doing while the conflict is before the world. So much for the general principles of the Protocol which underlie Locarno. Considering the grave and concrete issues at stake, their application in so clear and uncompromising a manner to the most sensitive zone in the world must be registered as a great triumph of statesmanship, most of the credit of which undoubtedly belongs to Germany and her leading statesman, Dr. Stresemann.

But the respective tendencies brought to bear by the several participants are no less significant. France, it will be noticed, is still obsessed by a guarantee-sanctions preoccupation. The fear of sudden attack is in her brain. Though having secured the written pledge of Great Britain and Italy in case of breach or unprovoked aggression, she leaves open the possibility of starting off on her own as soon as she is satisfied that a breach or aggression has been committed. This guarantee-sanctions spirit governs both the main Treaty and the treaties which she has appended between herself and her two allies. Yet it should be noted that in what concerns Czechoslovakia and Poland France is shouldering the responsibilities of international loyalties and friendship with a handsome generosity, for there is no question that, with the main Treaty underwritten by Britain and Italy in her pocket, France could have been quite safe had she left her friends to the tender care of Germany.

The second point which deserves attention is that Germany, by declaring her frontiers with Belgium and France inviolable and not so her frontiers with Poland and Czechoslovakia makes Europe's faith in her own stability lose in the east all that it gains in the west. The pious language of the preambles to the Germano-Polish and Germano-Czechoslovakian Conventions does not suffice to hide away the gap. Nor is our feeling made more comfortable by the fact that, on joining the League, Germany assumes the obligations of Article 10 which binds her to respect the territorial integrity and existing political independence of all the Members of the League; for this Article protects the west as well as the east and if Germany means to respect it it is not easy to see why she should have declined to recognize the inviolability of her eastern frontiers in the same breath with that of those of the west though of course she need not have pledged herself to maintaining the status quo. Inviolability to attack does not mean permanence in law. Dr. Beneŝ in his statement to the Permanent Parliamentary Commission of his country (October 30th, 1925) explains this difference in the treatment meted to east and west by the refusal of Great Britain and Italy to guarantee any frontier other than the western but it seems that if Germany had been willing to negotiate with Poland and Czechoslovakia a treaty similar to that concluded with Belgium and France, such a treaty, even without an

Italo-British guarantee would have improved in no small degree the political situation of Europe. No doubt such a treaty was too much to expect in view of the state of political opinion in Germany but the fact as it stands, coupled with the peculiar wording of the German Conventions with Poland and Czechoslovakia, leaves an unpleasant cloud of uncertainty hovering over the east of Europe.

But the most curious attitude of all is that of Great Britain.[1] Germany, after all, was just convalescent from a war in which she had suffered dreadful losses. In stabilizing her western frontiers she accepted a sacrifice which was bound to weigh heavily on her pride and hope; her inability to extend the same treatment—at any rate explicitly—to the east was in the circumstances but natural. Great Britain was not in such a case. She came to Locarno as an honest broker between the parties, a broker moreover ready to contribute in kind to their settlement. What was in fact the value of her contribution? Exactly this: that while according to Articles 10 and 16 of the Covenant she was not *legally* bound to coöperate with her armed forces in repelling an act of aggression against France or Belgium (or against Germany, once Germany had joined the League) she explicitly accepted such a responsibility in Locarno. That in so doing she did something is obvious, since her Locarno partners have expressed their gratitude to her. But is there an honest and in-

[1] Italy followed Great Britain. But of course no one expects Italy in her present mood to take a leading part towards the construction of a world of reason which her own great men foreshadowed in other brighter days.

formed Englishman who thinks that Locarno has added much, if anything, to the actual responsibilities of Great Britain? In my opinion, Articles 10 and 16 combined with the vital interest which Great Britain feels in the preservation of the peace of the Rhine suffice to answer in the negative. A war on the Rhine is a war in England and Great Britain knows it full well. Her underwriting of the Treaty of Guarantee (of Locarno) added nothing to her pre-Locarno commitments.

On the other hand, the careful limits which she set to her contribution cannot but be read in a light detrimental to the sense of confidence which is the true need of the world and of England herself. There are two directions along which Great Britain's abstention in Locarno was, to say the least, unfortunate. The first is her refusal to guarantee an eastern treaty analogous to the western Treaty of Guarantee. What was her risk? The argument invoked above may be repeated here *mutatis mutandis*. Articles 10 and 16 commit Great Britain to a most active and direct part in guaranteeing the frontiers of Poland and of Czechoslovakia as they do in the case of any other Member. Great Britain is the leading Permanent Member of the Council. Such a position of privilege entails corresponding responsibilities and no honest commentator of the Covenant can deny that the responsibilities arising out of Articles 10 and 16 are of the very first importance. Now, it is evident, particularly in view of the Franco-Polish and Franco-Czechoslovakian commitments, that an attack on those frontiers could not remain localized but would bring about a regular European war into which Great Britain would be fatally precipitated. In refusing to guarantee an eastern pact Great Britain casts a shadow over Articles 10 and 16. No doubt it may be argued that legally these two Articles do not go so far. But we are dealing with faith which is one of the most delicate of imponderabilia in politics and Great Britain's action in this case, following closely upon her decision not to ratify the Protocol, was bound to result in disastrous moral effects. The first was a general and diffuse weakening of the Covenant guarantees; the second an encouragement to those who feel that the Eastern European settlement is too precarious. These two effects, combined with the fatal solidarity which links together European affairs, constitute a far greater risk of war for Great Britain than a definite pledge to go to war if trouble arose would have been, while such a pledge would have removed a violent solution of the Eastern difficulty from the field of practical politics.

Moreover, curiously enough, neither Great Britain nor Italy is mentioned at all in Article 2 of the Treaty of Guarantee, which they both signed, whereby: "Germany and Belgium and also Germany and France, mutually undertake that they will in no case attack or invade each other or resort to war against each other." Now why this self-effacement? It seems that the names of Italy and Great Britain, two ex-enemies of Germany, would have been at their place in this remarkable text. To guarantee that others will not fight is admirable, but to pledge oneself not to fight would have been more admirable still. The determination to evade all self-denying ordinances, all bounds to her international freedom of action, seems evident on the part of Great Britain in Locarno. And here again, this example coming as it did from the apex of international society was to have deplorable effects on the morale of the world.

Chapter IX

THE RETURN TO THE DIRECT METHOD

THE PREPARATORY COMMISSION

THE Sixth Assembly had behind it the death of the Protocol and ahead of it the birth of the doves of Locarno. It had to weep with one eye and to be merry with the other. In these exacting circumstances, it chose for its spokesman the only man nimble enough for the task. Señor Quiñones de León, Spanish Ambassador in Paris and the representative of Spain in the Council and in the Assembly, is a living proof of the fact that the diplomat is not made but born. He is one of the few Spanish ambassadors who do not belong to what Foreign Offices know as "the Career" or "the Service." But he is a diplomat for all that. So that the Sixth Assembly approved the draft resolution which he proposed to take stock of the past and to prepare for the future. Not that what was then known as the Spanish Resolution means anything in its actual words. But then the actual words of League Assembly resolutions, like the actual words of prayers, incantations, love-letters and other important utterances are as irrelevant as the chemical formulæ of medical prescriptions. What matters is their effect on the body politic, religion, magic, amorous or physical on which they are expected to act. Señor Quiñones de León's resolution was drafted in terms of so magical a power that the grave divergencies of the first days of the Assembly were merged into an exact concord and frowns flourished into smiles. The French wanted some kind of revival of the Protocol; Sir Austen Chamberlain was anxious that nothing should be done which might impair or even handicap the happy event which he was expecting in Locarno; the Resolution handicapped nothing, while, if it did not actually revive anything, it prevented the revival of nothing. The Assembly moreover discussed with its usual thoroughness a most important matter: was it better to start preparations for a disarmament conference straight away in anticipation of the happy effects of the coming Locarno agreements on the feeling of security, or should we wait till the wings of the Locarno doves had cooled our feverish heads with the gentle gales of peace? The Assembly decided to invite the Council to start work at once. This decision implied notable changes both in method and in the constitution of the organs which were to carry out the work.

The Temporary Mixed Commission had disappeared a year earlier. The Council, dominated to an extraordinary extent by the opinions of their military advisors, the sum total of which compose the Permanent Advisory Commission on Military, Naval and Air Affairs, had never been able to show much sympathy for a Commission such as the "Temporary," created if not in actual antagonism at least as an alternative organization to the permanent and military body. The "Temporary" moreover had fulfilled the purpose for which it had been created. The Treaty of Guarantee was its direct, the Protocol its indirect, offspring. Disarmament had now entered into a more official phase and what was wanted was a committee composed of accredited government representatives with powers to negotiate. During 1924-25 the work of disarmament was theoretically entrusted to a commission described as the Coördination Commission. It was a lamentable failure from the very outset, owing, not to its personnel—for after all the men were always the same whatever their status—but to a defective constitution. Its nucleus was the so-called Committee of the Council or Council in Committee, a body composed of Council-member-understudies and which did not seem to know exactly how far it was the Council itself and how far it was a mere advisory committee to the Council. Round this vaguely constituted body, composed at any rate of government representatives, the military, financial, economic, labor and employer experts of the extinguished Temporary had been gathered in a no less vague and shadowy capacity, for no one knew exactly how far they could vote nor even how far they could discuss what the exalted members of the Council Committee had decided. The Commission was an interesting though unsuccessful experiment, interesting precisely because of its failure. It helped the Council to avoid not a few mistakes in the organization which it was to set up in pursuance of the decisions of the Sixth Assembly.

The Council had then to bear in mind:

—That the work was to be mainly political and kept in hand by responsible government representatives.

—That many questions would be raised which would necessitate technical debates for which the government representatives would have neither the competence nor the inclination nor, last but not least, the time.

—That there were undoubted advantages to be derived from keeping in touch with certain experts who had participated in the disarmament work of the League from the beginning—thus for instance the nominees of the Labor and Employer Groups of the International Labor Office.

The solution adopted met all these requirements adequately. A Preparatory Commission for the Disarmament Conference was set up, composed of the representatives of:

(a) The Governments of the Nations represented in the Council.

(b) A certain number of other Governments adequately selected by the Council to make the Commission fully alive to all local problems presenting distinctive characteristics.

The Commission was provided with two advisory technical bodies:

(a) The Permanent Advisory Commission for Military, Naval and Air Matters, normally composed of the military, naval and air experts of the Council Members but which when acting as the auxiliary organization of the Preparatory Commission was extended to include similar representatives from all the Governments represented in its principal.

(b) A "Joint Commission" composed of experts from the Economic, Financial and Transit organizations of the League and of nominees of the Labor and Employer Groups of the International Labor Office Governing Body.

The United States of America and the Union of Socialist Sovietist Republics were invited to join this organization. The United States of America accepted and the Soviet Union also joined as soon as its difficulties with the Swiss Confederation enabled them to tread on Swiss territory with self-respect. But the coöperation of the United States of America had to be paid for with a heavy sacrifice. The American Delegation expressed their stern determination not to coöperate with the Permanent Advisory Commission on Military, Naval and Air Affairs which was a League organization and therefore untouchable for American people. This was a serious difficulty. The League however rose to the occasion and, with a fine sense of generosity and of the importance to be attached to the coöperation of the United States in the gravest of all the world problems, suggested that the technical Military Commission, while remaining identical in its composition, secretariat and powers, should be re-named "Sub-Commission A." The American Delegation responded with an admirable spirit of conciliation to this generous offer and the crisis was averted. The Commission was able to come to business.[1] But what was that business to be? The

[1] A Sub-Commission B. had also to be set up because the American Delegation refused to recognize the Joint Commission, also tainted in their eyes with too close an acquaintance with the League of Nations. Sub-Commission B. dealt theoretically with economic and

matter was the object of a long and passionate debate in a session of the Committee of the Council, which had been entrusted with the duty of drawing up the agenda of the Permanent Commission. Needless to say, the protagonists were France and England; needless to say, the respective positions were the same. Lord Cecil, this time a fully accredited British representative, wished to concentrate on disarmament, i.e., wished the Commission to adopt the direct method. M. Paul-Boncour, speaking for France, endeavored to widen the scope of the enquiry in order to lead to the inevitable conclusion that disarmament was dependent on a system of international coöperation for maintaining the peace of the world. The setting was different but the dialogue was the same. "Disarmament," said Great Britain. "Security," France answered. In actual fact, the argument manifested itself in three ways:

A difference as to what it was that was to be limited: "Peace armaments," said England, "War armaments," said France;

A difference as to whether the efficiency of the system of sanctions should or should not be improved in order to stimulate disarmament;

A difference as to a system for the international

financial matters. It never did a stroke of work and was a mere fifth wheel put there merely to save the face of the American Delegation. It is a curious example of the disadvantages to which a nation will submit for the sake of prejudice that the United States of America denied herself the opportunity to work in the Joint Commission where much of the best disarmament work was done merely owing to its, may we say, bigoted objection to the name and some of the outward aspects of the League.

supervision of the observance of the Convention by all its signatories.

Traces of this duel remain in the program of work which the Committee of the Council finally drafted. This program was the outcome of a compromise between drafts presented by Lord Cecil and by M. Paul-Boncour completed here and there with ideas from a memorandum presented by Señor Cobián, a Spanish delegate. It contained seven questions: the first on definitions: what are armaments? What are the elements of war power and those of the different kinds of arms in time of peace? The second on what is to be limited. Peace strength or war strength? What is, and what forms can take the reduction or limitation of armaments? The third on the standards by which armaments can be measured: the fourth on whether there is any method for ascertaining that a force is organized for aggression or for defense. The fifth on the principle which might be used as a basis for a scale of armaments; here, amongst such criteria as population, resources, geographical situation and what not the French succeeded in inserting the following paragraph: "the degree of security which in the event of aggression a State could receive under the provisions of the Covenant or of separate engagements contracted towards that State."

Not content with this, they asked that the Commission should study the measures which might increase the efficiency of the League sanctions against the aggressor. The perseverance, nay, the persistence of the French

General Staff intent on extracting the last ounce of military efficiency out of the Covenant was admirable. Lord Cecil held his ground. In the end, a compromise was drafted in a curious form which betrays the impatient and exasperated surrender of a parent to an insistent and unreasonable child: "Can the reduction of armaments be promoted by examining possible means for ensuring that the mutual assistance, economic and military, contemplated in Article 16 of the Covenant shall be brought quickly into operation as soon as an act of aggression has been committed?"

The sixth question deals with aircraft. Is there any device by which civil and military aircraft can be distinguished for purposes of disarmament and if not how can the value of civil aircraft be computed in estimating the air strength of a country? This question was most interesting because it originated in the British delegation, which of course means in the General Staff of the British Air Force, revealing the misgivings with which British airmen saw the formidable strength of France's air defenses. But in putting this question, the British Delegation ran counter to their own principle, i.e., that it was useless to enter into a discussion of civil strength convertible into military strength and thereby gave the French an excellent argument for their war potential controversy. The French, singularly ungrateful, pocketed the advantage and added insult to injury by avenging at sea the British onslaught in the air; they suggested a rather searching, in fact positively indiscreet question as to the military value of commercial fleets, a question which, after much gallant argument, was reduced under British pressure to the following form: "Is it possible to attach military value to commercial fleets in estimating the naval armaments of a country?"

A seventh question bearing on the possibilities and virtues of regional disarmament closed this comprehensive program.

Seven is not a bad number. It can boast of an esoteric pedigree at least equal to that enjoyed by *one* and by *three;* yet this illustrious number failed to satisfy the Preparatory Commission and the first result of its debates was not to answer the questions put to it but to add to their number. A French proposal was examined, directed of course towards a definite study of means for increasing the efficiency of the Covenant as an instrument of security; its object was

(1) To establish methods or regulations which would facilitate the meeting of the Council in case of war or threat of war.

(2) To enable the Council to take such decisions as might be necessary to enforce the obligations of the Covenant as expeditiously as possible.

(3) To investigate procedure for the rapid drafting of recommendations regarding the military assistance provided for by Article 16 of the Covenant and measures for preventing hostilities.

(4) To study measures which would enable the Council to give most rapidly such economic and financial help as might be necessary to a State which had been attacked.

A most valuable rider to this proposition and one of

the most sensible contributions made to the work was presented by the Finnish Delegation: that a study should be made of the means whereby financial assistance could be provided when an emergency occurred to a State victim of an attack. A Polish proposal was also examined suggesting a definite organization of regional assistance in combination with regional disarmament.

It will be noticed that the Commission, though definitely created in order to tackle the problem of disarmament direct, could not get away from the problem of security. The insistence of the French was no doubt the determining cause of this recurrence of the theme of security right across the symphony—or rather polyphony—of disarmament. But who could deny that the relation between the two is inherent in the problems at stake? The most dramatic demonstration of this objective law, i.e., the mutual intimacy of the two problems of disarmament and security, was still to come. The Preparatory Commission however could not shirk the main task for which it had been appointed. Had it done so the German Delegation would not have tolerated it. Germany had by now joined the League thereby increasing security to a considerable extent, particularly after Locarno. She could claim the right to ask for a corresponding measure of disarmament. The Germans insisted time and again that, as the preamble to Part V of the Treaty of Versailles proved, the disarmament of the defeated powers was in itself a factor of security which demanded a corresponding element of disarmament on the part of her ex-enemies. Nor, in all fairness, can it be said that the members of the Commission sought to shirk the fulfillment of their main task. Faced with the complications which the security problem brought to bear upon it the Commission adopted a practical method: it split the work; it kept Disarmament proper and sent back the questions more directly concerning Security to the Council Committee. In this way, the problem, which in its widest sense had been reduced to an organic unit in the Protocol, was now divided as follows:

(1) Problems of arbitration, conciliation and judiciary settlement, studied by the successive Assemblies and eventually by the Commission on Arbitration and Security created later.

(2) Problems of security, studied by the Council Committee, its advisory organizations, and the Committee on Arbitration and Security.

(3) Disarmament proper, studied by the Preparatory Commission itself.

Chapter X

PEACEFUL SETTLEMENT

OF the three parts which compose the Protocol, Disarmament is but a consequence and Security but a state of mind. "Arbitration," i.e., the peaceful settlement of all disputes whatsoever is not only an indispensable condition for Security and Disarmament but also an aim in itself and, it may even be argued, a truly essential aim of the League of Nations. When therefore M. Unden, the Swedish delegate in 1925, having taken note of Great Britain's refusal to ratify the Protocol, proposed to the Assembly that the Council be asked to resume the study of the principles of compulsory arbitration set forth in the first part of the Protocol, he was like a true pilot setting the new course for the World Ship. His proposal, however, was considered too bold. The Japanese moreover were particularly anxious to advance the claims of Conciliation, probably owing to the fact that Arbitration and Judicial Settlement break their teeth against the hard granite of "domestic jurisdiction." Other delegations were no less anxious to promote a kind of general enquiry into the progress of peaceful settlement in the world before new proposals were made for its furtherance. The Council was thus invited to undertake the study of the question in a general and non-committal way.

A survey made by the League Secretariat puts at 85 the number of arbitration, conciliation and mixed (arbitration plus conciliation) treaties registered with the Secretariat at the date of February 1st, 1922. The number of nations in the world is about 60. If all of them were linked up two by two with treaties of this kind there would be 1,770 of them. We are therefore a long way yet from such a fool-proof system of peaceful settlement. But of course a net-work of treaties of this kind would be but a clumsy substitute for an universal convention which more than once has been proposed and more than once rejected in Geneva. A remark must be made in alleviation and another one in aggravation of the position thus revealed. It is evident that there are many theoretically possible treaties with but a negligible practical importance: thus a treaty of compulsory arbitration between Latvia and Paraguay or between New Zealand and Siam would not materially alter the sense of security nor even particularly enhance the moral tone of the community of nations. On the other hand, due account must be taken of the fact that a certain number of these treaties do not carry peaceful obligations very much farther than the Covenant. According to an American specialist,[1] there are however no less than 25 of these treaties which provide for compulsory arbitration of all disputes whatsoever. It is an important fact, and one which English-speaking readers should note, that though some of these treaties have been concluded by

[1] Mr. Noel Field in a pamphlet prepared for the National Council for the Prevention of War in 1926.

great powers, England is a party to but one (with Uruguay) and the United States of America to none whatsoever.[1]

On the whole, it cannot be doubted that the movement towards peaceful settlement received a powerful stimulus from the work of the Temporary Mixed Commission which ultimately culminated in the Protocol. There was even a danger lest this movement, deprived of its centralizing and unifying agent in Geneva, might lead to a somewhat chaotic "growth" of bilateral and multilateral agreements. This feeling however has been exaggerated, probably in order to justify action of some sort when the only action worth undertaking was out of the realm of immediate possibilities. For, what was the position? The problem of the relations between law and force had been studied. It had led to the Protocol and in particular to its first part. Great Britain with disarming frankness and other nations less openly had refused to consider compulsory arbitration on all questions and the nations of the world, in the absence of a universal solution, went their way seeking local solutions along the line of least resistance. True, this process may lead to overlapping, to waste, and even to a certain number of incompatibilities in some definite cases; but it is difficult to see how any grave danger might arise from unmethodical efforts of arbitration, conciliation and judicial settlement of disputes.

Nevertheless, the feeling grew in Geneva that some-

1 This statement would have to be happily qualified if the Senate ratified the truly statesmanlike treaties prepared by the Pan-American Conference in December 1928-January 1929.

thing was needed in order to bring some unity and some order into this most encouraging movement towards the peaceful settlement of disputes. And thus it is that when the Commission on Arbitration and Security was created in 1927 one of the first tasks which it received from its principal—the Preparatory Commission—was the study of the measures which would make it possible for the League of Nations to promote and to coördinate special or collective agreements on arbitration and conciliation.

Quite rightly the Commission interpreted its task in a purely practical and utilitarian way. Since the object for which it had been created was to pave the way for an easier, or at any rate less difficult, agreement on disarmament, it did not waste its time in examining the best theoretical method for solving all conflicts by peaceful means; it concentrated on the forms of international conciliation, arbitration and/or judicial settlement which would be acceptable to States. The work of the Committee led to three draft general conventions; and three draft bilateral conventions. In each case (general or bilateral) the three types are respectively:

a. Pacific settlement of all disputes. The League disputes are submitted compulsorily to a judicial or arbitral settlement and optionally to a preliminary procedure of conciliation; the non-legal disputes are submitted compulsorily to a procedure of conciliation, failing which they are submitted compulsorily to an arbitral tribunal composed of five members.

b. Conciliation, arbitration and judicial settlement.

The first category of disputes, namely legal disputes, is dealt with as in Convention A. But the second, the non-legal ones, if and when conciliation fails, is left to the more elastic procedure of Article 15 of the Covenant completed by Article 17 if one of the parties concerned is still outside the League of Nations.

c. The conciliation convention. In this type all disputes are to be submitted to conciliation.

Nothing more elastic, more respectful of the conservative feelings of some States could have been devised. The path of reasonableness, the true path of renunciation of war, which is the path of acceptance of justice, is made easy for those who dislike it with an admirable spirit of patience and consideration for the weaknesses of the strong. For, it must be noted, it is the strongest who are the weakest. Thus, of the Big Powers, only Germany has subscribed to the optional clause of the Court Statute, accepting the Court compulsory jurisdiction.[1]

The Committee went out of their way to remind States that the clause may be accepted with specific reservations excluding certain points from its operation. But the fact remains that the Great Powers do not bind themselves. Now, this is one of the worst features in the situation. It is surely unpleasant to see that when small nations without a judge in the Hague ac-

[1] The position of France is not clear. She accepted the clause subject to the Protocol entering in force. But the Protocol being legally dead, France's acceptance would seem to be null and void. Yet her representatives have more than once referred to France as having signed the optional clause. Spain has signed and ratified the optional clause of compulsory jurisdiction without reservations (September, 1928).

cept the jurisdiction of the Court and trust it, and while Germany, with a number of questions pending on which she might some day wish to seek a solution by force of arms or even by the operation of political power, also subscribes to the compulsory jurisdiction of the Court in which she has as yet no judge, countries such as the United States of America, Great Britain, France, Italy and Japan with judges in the Court refuse to bind themselves. The Court has proved its ability and its qualities. It has shown itself impartial, competent and dignified. Its compulsory jurisdiction, moreover, would not cover political questions, i.e., questions on which there were no legal or contractual texts to interpret, no facts to ascertain; there seems to be no other reason for withholding adhesion than the desire to maintain an intact and unfettered freedom of action in order to bring the power of the nation to bear even on problems recognized as having a judicial as opposed to a political character. This deplorable example coming from the top is one of the chief causes of stagnation in the evolution of international life towards higher ethical levels. It must be considered as one of the main obstacles on the path to disarmament.

Chapter XI

SECURITY

SECURITY is the ideal of the insecure. It is therefore a purely subjective ideal and as such it has proved most fertile in the international world, for it has given rise to the most varied forms of argument and to the most ingenious and self-renovating proposals.

It began to manifest its creative capacity at the Peace Conference with the suggestion that an Anglo-American pact should be signed guaranteeing France against attack. Later on it inspired the articles of the Covenant dealing with war, threat of war, and sanctions. It impressed its views on the discussions which led up to the Treaty of Guarantee. It reached its climax with the Protocol. But when, the Protocol shelved, the League endeavored to capitalize Locarno in terms of disarmament, security, which some thought satisfied for the time being with the serene atmosphere of Locarno, showed again its anxious face, and its arguments took not one but several forms.

First, it was asked that a study should be made of the means whereby the relevant articles of the Covenant might be strengthened so as to increase the sense of security and thereby lead to further disarmament beyond that which might be consented on the strength of Locarno and of the Covenant. Then, right in the midst of disarmament proper it was pointed out that a reduction of actual armaments without due consideration of potential armaments would act unfairly against nations economically and financially weak. The argument cuts in both directions: it renders singularly complicated all discussions of a technical nature as to what is to be limited; thus the question of war potential is brought to the forefront; this question has been the object of much humorous comment by people who did not understand it or who did not wish to understand it; it has often been misrepresented as an attempt to limit the economic and financial power of nations; because a manufacture of sewing-machines, it was argued, can be turned into a manufacture of machine guns it is preposterous to suggest that sewing-machine manufactures should be limited. Of course it is preposterous, but no one ever suggested such a thing. Obviously the economic and financial power of a nation is amongst the chief sources of potential military power which the nation possesses. It is evident that a nation with a powerful iron and steel industry, with numerous motor-car and sewing-machine manufactures, can reduce its artillery and its rifle brigades with an easier heart than a nation whose main production consists in tomatoes or cane sugar. But no one suggests that in order to make disarmament possible the first nation should reduce its iron and steel furnaces. What is asked is that countries economically strong should recognize that the more the world disarms the more, all other things being equal, grows their own power; and, that being recognized, it is only logical to conclude that in all fairness something must be found to compensate other nations for the loss of relative power which they incur in disarmament. This something is obvious, and the Security School sees it with its usual acumen: that all power to coerce should henceforth be put at the disposal of the community and no longer be wielded by the unlimited sovereignty of the powerful nations. Hence that most admirable of definitions of disarmament: disarmament is an agreement between all the nations as to the uses to which they will put their armaments.[1] In actual fact this argument leads to the same conclusion as the first. Something must be done straight away but we might enquire as to how much could be done if we strengthened the Covenant articles which deal with international coöperation for keeping the peace. Security however had still to suggest two other definite problems, both raised in the course of the work of the Preparatory Commission: one was the question of Chemical Warfare, the other that of Civil Aviation. Both are in their essence problems of war potential, but by the exceptional importance of the particular weapons in question, both were bound to receive a special treatment by a commission on which technical military thought exerted a predominant influence.

•
• •

The question of the actual value of the articles of the Covenant is almost as old as the Covenant itself. An

[1] This definition is the more valuable for coming from an out-and-out believer in what I have described here as the pacifist school, Professor Hull.

examination of the varied fortunes which the several articles of the Covenant have undergone under the tender cares of statesmen and jurists would be out of place here. Our concern is not with legal texts and theories but with the tendencies at work as they operate in those articles more particularly connected with the problem of security. They cover the series between Articles 10 and 21. Here as everywhere the tendencies may be reduced to two main forces plus a certain number of eddies. The main forces are: that which points to a limitation and if possible a reduction of the meaning of the Covenant, and that which would dot the i's and cross the t's of the Covenant, of the rights it defines and particularly of the obligations it imposes. There is no question that the early campaign against Article 10 leading up as it did to a restricting interpretation was one of the causes of the present skepticism as to the practical value of the Covenant. Nor is theoretical interpretation the worst evil in this respect. The fact that Canada should have been the initiator of the movement, nay the State to propose that the articles should be altogether suppressed, is highly significant. Here as in many other cases, the concern of not a few League Members is lest they may be put by the Covenant in a position antagonistic to the United States of America. Add that the Article if rightly enforced would have stood in the way of "enterprising" nations other than the United States of America. The result is that Article 10 stands, though somewhat weakened (more in its spirit than in its actual meaning) by interpretation and that moreover events have reduced its meaning to very little indeed. There are at least two concrete cases in point: one, that of Nicaragua, in which a League Member has evidently lost both its political independence and its territorial integrity without calling forth any help from the League; the other is that of Albania, a country whose political independence has been much reduced by the conclusion of a treaty with Italy which can hardly be deemed to be in harmony with the Covenant. Nor is the Italo-British Treaty over the head of Abyssinia a more palatable example. In the three instances the proof that the letter of the case is compatible with the letter of the Covenant is not altogether beyond the means of a well-appointed jurist; in the three examples the spirit of Article 10 of the Covenant is evidently violated.

Being in the nature of a general principle, Article 10 was bound to deteriorate in this early stage of the World-Community, when the general interest not being sufficiently felt by all, everybody's business is nobody's business. But while "enterprising" powers too fond of adventures and prudent nations too much afraid of them watered it down, nations bent on security concentrated their efforts on Article 16. This Article however had also been closely watched by the powers desirous of maintaining as full a freedom as possible within the Covenant. The Assembly of 1921, following up the labors of a "blockade" committee, had suggested a series of amendments to Article 16 the general tenor of which was towards dilution. Further, in anticipation of possible delays in the ratification of these amendments, the Assembly had adopted a resolution whereby the amendments in question were recommended to the Council and to the Members of the League as "rules for guidance in connection with the application of Article 16." The question remained in vague abeyance. It is there still. Yet, the general consensus has given a kind of moral ratification to two general principles: the first, embodied in the 4th resolution of 1921 is to the following effect: "It is the duty of each Member of the League to decide for itself whether a breach of the Covenant has been committed. The fulfillment of their duties under Article 16 is required from Members of the League by the express terms of the Covenant and they cannot neglect them without breach of their treaty obligations."

The second flows from the terms of the Article itself and particularly from a comparison between its first and its second paragraphs: it amounts to a difference in degree as to the economic and financial measures of coercion (first paragraph) and the military measures (second paragraph) to be taken against a Covenant-breaking State; while the obligation to apply the first, known as the economic and financial sanctions, is automatically assumed by League Members as soon as they acknowledge the existence of a breach, military cooperation in sanctions depends on the sovereign decision of the State concerned.

Both these principles, generally admitted as they are to-day, weaken the Article in so far as it constitutes a deterrent against would-be Covenant-breakers. Both were the object of special attention on behalf of the Security School. The Treaty of Guarantee and the

Geneva Protocol had no other aim. The Locarno System was devised as a remedy for this defect in a definite area of the world. Not content with this triumph, the French succeeded in raising the question again before the Preparatory Commission. Amongst the concrete proposals which they put forward under this head, the following was to attract special attention: "That methods or regulations should be investigated which would . . . enable the Council to take such decisions as may be necessary to enforce the obligations of the Covenant as expeditiously as possible."

This point, when taken up by the Committee of the Council, was entrusted to Senator De Brouckère, a Belgian senator who combines a lucid mind with political wisdom, a happy though rare combination. The effect of his report was to shift the question from Article 16 to Article 11.

Now, the difference between these two articles is that between cure and prevention. While Article 16 seeks to meet the evil of war by measures of a grave character—indeed so grave a character that some are tempted to apply to this Article the Spanish saying that the remedy is worse than the evil—Article 11 provides for means whereby the evil may be averted ere it is too late. It is therefore a fundamental article and one drafted in a most statesmanlike spirit.

The conclusions of Senator De Brouckère as adopted by the Council Committee and later by the Council and the Assembly need not be outlined here in detail. They do not add anything to the substance of the Article, as indeed they could not do without going through the tedious process of amending the Covenant. They constitute a kind of set of rules or rather a schedule of suggestions which without limiting in any way the wide freedom wisely granted the Council under this Article, may give it guidance and suggestions to deal with specific cases.

Special mention must be made however of the growing importance granted to "measures of conservancy." Senator De Brouckère's report refers to the previous work done in the matter and rightly shows that the Council's adequate use of the powers which Article 11 grants it in this respect may prevent many a disaster. This opinion is strongly endorsed by the Commission on Arbitration and Security which recalls that "valuable suggestions on this point are to be found in the Locarno Agreements. These Agreements provide that, if a question covered by the Agreements is laid before the Council, the latter shall ensure that suitable provisional measures are taken; and that the parties undertake to accept such measures, to abstain from all measures likely to have a repercussion prejudicial to the execution of the decision or to the arrangements proposed by the Council, and, in general, to abstain from any sort of action whatsoever which may aggravate or extend the dispute."

Proceeding along these lines of thought, the German Delegation to the Commission on Arbitration and Security presented a number of suggestions designed to strengthen the means of preventing war.[1]

[1] "I. In case of a dispute being submitted to the Council, the States might undertake in advance to accept and execute provisional recommendations of the Council for the purpose of preventing any

These suggestions are evidently one of the most substantial contributions towards what the French admirably describe as the organization of peace. Coming from the German nation, they should be appraised not merely as an intellectual but as a moral contribution of the very first order, a conclusion which applies with particular force to the Draft Treaty which the German Delegation submitted in elaboration of the suggestions themselves. Nevertheless, this truly statesmanlike proposal did not meet with all the success one might have expected. The sense of the Commission was undoubtedly expressed by its spokesman M. Rolin-Jaequemyns. It is cautiously conservative. Its gray-blue arguments reflect the shadow of Great Powers' preoccupations. We read the lines and find the usual political "wisdom"; we read between the lines and see more or less what follows:

aggravation or extension of the dispute and impeding any measures to be taken by the parties which might exercise an unfavorable reaction on the execution of the settlement to be proposed by the Council.

"II. In case of threat of war, the States might undertake in advance to accept and to execute the recommendations of the Council to the effect of maintaining or re-establishing the military status quo normally existing in time of peace.

"III. In the case of hostilities of any kind breaking out without, in the Council's opinion, all possibilities of a pacific settlement having been exhausted, the States might undertake in advance to accept, on the Council's proposal, an armistice on land and sea and in the air, including especially the obligation of the two parties in dispute to withdraw the forces which might have penetrated into foreign territory and to secure the respect of the sovereignty of the other State.

"IV. The question should be considered whether the above-mentioned obligations should be undertaken only in case of a unanimous vote of the Council (the votes of the parties to the dispute not being counted), or whether the majority, simple or qualified, might suffice in the matter. Furthermore, it should be considered in what form the obligations would have to be drawn up in order to bring them into conformity with the Covenant."

—Italy's anxiety lest such "conservatory" measures deprive her of a hard-won frontier superiority over her north-eastern potential adversaries.

—France—yes France or at least her military opinion has changed since the days of the Protocol. Then France was obsessed by the possibility of a German lightning attack, and conservatory measures were important while the conflict was in a bad way, particularly as her own normal military establishment was strong enough for any emergency. This is no longer the case and will be less and less so as democratic pressure brings down the technical efficiency of her preparedness below what her experts consider safety-point. In the future then, if the Council was to receive powers preventing the war instrument to be tuned up while the conflict was in progress, France might find herself insufficiently defended if and when conciliatory measures failed.

—Great Britain, finally, shuns general agreements. The English gentleman insists on choosing those with whom he will condescend to treat. Whenever general agreements are mooted, we find somewhere a paragraph inspired in this British sense of isolation and fastidious choice of partners. Here is the corresponding paragraph in the Rolin-Jaequemyns report:

"At the same time, it must be borne in mind that important projects undertaken by the League have failed chiefly by reason of their general character. Some States might feel doubtful whether their vast, numerous and varied interests would permit of their assuming a general undertaking in regard to all States without exception, even if the undertaking appeared acceptable, or had already been accepted, in regard to specific States."

Nothing daunted, the Germans presented the Draft Treaty embodying their proposals, wisely postponing however their suggestions as to the conservation of the status quo during crises. Their reasons for so doing are couched in a language which deserves to be reproduced:

"As the Committee was unable to reach agreement on this point, it thought it preferable not to take the German delegation's second suggestion into consideration for the time being. This delegation thought that better results could be achieved when further progress had been made in the work connected with the limitation of armaments, and reserved the right to revert to suggestion No. II in due course."

Such was the ulterior development of the sum of the suggestions of the Council Committee on Article 11. But the work of the Council Committee did not stop there. Article 11 is essentially an article of action. It seeks to forestall emergencies and if necessary to meet them. It is therefore of the utmost importance that it should be made efficient. In a well-organized community, the crack service must be the fire brigade. Article 11 is the fire brigade of the Covenant. The Committee realized this fact to the full and appropriate studies were undertaken to ensure that in actual practice the working of Article 11 was as smooth and expeditious as is compatible with the complexity of the League.

The Committee had before it a recent case in which the League machinery had been called into play and had succeeded in putting down the flames of war in the Balkans. The commission of enquiry sent by the Council to investigate the Greco-Bulgarian dispute reported that in such cases "the saving of a few minutes may prevent a catastrophe. In the present circumstances, which are exceedingly favourable—in that the President of the Council received a telephone message one hour after Bulgaria's appeal had been received by the Secretary-General—a military operation which might have had the most dangerous results was only just prevented." The Commission devoted a special attention to the matter of communications.[1] It became evident soon that, important as good railway services were between Geneva and the main European countries where Council representatives happened to reside, special attention had to be devoted to two special kinds of communications: aviation and wireless.[2]

[1] By the curious irony of life the boat which conveyed Senator De Brouckère, President, and the writer of these lines, Secretary, of a sub-committee which was to meet in London in order to study this point, i.e., the improvement and efficiency of communications to allow the Council to meet urgently in case of emergency, left Antwerp one evening at seven o'clock for London and was still in the Scheldt at seven o'clock next morning. The distance Antwerp to Harwich which usually takes ten hours took us twenty-four owing to fog. The Sub-Committee had to be adjourned by as much. It shows that the refusal of the British Government to countenance the Channel Tunnel proposal, whatever its (secret) merits from the defense point of view, might be dangerous from the point of view of a more general security.

[2] The matter has been admirably summed up in a resolution adopted in 1928 by the Commission on Arbitration and Security which inherited this subject from the Council Committee:

"The Committee on Arbitration and Security . . . directs attention to the following passage in the Report of the Committee for Com-

The studies undertaken aim at ensuring a free international aerodrome and a free international wireless station in Geneva in such conditions that in time of emergency Swiss neutrality may not be a hindrance to the working of the League organizations dealing with the crisis.[1] They have led to definite negotiations whereby the League would have certain rights of use over the Cointrin Aerodrome, close to Geneva, and a powerful wireless station will be erected to be put at the

munications and Transit, dated March 1927, which was submitted to the Council and the Assembly:

> "'. . . that at a time of general emergency—for example, immediately before mobilisation and, above all, during the actual period of mobilisation—the total or partial taking over by the State of the means of communication must inevitably mean that, in many cases, communications of importance to the League might be rendered less rapid or less certain despite the successful application of the measures laid down in the report approved by the Council at its December session, unless some special means, independent of the general system of national communications, . . .'

"Considers that the systematic study of the means to be employed by the organs of the League to enable Members to carry out the obligations devolving upon them in virtue of the different articles of the Covenant requires that communications for the purposes of League action in case of emergency should have every guarantee of independence and should be as little affected as possible by the disturbance which a state of emergency will necessarily produce in the regular working of the communications controlled by the different Governments; . . ."

[1] By a concession which true internationalists must deplore the Council admitted in March, 1920, that Switzerland was entitled to remain neutral in the military sense while partaking in economic and financial measures under Article 16. This could hardly justify neutrality towards the application of Article 11 in time of emergency, but the League is entitled to secure its own independence in the matter. The difficulties experienced in obtaining Russian coöperation with the Disarmament Commission while the Swiss-Soviet dispute lasted would suffice to explain why the League should be specially careful in this connection—helpful and even generous as the Swiss authorities were in their interpretation of their duties towards the League with regard to the Soviet attitude.

disposal and under the control of the League in time of emergency.

* * *

So much for Article 11. As for Article 16, M. De Brouckère's report adumbrated further work on it. Little could be done in the field of interpretation. Moreover, since the study of this article had been suggested by the French Delegation, it was evident that the stress was to be laid on preparedness to be applied with due efficiency. Nothing could be done from the military point of view. It is, we know, the weakest aspect of the Article that the obligations of a military character incurred in it are but vague and elastic. But even if they were as definite as the French General Staff should wish it is beyond the power of the most brilliant strategist to prepare for all the cases of sanctions which the League may theoretically have to apply.[1] The attention of the Commission was thus left to concentrate on economic and financial sanctions. The appropriate committees were consulted: both the Financial and the Economic Committees of the League reported that no special measures could be taken beforehand beyond the collection of a certain amount of international information. But in the course of these

[1] The mail-bag of a League Disarmament Director is a mine of felicitous suggestions on this as on many other points from voluntary collaborators. I once received a neat little plan of universal disarmament from a French naval officer, I am glad to say, retired. He had a definite legal scheme of operations against every nation of Europe and out of Europe which would place itself in the position of the aggressive State; with heavy punishment, too, such as loss of territory, reparations and so forth. One only nation had been forgotten: France.

studies, the League Disarmament Organization was led to examine a Finnish proposal which deserves special attention.

SCHEME OF FINANCIAL ASSISTANCE TO STATES THREATENED WITH AGGRESSION

The Finnish Government reasoned as follows: You want us to disarm. But we are not armament manufacturers and moreover we have a long and defenseless frontier with a neighbor which does not belong to the League of Nations, which is very powerful and which holds opinions out of sympathy with ours. We are desirous to save the considerable expense of renewing our obsolete war material and we wish to reduce our military burdens. But if, having done so, we were confronted with imminent danger from Soviet Russia, we would have suddenly to re-arm. This we would not be able to do without importing our armaments which in its turn implies heavy loans abroad. Now, a State on the eve of war borrows on ruinous conditions. We ask that here and now in time of peace the League prepare a scheme whereby a State threatened by aggression may borrow not on its own credit alone but on the credit of the League at normal rates.

The idea was clear and statesmanlike. It was in fact a definite example in the special field of finance of the idea underlying the French case in the war potential controversy, for it amounted to this: If you want small States to disarm, you must pool and put at the disposal of the world the war potential value of the credit of the several States.

The Finnish proposal was rapidly taken up by the other members of the League Disarmament Organization. It was of course referred to the Finance Committee which prepared a scheme, the general features of which are the following:

The State which was the victim of aggression would be assisted by the League to obtain a loan on the money market in the ordinary way. The assistance would take the form of a guarantee for the loan. This guarantee would be given by the States participating in the scheme, perhaps in the same proportions as their contributions to the League. The Convention establishing the scheme would fix a maximum limit for the guarantee. If this maximum were fixed at fifty million pounds, and if all the Members of the League participated, each State would be called upon to guarantee the interest on and amortization of a sum equal to about fifty times its annual contribution to the League. The signatories of the Convention would deposit general bonds of guarantee with the Secretary-General or the Trustees (who would be appointed by the Council). When a State which was a party to the Convention was attacked and asked for financial assistance under the terms of the Convention, the Council of the League would, on the advice of the Financial Committee, decide how and to what extent the request should be complied with, and would fix the amount of the loan. For this purpose the signatories would exchange the general bonds for "specific bonds of guarantee" to the amount required, but not exceeding the total of their guarantees. The "specific bonds of guarantee" would be drawn up in a form generally corresponding to that of the bonds deposited with the trustees for the Austrian Reconstruction Loan, and the procedure of their operation would be the same. Should the attacked State default, the "specific bonds" would be presented to their signatories. The Committee further proposed to strengthen the scheme by establishing a supplementary guarantee whereby a small number of signatories holding a very strong financial position would guarantee the signatories of the specific bonds for the entire amount. If necessary, they would temporarily furnish the funds required for the payments to be made. Each Government signing the supplementary guarantee would undertake to facilitate the public issue, in its country, of loans floated under the Convention.

This ingenious scheme raises several problems. The first is the definition of aggression. As matters stand, each State remains the ultimate judge of aggression under Article 16. A convention of financial assistance could not work with any degree of efficiency unless the Council could apply it on its own authority. At first sight, it seems as if the difficulty could be solved by applying Article 4, paragraph 5 of the Covenant.[1] But the Financial Committee of the League are opposed to this solution on grounds of efficiency, since it is evident that if all the guarantors were to sit on the Council the Council would become an unwieldy body just when its urgent decision is wanted. The matter is still open and

[1] Any Member of the League not represented on the Council shall be invited to send a Representative to sit as a Member at any meeting of the Council during the consideration of matters specially affecting the interests of that Member of the League."

will remain so for some time to come like all questions touching upon sovereignty.

A second and a most important point is that the scheme of financial assistance should not be considered merely as an adjunct to Article 16, i.e., as a part of the systems of sanctions against the aggressor and of help to the attacked, but that it should also be applied in connection with Article 11, i.e., when the Council is dealing with a conflict which might, if allowed to drift, degenerate into war. It is obvious that if, under this scheme, the Council raised a loan to hold at the disposal of the prospective victim, much wisdom might be obtained in the would-be aggressor by a process of spontaneous generation. The general trend of expert and political opinion is strongly in favor of such an extension of the scheme.

In view of the evident advantages which such a strengthening of Article 11 would entail it is therefore unfortunate that the British delegation should have insisted at every step that Great Britain could only approve the scheme on condition that it should form part of an adequate measure of general disarmament. This attitude is evidently one of power and not of cooperation. It means that the British Government wants to keep a trump card (its financial power) to weigh on the Disarmament Conference, i.e., to obtain from the Disarmament Conference an "adequate" superiority in British (relative) arms. The reader will find in the first part of this work reasons for sparing himself any surprise at this attitude. But we may deplore what we understand. A scheme such as that prepared by the Financial Committee would do much—more perhaps than any other suggestion made to date—to improve the moral atmosphere of the world, ultimately bringing about disarmament. It is a good in itself, independent of disarmament, and its adoption should not have been subordinated to any conditions whatsoever.

Chapter XII

CHEMICAL WARFARE AND CIVIL AVIATION

1. CHEMICAL WARFARE

THE question of Chemical Warfare has been taken up in Geneva from three different points of view which we may enumerate in an order of growing relevancy:

(a) from the point of view of the people who want war to be less inhuman,

(b) from the point of view of the people who want to impress mankind with the horrors of war,

(c) from the security point of view.

Though in practically every debate the three orders of arguments appear almost inextricably mixed, the three tendencies pull each its own way and lead each to its own results.

Sentiment. The wind of sentiment blows from the Anglo-Saxon world. When it prevails, it soon has its effect on the others and all faces lengthen accordingly whatever their original condition; but the wind is Anglo-Saxon for all that. Chemical Warfare was first presented under the inhuman and repulsive light which it has by Lord (then Robert) Cecil. In his mind something might be done to enlist the sympathy of scientists. His idea was that by securing full publicity for chemical inventions all nations would be put on an equal footing in the matter of Chemical Warfare and the value of this form of warfare would correspondingly fall. The suggestion was put to the League Committee on Intellectual Coöperation which reported that it was impracticable.

The next whiff of sentiment came from the United States. The League had called a conference to conclude a convention putting the international trade in arms under international supervision. The United States, which had officially coöperated in the preparatory work, was represented by a brilliant delegation headed by the Hon. Theodore Burton, chairman of the Foreign Affairs Committee of the House of Representatives. The agenda was clear and the American Government knew it. Nevertheless, the American delegation sprang on the Conference a proposal amending the Draft Convention to the effect that the international trade in chemical warfare materials and implements should be prohibited. The Conference was somewhat surprised. But League Members have come to realize how difficult it is for a State not fully trained in the methods of international coöperation to observe the rules on which the League is run, and, though the proposal implied a serious alteration in the agenda, it was considered. Two objections were raised at once: the first came from those who think that the League should not meddle with the laws of war any more than a government should meddle with the laws of dueling or with the rules of assaulting and housebreaking; for the League of Nations to say: "Thou shalt not wage war with chemicals" is tantamount to a government enacting that "no one shall murder with arsenic." The League moreover should not make laws which it knows will not be respected. Nothing weakens the authority of the legislature as much as legislation taken in disregard of custom. This argument, which might have appealed to a distinguished legislator of the land of prohibition, had but little effect. Not so the third objection, which was not long in making itself felt. It came from the countries which do not own chemical industries nor indeed any elaborate plant for chemical research: "We sympathize with your aims and believe in your motives," these countries said, "but how are your proposals going to work in actual practice? You want to prohibit international trade in chemical warfare material and gases; but, as long as you do not prohibit the manufacture thereof at least with an equal amount of efficiency, your proposal amounts to reserving chemical warfare for the exclusive monopoly of the manufacturing nations." The American delegation was honorably quick in altering its proposals to suit this reasonable view—so reasonable in fact as to have deserved anticipation. Several formulas were examined and in the end the nations present at the Conference were invited to sign a protocol declaring chemical warfare to be an international crime which none of them would commit. They all signed. Nations in Geneva and out of it are always willing to oblige the United States. And then, it is always safe to sign with the United States. The Senate refused to ratify.

Anti-War Propaganda. Meanwhile Lord Cecil's mind had evolved towards more fertile thoughts. It occurred to him that, since the war of the future was bound to make ample use of chemical warfare, this fact might be a useful weapon of anti-war propaganda in the hands of competent people able to picture with authority and vividness the horrors that lay in store for a world which allowed itself to drift into war. The usual machinery of committees was put into operation and a final report emerged. "Emerged" however is not quite accurate. The report received that "secret publicity" which is obtained by official documents when they fail, as they nearly always do, to appeal to the imagination. It is doubtful, moreover, whether Lord Cecil's plan was well grounded in human psychology. The very fact that a mankind which has lived through the horrors, and perhaps worse still, the painful and tiresome drudgery, of the War should need to be reminded of its terrible ordeals shows that neither horror nor drudgery shall ever suffice to stay the hand of mankind lifted against herself in murderous folly. The war-mind is a kind of madness, and all forms of ugliness and distortion are more likely to help than to hinder it. Hence, incidentally, the mistake of those who hope to abolish war by making it more and more horrible. Fear is too much akin to war. Let us not seek an ally in fear. The true path to peace is through reason. Our imagination must call forth plans of reason, ideas and ideals of reason in order to build up a stable peace.

Security. And so, on to the third attempt at dealing with Chemical Warfare, also under the leadership of Lord Cecil. (May we pause to admire the perseverance, the singleness of purpose and the creative mind of this true world-citizen, always ready to try a new line of attack through the intellect for a problem on which his heart is firmly set.) The Preparatory Commission was this time asked to study two questions:

(a) Whether it is possible to turn chemical industries from peace purposes to war purposes in a short time.

(b) Whether in the affirmative this can be prevented.

Thus understood, the question is of the utmost importance. For while we know that the League of Nations can deal effectively with disputes on condition that the parties keep their heads, it is very difficult to keep one's head knowing that our neighbor is feverishly manufacturing gas to asphyxiate us out of the use of it. Moreover, the world is quietly carrying on a chemical armament race the basis for which is no other than the flourishing state of the German chemical industry. The French General Staff are nervous at the immense aggressive capacity of the German chemical plant. England has declared her own chemical industry a *key* industry (the impeccable elegance of English euphemism should be admired in the midst of the closest argument). The United States cannot of course lag behind their European cousins if only for the sake of equality. (Oh, Equality, how many sins are committed in thy name!) And so gas is made right and left while protocols abjuring it as a weapon of war are signed left and right. Lord Cecil saw that the true difficulty was in the convertibility of chemical industrial power into chemical warfare power. He rightly proposed that this difficulty should be studied by the League.

But when the question reached the appropriate Commission—of which more hereafter—another item had been added to it: briefly put, it amounted to an enquiry into the possibility of setting up an international system of complaint and enquiry into alleged violations of a convention prohibiting Chemical Warfare. The Commission which considered this question in its technical aspects was composed of a nucleus of what was known as the Joint Committee plus a certain number of experts chosen by the Commission and paid from League funds. In actual fact, the choice was made by the usual method, i.e., in consultation, though unofficially, with the offices of the respective countries; yet it is well to bear in mind that the chemical experts selected were in Geneva as international and not as national experts. It was a curious Commission in more ways than one: the Italian expert was the only one who could be described as an Italian *tout court*. The British expert had a French name; so had the German; the American expert had an Italian name and was Cuban born; the Frenchman turned out to be an Alsatian who spoke French with a German accent. If ever a Commission met under good auspices to do international work the Chemical Warfare Commission was it. What about results? Not so bad as results go. But the report which they produced should be read between the lines. The Commission had no difficulty in answering the first point. Chemical factories can be turned from peace to war purposes immediately in the case of gases such as chlorine and phosgene which are normally manufactured in time of peace; in a few hours or weeks in the case of other gases; and at most in a few months in the case of new products. But what about the methods for avoiding it? Here M. Jouhaux, who sat as one of the Joint Committee members, endeavored to lead the way to the only reasonable solution in sight: an international chemical cartel which, being manned and managed by international employers and experts would see to it that none of its branches went astray. A curious scene followed. Of the chemical experts present only one, the Frenchman, was a business man; the others were theoreticians, laboratory experts or professors; these intellectuals unanimously declared that "the industry" would find M. Jouhaux's plan unacceptable; the business man quietly declared himself ready to accept it straight away. He favored a loosely knit federation of national industries which would submit when necessary to the inspection of a "syndic," and when the American expert objected to the plan on the grounds of national sovereignty and industrial secrecy the French expert retorted that the French manufacturers had accepted that their works should be inspected by American customs officials who came to visit their works in order to control costs, so that what French sovereignty and French industrial secrecy had given up to help the American Treasury, American sovereignty and American industry would certainly sacrifice to help the peace of the world. The argument is here re-told for the sake of its inherent value, but as a matter of fact the Commission did not go beyond a timid adumbration of international understandings which would apportion the quantity of each gas to be produced in every manufacturing country according to the requirements of legitimate use. The question of control was treated with a little more courage: the Commission considered two kinds of infractions: by firms and by States. The first, it said, could be dealt with by the machinery of the industrial cartel envisaged. The second would require an international commission or preferably a single enquirer. The Commission did not see any difficulty in accepting such a procedure—an opinion of course limited to the strictly technical aspect of the question and leaving aside all its political implications and complications. Despite this reservation the American expert preferred to keep out of this part of the report. He was quickly followed by his Italian colleague.

What is the conclusion of this episode? The same which we have met and are to meet so many times: that the questions of disarmament resolve themselves into questions of security and the questions of security into questions of international organization.

2. CIVIL AVIATION

Such is of course the solution which occurs to the mind when we try to grapple with the problem of Civil

Aviation. The importance of this problem is crucial. It flows from the following chain of facts:

The immense majority of nations do not consent to separating land, sea and air disarmament.

Air disarmament is impossible unless something is done to allay the fears of air-disarmed nations lest their rivals use their civil aviation for war purposes.

Therefore, without an adequate solution of the problem of Civil Aviation no air disarmament; without air disarmament no general disarmament.

That the problem is real can be shown in a manner similar to that used in connection with Chemical Warfare. (There is between these two problems a curious parallelism, apart from the obvious fact that the Chemical and the Air Arm, by combining their separate forces, multiply their efficiency to a terrifying degree.) Thus, just as every important nation grants special attention to its chemical industries with an eye on war potential, so every nation sees to it that its civil aviation is in a flourishing state—on the advice of the General Staff. The question arose in the course of the technical investigation carried out by the Expert Military Commission of the Preparatory Commission in connection with the possibility and forms of Air Disarmament. The Air Sub-Committee felt overwhelmingly military and declared itself incompetent to deal with civil aviation. A special Commission of civil aviation experts was therefore summoned. Here again, be it noted, this Commission was not composed of official representatives of national interests (which was the case with the Military Air Sub-Committee) but of men selected by the international organization on their own personal competence. When Senator De Brouckère who presided over the Military Committee in Geneva opened the sitting of the Civil Aviation Committee in Brussels, he was however able to greet in the room most of his Geneva friends. Some had come as advisors to their co-nationals (supposed to be internationals); others had not troubled to sit behind a civilian and had assumed civil competence by an act of their own. Fortunately there were one or two genuine representatives of civilian aviation. The Committee had the good fortune of securing the services of Mr. Guggenheim who brought to its work an unrivaled experience of civil aviation in the wide field of the United States. A Dutch manufacturer member of the Committee roundly declared that the military protection which nearly all civil aviation "enjoyed" in the form of War Office grants was a nuisance for it prevented the free development of civil aviation along its own lines, i.e., safety and efficiency, keeping the attention of manufacturers, designers and inventors concentrated on speed. Here again the report should be read between the lines. Had the Committee been freer from Government shackles it would have expressed bolder views. As it is it recommended that civil aviation be developed independently from military aviation and under separate leadership;[1] that Governments abstain

[1] Hardly had it made this suggestion than the Committee was bound to conciliate its English and its Italian members by adding a footnote which amounts to a withdrawal to the effect that they did not mean to allude to the cases in which both air services are under only one Ministry. As a matter of fact France has now imitated

from exacting military qualities in civil aircraft and that the use of military aircraft in civil lines be avoided; that pilots for civilian work should not be required to possess military training; that no encouragement should be given to civilian lines established for military purposes; finally that economic understandings between the several national enterprises should be encouraged. The whole report is written in a timid vein but this last recommendation is the most timidly expressed of all. Had not the word "national" remained in its first sentence to the effect that in most cases civil aviation has taken a national character, the original tendency of the proposal would be unintelligable in its present form. It was watered down at the request of the Italian experts. Its spirit was obvious. The difficulty is one of confidence. Some nations fear lest the civil aviation of their neighbors may be developed as a war weapon. Now it so happens that, at any rate in Europe, it is hardly worth while flying unless one is to cross one or more frontiers. Aviation in Europe is essentially international. Why not make it international in its organization and staff? That is surely the only reasonable way of dealing with all its problems, technical, economic and political. For a network of lines owned and manned internationally could never be organized against any one nation.

It will be seen that as in the case of Chemical Warfare or of Financial Assistance or indeed of any other

Great Britain and Italy in a move which, despite the courteous denegations of the Committee's footnote, is evidently against the spirit of its debates.

problem which may be studied on these lines the case of Civil Aviation has led us to the conclusion that a problem of Disarmament resolves itself into a problem of Security which in its turn leads to a problem of International Organization.

Chapter XIII

TOWARDS A CONVENTION

MEANWHILE the work of disarmament proper was entrusted to that body euphemistically decribed as Sub-Committee A. in order to spare the modesty of the American nation. Sub-Committee A. was composed of all the military experts of the delegations. It was a group of fifty or sixty men, soldiers, sailors and airmen. The task which had been put before them was particularly arduous. They were not to draft a convention. That stage had not been reached yet. They were to provide answers to questions some of which were general and abstruse, others narrowly technical, yet, on the whole, questions on which a *single-minded* committee of three men would have provided an answer within twenty-four hours. The Sub-Committee worked hard from May 17th till November 5th. In this period they spent about 3,750,000 sheets of roneo paper, i.e., enough to enable the Polish or the Swedish delegation to walk home on a path made of League paper; and their findings were recorded in a voluminous book so crowded with minority reports, reservations, counter-reservations and explanations as to be almost unintelligible without the help of a specialist.

But the cause of this signal failure of Sub-Committee

A. is honest. There was no lack of intelligence in the Sub-Committee. Far from it. If anything, that elusive commodity was rather over-abundant than scarce. But a body of military experts could not be expected to provide unanimous solutions on problems which—however theoretical and detached in their outward form—were all vitally connected with military power. The matter has been discussed in general terms in the first part of this work. The report of Sub-Committee A. provides an admirable illustration of what was then said as to the rôle of military experts in disarmament discussions. One or two brief examples may suffice to bring out here the striking nature of the results obtained. The question: What is war material? came to be examined. The lay mind may perhaps imagine that such a question is idle. It is not. A gun is war material. So is a gun carriage. So is a gun carriage wheel. What about the grease for the carriage wheel? It is indispensable for the wheel, therefore for the carriage, therefore for the gun. A military kitchen is war material. What about a military bed? Is a uniform war material? And what about a pair of military shoes? The Commission examined the matter and penetrated into a regular labyrinth of subtleties and distinctions with the result that they declared that while the steel and the wood necessary to manufacture a rifle were war material, the complete rifle, if stored up in an army depot and not in actual service, ceased to be war material and became an inoffensive object of peace.

But why, you may ask, spend so much subtlety on mere definitions? And you touch on one of the characteristics of military debates. The military mind is used to the gradual conquest of *positions*. The soldier begins by taking a first line of advance; he fortifies himself there; with the advantage thus acquired, he attacks the second position and so on to the final planting of his flag on the very summit which was his aim from the very beginning. The masters of this strategy are of course the French. Their admirable method, their dogged perseverance, their intellectual capacity for classifying questions by order of logical precedence, enables them to fight their way in debate step by step. Time and again in Geneva a resolution presented, pressed and wrenched from a Commission by a strong French delegation is seen to blossom forth months or years later in altogether unexpected consequences—unexpected, that is, by all but the French. This tendency which is pretty general in the French is naturally akin to a military psychology, and Sub-Committee A. took the French hint with the utmost alacrity. So that the questions submitted to them were treated exactly like successive lines of trenches for dialectical fights; generally speaking these lines were: first definition; then comparability; then limitation or reduction. In each of these lines the battle was fought on strictly national grounds; each delegation was always ready to vote for the general principle, if, when applied particularly, it resulted in an increase of the delegation's own relative armaments.

Such is the background which gives its dramatic and even its comic value to the famous duel on naval categories. It began on the trench of definitions. Could naval units be defined on separate categories? The English, the Americans and the Japanese wanted navies limited by categories; the French, the Italians, in fact practically every other naval power preferred the total tonnage method. But this was the summit to be conquered. The first trench to be won was definition. The Naval Sub-Committee fought Homeric fights on that trench. One day the British naval delegate with that frank somewhat bald sincerity of his nation and profession put the matter in a nutshell. "Is it possible," he asked the Sub-Committee, "to classify naval ships in categories which the expert can discern?" and he asked for a division. The Naval Sub-Committee voted and there was a majority of noes. To add insult to injury, the French delegation hurried to another room to fetch a Czech general who, as the "naval" representative of his land-locked country, had a right to vote. I turned to my English friends in the Committee and sought to allay their feelings by comic relief: "It serves you right. Why did you allow Shakespeare to give Bohemia an access to the sea?"

And yet those five months of hard work and Homeric battles were not altogether lost. To begin with they enabled every delegation to realize the weakness of its own case. For, absurd as many a national argument may seem to the international observer, most national arguments are held in perfect good faith. The Commission was at least biting into the very bones of the difficulty. The process of mutual education was painful but it bore fruit. Then, the technical phase had to be gone through. Had the politicians tried to solve the problem without giving the experts a full say, the result would have been received with hostility in every Fighting Department (Defense Department I believe they prefer to call themselves) of every nation, which, given the sheepish, unenlightened state of public opinion in the world, would have been fatal. Finally the fact that this military technical work was over, drove the Plenary Commission to the wall. It could adjourn no longer. All preliminaries had been duly performed. All previous questions answered. Nothing remained but to work and deliver the goods. Were any goods to be delivered?

When the Commission met in March, 1927, two substantial reports lay before each delegate: that of Sub-Commission A., on military, naval and air questions; that of Sub-Commission B. on the economic and financial aspect of the problems raised. Two courses lay open: the first was to take up the same questions all over again from a political and synthetic point of view and report to the Council thereon; the second to consider the two reports as reference documents and to go straight ahead with the work of drafting a convention. The Commission took the bolder course and Lord Cecil made this happy choice inevitable by submitting to it a draft convention on behalf of the British Government, a move which was immediately followed by M. Paul-Boncour who presented another draft convention on behalf of the French Government.

The work was not however as near completion as this wealth of ready texts might suggest. Far from it.

In fact these draft conventions were but empty frames in which it was proposed to insert future disarmament; neither the English nor the French draft mentioned or adumbrated a single figure. The drafts were mere forms destined to put before the Commission the several rules of disarmament on which agreement was necessary in a form approaching that which it was contemplated they should ultimately have. Nothing could illustrate more eloquently the baffling difficulty of disarmament than the fact that, though not one single figure was mentioned or even thought of, the debate on these blank conventions led to an impasse and that later meetings of the Commission have been unable to bridge over the differences revealed in this modest preliminary stage of the work.

The discussion which followed centered round four main problems: men, material, money and control.

Men. The English and the French proposals differed amongst others in the following respects:

While the French proposed to limit all effectives, the English suggested that land effectives only should be limited. This was not altogether unexpected in a naval nation.

While the English wished to limit trained reserves the French wanted them left out of account. This was not altogether unexpected in a military nation.

As to the first point the British delegation, together with the American delegation which had taken a similar attitude, was won over to the general feeling of the Commission which naturally objected to any discrimination in favor of naval or air effectives.

The second point remained one of permanent difference between France and England. It was to be one of the objects of the famous Franco-British Naval Agreement of 1928, of which more hereafter.

Material. This matter was discussed under three separate heads: land, sea and air.

Land war material. The British draft was silent. The French draft sought to limit war material (of all kinds) by determining a treaty maximum for the expenses in manufacture, purchase and upkeep for the duration of the treaty. As a result of the debate two texts remained before the Commission: the French text embodying the idea of total budgetary limitation for the period of the treaty and a German proposal limiting war material in service and in military stores under a special schedule.

A Dutch draft stipulated that the High Contracting Parties must set down and communicate to the League before March 1st every year a detailed statement of their arms, ammunition and material distributed under a certain number of specified heads. Definite objections were raised to this as well as to the German proposal by the Japanese and Italian delegations.

Sea war material. This was one of the points on which the Conference broke down. Originally the British and the French drafts differed considerably: the British would limit the tonnage of every category of ships; the French only the total tonnage. There was a gallant effort of conciliation on both sides. In the end the English had not budged—extremely conciliatory as they had been on various other points in discussion particularly on effectives. Yet the French had met them more than half way on this matter of sea war material. Their proposals comprised limitation of total tonnage, limitation of tonnage by categories of which there would be four (battleships, aircraft carriers, surface ships of less than ten thousand tons and submarines), changes of tonnage distribution within the total maximum to be subject to one year's notice before beginning building. The British declined to accept this very reasonable proposal. The Italians on the other hand, whose initial position was identical with that of the French, found this proposal too conciliatory and did not go beyond a six months' notice of construction within a general maximum but without any definite limits of category.

Air war material. There was a considerable and significant difference in the initial proposals. While the French stipulated a limitation of aircraft belonging to land, sea or air services, the British draft only covered aircraft attached to land bases or in use with land forces so that naval aircraft was not limited at all. The final draft however was unanimous in fixing a maximum to the total number, power and (in the case of airships) volume of aircraft in service with all forces whether military, naval or air.

Money. The British draft was silent about limitation of military, naval and air budgets. The French proposal provided for maximum figures to be inserted in the Convention. Opposite the space in which its draft article on this matter was inserted there stands a declaration by the British, Italian and Japanese delegations to the effect that budget limitation should only be effected by means of publicity, as well as a reservation by the American and German delegations directed against the insertion of any provisions whatsoever concerning military expenses.

Communication of military, naval and air budgets to the League was however accepted by all. This communication was to be couched in the form of a model statement on a uniform basis which was prepared by a commission of experts on budget matters. A similar communication was to be made of sums spent in military, naval and air appropriations during the preceding year.

International supervision. The British draft went a long way to conciliate American opinion and was discreet in its use of the machinery of the League of Nations; the general supervision of the Convention was entrusted to the following High Contracting Powers: Germany, the United States, Great Britain, France, Italy, Japan and the remaining members of the League Council. Moreover all contracting parties are to agree to coöperate in any measures necessary to uphold the Convention in case of violation.

The French draft is far more elaborate. A Permanent Disarmament Commission is set up composed of representatives of

(a) The Members of the Council.

(b) The United States of America and the Union of Socialist Sovietist Republics.

(c) Other Nations to be chosen by the Conference.

This Commission acts as a clearing-house for all the

information which the High Contracting Parties must provide. It prepares a yearly report which must be published and distributed to all Contracting Parties. It can hear any party which claims that new circumstances have arisen altering its national security and must report to the Council thereon; it may by a two-thirds majority decide that an enquiry is necessary and even, by the same majority, that it must take place on the spot, in which case the High Contracting Parties undertake to allow it to operate in their territory.

In the matter of derogations, the British draft provides for three cases under which a Contracting Party may increase its armaments beyond the maximum laid down in the Convention: (a) war in which the party is a belligerent; (b) threat of rebellion, or unforeseen circumstances implying serious military operations; (c) authority of League Council. After discussion the British delegation accepted to drop the case of unforeseen circumstances but maintained the remaining cases.

The French draft admits only one case of derogation: unjustified aggression. But even this case is subject to the general obligations of the Covenant and to the Council's decisions.

•
• •

Such is, baldly told, the story of the March-April meeting. But its true history is of course much more instructive and complex. For the first time perhaps a fully responsible official Commission came at close grips with the problem of disarmament and the result was what might be expected: disarmament revealed its true nature as a mere symptom of politics, i.e., of power. The debates of the Commission forced every Nation to take the attitude which the requirements of her power dictated.

This will perhaps stand in a clearer light if the general principles on which a Disarmament Convention should stand are first outlined in each case:

I. Men. In the matter of men what would appear to be the general principle is that a country should be well defended while having no aggressive capacity. The number of men under arms or immediately available should be the primary consideration. We know that the first difficulty is in defining a unit that can be comparable. The Convention adopts what amounts to the unit proposed in Señor Cobián's memorandum, the man-day. But the main difficulty is in defining who are the men to be counted. The British draft was stern on limitation of man-power whenever armies were concerned, but when it came to navies the thing became "unpractical" or "unnecessary" or even "illogical," which is surely a weak argument on English lips. This attitude became apparent time and again. When trained reserves were discussed, the French brought forward the machine guns of their logic and directed a murderous barrage fire at the Merchant Marine seamen of all categories, whom they rightly considered as "reserves" no less "trained" than their civilians who had passed through the army. When the British claimed that the N.C.O.'s and Commissioned Officers of the army should be limited the French pointed to their own draft in which this limitation had been provided for along with that of all kinds of naval officers which the British had forgotten and whose limitation they gallantly resisted. Arguments were excellent on both sides but who can doubt that they were thought out after and not before the conclusions which they were supposed to uphold? The French moreover were no less nationalistic in their position. They stuck to their trained reserves like one man. It is true that literally speaking their proposal fits the general principle more closely. What matters is the limitation of aggressive force and not the limitation of the force which a nation may call to carry on a defense after she has parried the first onslaught of the enemy. But France's insistence on maintaining her trained reserves intact is but the counterpart of England's anxiety to maintain a predominant naval force. Neither is building up a comprehensive scheme of disarmament. Both are thinking of power. In the case of France, her thoughts of power are stimulated by German opposition. Deprived of the standing citizen army by the Peace Treaty, Germany smarts under a military machine which not even her skill can turn into a manufacture of trained reserves as efficient as the French. What is then the position? Theoretically that France possesses an aggressive power towards Germany which Germany lacks towards France, with reasonable chances that in a protracted war the trained reserves of France would be superior to the trained reserves of Germany (of course when the German reserves trained by the last war have all been eliminated by age). In practice, the position is complicated by the existence of the Covenant and of the Locarno Agreements, as well as by the obvious fact that France is not likely to embark on a scrap with Germany. But the crux of the matter is in peacetime power. The military superiority of France allows her to speak with more assurance and Germany, rightly resenting her inferiority, attacks the principle of trained reserves because these trained reserves constitute a background of power which France can use to have her voice prevail in the world's counsels just as the British fleet is the basis of English weight in the international world.

II. Material. The question of war material is extremely complex. The German delegation insisted that war material should be limited to figures to be set down in the Covenant. Other delegations, for instance the Belgian, considered that it was useless to stipulate a limitation which could not be easily verified and they concluded that war material cannot be usefully limited. It would be difficult to judge the merits and demerits of the case but this may be said at once that the proposal to limit war material came from a nation which has been suspected for years of concealing war material. We have no right to assume that such suspicions are justified or unjustified but the fact that they exist suffices to prove right those who pay but little attention to the value of a merely verbal limitation laid down in a treaty without adequate measures for guaranteeing that the limitation passes from words to deeds. The problem as a matter of fact would not appear to be altogether insoluble. Two solutions have been adumbrated and if both were simultaneously applied there does not seem to be any reason why the limitation of material should not be as efficient as might be reasonably expected.

The first solution is the strict regulation of both manufacture and trade in arms combined with the gradual elimination of existing stocks through use, wear and tear, and obsolescence. This is the most natural method whereby the difficulty of calculating existing stocks may be eliminated. New stocks would then be known by simple arithmetical operations with the figures of manufacture, export and consumption. This method depends therefore entirely on the existence of two auxiliary conventions: one on international trade in arms and another on the manufacture of arms. We might then here open a parenthesis in order to deal briefly with these two subjects. Both moreover are mentioned in the Covenant on their own merits and apart from their importance in connection with general disarmament.

The supervision of the international trade in arms is provided for in a somewhat vague paragraph of Article 23 which must be read in combination with the covering preamble at the head of the whole Article:

"Subject to and in accordance with the provisions of international conventions existing or hereafter to be agreed upon, the Members of the League:

. . . (d) will entrust the League with the general supervision of the trade in arms and ammunition with the countries in which the control of this traffic is necessary in the common interest."

This sentence admitted a wide range of interpretations from that which would limit its scope to keeping comfortably unarmed a certain number of peoples held in tutelage, to a bold and universal conception which would extend supervision to all international trade in arms whatsoever. In actual fact its meaning evolved from the former to the latter through the sheer virtue of the spirit of Geneva and the requirements of the case. The St. Germain Convention signed in 1919 as one of the by-products of the Peace Conference was mostly concerned with the "special" traffic. Despite repeated requests from the League the United States of America refused to ratify it, amongst other reasons because it was too closely bound up with the League machinery. The League invited the United States to coöperate in the drafting of a new convention and this time the Commission (it was the Temporary Mixed Commission then in charge of this work) had before it two drafts both of which went a long way towards establishing an international supervision over all movements of arms which crossed a frontier.[1] The outcome of the Commission's work and later of the Diplomatic Conference called in May, 1925, to settle and sign the final draft, was a convention enacting that all exports should be subject to a license of the exporting country, that export licenses should be granted only for export to governments and that full data as to exported

[1] These two drafts had been presented respectively by Admiral De Magaz (a Spanish member) and by M. Jouhaux (one of the Labor members of the Commission.)

articles should be sent to Geneva or alternatively published. There were, as usual, interesting national positions to observe. Thus, the Spanish-American members of the Conference objected to the stipulation that the government to which arms could be exported would be that recognized by the government of the exporting country. They wished to stipulate that the government receiving the arms would have to be recognized as such by the majority of the contracting parties, a claim which they subsequently abated to recognition by three signatory governments; the American delegation however, on whose initiative the original form had been inserted, preferred to retain it. The question at stake was clear. Washington wanted to remain free to recognize—and arm—whom she wished in Spanish-America; the Spanish-American governments wanted some collective guarantee. An ingenious formula was found, more satisfactory no doubt to the United States than to the Spanish-Americans: it was decided not to speak of recognition at all. One advantage remained: the exporting country was deprived of its latitude to arm impartially more than one party in a civil war. Had a convention with such an article been ratified it is probable that the trouble in China would have lasted a shorter time. This story is told for the sake of illustration, for as a matter of fact, the Convention, though not quite dead, is frozen out of activity by the cold attitude of the American Senate towards it. France and Venezuela are the only powers which have ratified it. The attitude of the United States is crucial because all the manufacturing powers fear that if ratification does not take place simultaneously in all of them the effect of the Convention will be to transfer trade from the bound powers to the powers which remain free. Such is in particular the attitude of Great Britain whose government has circularized a certain number of producing powers to that effect. The outcome of this step, if any, is not known. France has acted in a bolder way; she has ratified, subject to the ratification of other producing powers, a decision which transfers responsibility for her application to the Convention to the powers who refuse to ratify, in actual fact to Great Britain and the United States.

The state of suspended animation which afflicts the Convention on International Trade in Arms is in part the cause and in part the effect of the poor progress made in the preparation of a convention on the manufacture of arms. The subject is introduced in Article 8 of the Covenant in the following terms:

"The Members of the League agree that the manufacture by private enterprise of munitions and implements of war is open to grave objections. The Council shall advise how the evil effects attendant upon such manufacture can be prevented, due regard being had to the necessities of those Members of the League which are not able to manufacture the munitions and implements of war necessary for their safety."

The Council had the matter studied from the very inception of its activities. The problem is not solved yet. It has moreover evolved. The first idea was prohibition of private manufacture; it was argued however that States not possessing armament factories would be put under the subjection of manufacturing States. This argument, so considerate for non-manufacturing countries, was curiously enough particularly in favor with manufacturing nations. In actual fact the non-manufacturing State is in any case dependent on the government of the manufacturer. Every one knows that arms are not exported without government consent and no manufacturer can afford to be on bad terms with his own government. The relations between government and manufacturer may be private and discreet as in Great Britain or blatant and public as in the United States, where the President has more than once put an embargo on exports of arms when they were intended for people he did not particularly like. The abolition of the private manufacturer would therefore make no worse the case of non-manufacturing countries; but it would have two serious drawbacks for the manufacturing countries themselves: it would force them to take official responsibility for the export of arms to nations in conflict and therefore would put their neutrality on a fragile and delicate basis; it would deprive them of a convenient and relatively cheap armament-producing plant. For armament firms can of course provide armaments to their own government at rates made cheaper by the fact that they sell armaments abroad generally at much higher prices and also that they can engage in other kinds of manufacture.

Be that as it may the League work soon gave up as impracticable the abolition of private manufacture and turned its attention to supervision. Meanwhile the Conference on International Trade in Arms had taken place and a strong current of opinion had manifested itself there to claim that as a measure of equality between manufacturing and non-manufacturing States the Convention on the manufacture of arms should apply to state as well as to private manufacture. The argument of the non-manufacturing States was unanswerable; the Convention on Trade bound them to report all their imports of arms and therefore all their purchases. But the manufacturing States could always escape such publicity by having their armaments made in their own State factories even if the Convention on private manufacture was signed and ratified by them. The problem defined in the Covenant was thus enlarged by its own inherent logic. For a time, this development resulted in greater slowness. The progress made by the question had never been remarkable. Draft after draft and preliminary study after preliminary study lay sleeping on dusty shelves quietly forgotten or dismissed with gestures of significant wisdom only to revive for a few days at Assembly time, when Señor Garrero, the representative of Salvador, who had specialized in the subject, forced the Assembly to declare aloud that it was time something was done. The Great Powers immediately determined to do nothing about it. One of the forms that nothingness may take is a Convention. A kind of draft was prepared last August in Geneva. It may be summed up in this way: it organizes supervision by means of secret publicity.

* * *

It is therefore apparent that the Big Manufacturing Powers and not a few of the Small do not wish war material limited by the first of the two methods suggested. Are they more helpful with regard to the second? This second method consists in a limitation of the sums to be spent on war material. It was advocated by the French. It is evidently practical and efficient. In the way in which the French presented it, it is moreover elastic and adaptable. Nations would declare at the Disarmament Conference what their total expenses on war material would be for the duration of the Convention and they would be allowed to spend every year the corresponding quote-part obtained by dividing such a sum by the number of years which the Convention was to be in force, with the proviso that sums unspent in any one year could be added to the expenditure allowed in the next.

The arguments opposed to this proposal are worthless. That some nations have to pay more than others for their war material is irrelevant since prices could be made comparable by reducing them to purchasing capacity and moreover States would name their own figure at the Conference. That prices might vary during the duration of the Convention is true but as we shall see later the French draft very wisely provides for a procedure which would enable High Contracting Parties to exceed their treaty maxima should circumstances make it necessary. In actual fact, it is significant that the adversaries of budget limitation should be nations whose strength is in wealth and notably the

United States of America, the most vigorous opponent of the idea, and England.

The above considerations apply of course to all kinds of war material and more especially to army ordnance and armament. The position as to naval material is well known. Behind England, representing the limitation by categories school, there stand the United States of America and Japan. The British draft was inspired in strictly national requirements. This was particularly the case with its naval clauses. A strict and detailed definition of categories is an indispensable condition for the British Admiralty to retain its control of the sea. For, as the delegations of the Great Naval Powers frankly admitted, by allowing other nations freedom in the distribution of their naval tonnage they ran the risk that one of them might concentrate all its tonnage in one particularly dangerous category such as submarines. The obvious war character of the argument should be observed as well as that this argument was used by the British delegation with regard to France, at the time, and still now, the nation which enjoys the most intimate friendship with England.

III. Money. There is no question that a thoroughgoing section on budget limitations should be an indispensable part of an efficient and successful disarmament convention. There are at least two reasons why this should be so. The first is that the limitation of budgetary expenditure on armaments would act as a deterrent against any indirect turning of the Convention and would provide an easy check of the way it was executed. Let us bear in mind that a Commission of government treasury officials declared itself in favor of an international model statement of defense expenditure; that all necessary adjustments as to exchange, purchasing capacity, etc., have been allowed and that no technical impossibility may be put forward against the measure. Possible and advisable from the technical point of view, the limitation of defense budgets is of the utmost importance from the political point of view: for the reduction or limitation of expenses is the most tangible proof of reduction or limitation of armaments which the man in the street can receive. It is indeed the only tangible sign observable by the layman and in so far as the layman is the tax-payer it is observable in the most pleasurable way. Hence it is obvious that the nations which in Geneva objected to this most important and beneficent way of limiting armaments cannot be said to have served the cause which they professed to have at heart. It is moreover particularly unfortunate that the opposition should have been led by the wealthiest of the nations, the United States which went so far as to refuse to coöperate in the Commission of treasury officials, and Great Britain which was unsympathetic and insisted that no limitation could be effective except by publicity, surely a pessimistic view. Germany also objected, which reminded many a Commission member that the German defense budget is the only element of German armaments which the Treaty forgot to reduce or limit. Here therefore as everywhere the discussion seems to have been inspired to a considerable extent by power rather than peace.

IV. General Clauses. A. Derogations. It would

be difficult in a work such as this to pass in silence over the singular character of the derogations proposed by Great Britain. The delegation sought and obtained from the Government that the most unacceptable of them should be dropped: unforeseen circumstances necessitating important military operations. It was obviously incompatible with Article 8 of the Covenant, which for a League Member at any rate must be the constitutional basis of all Disarmament work: "After these plans shall have been adopted by the several Governments, the limits of armaments therein fixed shall not be exceeded without the concurrence of the Council." But the first derogation is not very satisfactory either, for it is obviously conceived in terms of too sweeping and general a character, since it provides for a suspension of the Convention when the nation concerned happens to be engaged in a war without any qualifications. True, read in relation to the Covenant which of course remains in force it is, legally speaking, admissible, but it would have been desirable to strengthen the hands of the Council on the eve of a conflict and also to re-state in this appropriate place an important principle of our new international law, by submitting the possibility of re-arming to the authority of the Council to be given only if the war in question is justifiable. It was argued in Geneva against this view that a nation threatened by war or engaged in a war would re-arm, Council or no Council, and though the argument is unanswerable it does not in any way weaken the advisability of putting every possible obstacle on the path of a nation which wants to go to war against the general opinion of the world as voiced by the League of Nations' official organs. Here again we may observe the typical British tendency to remain free to act in case of emergency. It would be grossly unfair to put the British attitude at any lower level than that but unfortunately that level is bad enough seriously to hamper the true progress of disarmament in particular and of the League in general. It is precisely the tendency to act independently of the best responsible and official public opinion of the world which is nowadays the most serious obstacle on our path.

The tendency which inspires the French draft is not less typical. As usual the French mind is obsessed by the fear of aggression. An unprovoked attack means mobilization; mobilization means instant derogation: yet, and though the derogation is automatic, it is only fair to observe that the French draft is far more satisfactory than the British; the British draft provides a derogation for any war without any qualifications whatsoever; [1] the French draft allows a derogation only in case of unprovoked aggression. So that for practical purposes this article of the French draft amounts to a renunciation of the right to fight a permissible war. In view of the French attitude and reser-

[1] The argument that no one can suspect Great Britain from wishing to be free to wage aggressive wars is wholly irrelevant for the Convention does not cover Great Britain only but every nation; in the second place the other fifty-odd nations of the world cannot be expected to have the same confidence in Great Britain that Great Britain has in herself; and finally it is extremely difficult with the best possible intentions for any one nation to know exactly when a war that she wishes to fight is or is not aggressive.

vations in the matter of the Kellogg Pact, two hypotheses are possible: that the consequences of this article were overlooked at the time or that the officials who drafted this text were not on speaking terms with those who drafted M. Briand's despatches to Mr. Kellogg. Such things may happen in the best regulated administrations.

B. Supervision. This matter is one of the favorite grounds of argument between the so-called Anglo-Saxon and the so-called Latin. There are two extreme views: the "Anglo-Saxon," represented by the United States and by Italy; the "Latin" represented by France. More moderate positions are occupied on the "Anglo-Saxon" side by Great Britain; on the "Latin" side by Spain, Holland and Sweden.

Briefly put the Anglo-Saxon point of view is that treaties rest on mutual confidence and their fulfillment should not be supervised nor in any way controlled. The Latin argument is that trust is good but seeing for one's self is better. Behind these arguments, a more important issue is at stake. France as usual is after security. She wants her signature underwritten by as many signatories as possible, and if it must come to fighting she wants her armies helped by as many armies and navies as possible. But, this said, we must acknowledge that France seeks to allay her fears—legitimate after all—in the most constructive and statesmanlike way. Her motives may perhaps be national; her aim happens to be international. What she wants is a well-organized community before whose forum all complaints may be argued out, all fears may find a remedy, all infractions of the Convention and of the Covenant may be punished or, better still, prevented. Surely it is, to say the least, disingenuous to argue that the organization of so civilized and peaceful a community is undesirable because it would suit French national aims. The organization of the World Community should be discussed on its own merits. And it is significant that the nations which stand against it, what we are bound to describe as the reactionary nations, are those which feel in the growing and acquisitive stage of their development: the United States and Italy together with, to a much lesser extent, Great Britain. Their arguments against international institutions entrusted with the supervision of the Convention are the arguments of the feudal lord against the growth of a well-organized State.

Leaving aside moreover this higher plane of world political evolution, the question of supervision is of the greatest importance from the merely practical point of view. I honestly believe that the French did much harm to the cause by their obsession about sanctions and inquisitive control. The morbid and over-provident element which drove their effort in a military direction vitiated what was fertile and creative in the idea itself, i.e., the institutional tendency which inspired it. This institutional tendency should have been presented as a necessity implied in the very circumstances, legal and others, which determined the Convention. Efforts were made then to direct the movement along those lines by describing this part of the work as "Measures for the Administration of the Convention."

For a moment of reflection will show that some kind of permanent organization is necessary in order that a convention may work at all. If it is to be based on Article 8 of the Covenant—as it should be—it must be perpetual (though subject to revision every ten years) and its maxima must be respected subject to a decision of the Council. Now it is obvious that unforeseen circumstances may turn up. A new weapon, a radical change in military laws, a considerable alteration in the value of money, a dramatic change in the constitutional or political organization of a neighboring State and a score of other events might force this or that country to seek permission to go beyond its maximum. The stability of the Convention requires that such changes should be neither so difficult as to make a convention altogether impossible nor so easy as to make it a mere scrap of paper. The obvious solution is a permanent Disarmament Commission entrusted with the examination of such problems as they arise and a final decision of the Council on it all. This simple method of rendering the Convention efficient yet elastic was opposed by the reactionary nations in the same breath with the identical institution for control. A further proof that the main problem of disarmament, i.e., the transformation of national armaments from a matter of purely national into a matter of international concern, is still overlooked, while methods of arming are discussed under the popular name of disarmament.

Chapter XIV

A MASTERPIECE OF THE DIRECT METHOD

THE COOLIDGE CONFERENCE

IN the recess between the second and the third sessions of the Preparatory Commission, President Coolidge bethought himself of the advantages of a separate conference and he issued an official enquiry to the British, French, Italian and Japanese Governments (February 10th, 1927) in order to ascertain whether they would be disposed to empower their representatives at the forthcoming meeting of the Preparatory Commission to begin negotiations towards a limitation of naval armaments. Much as this step has been commented upon since it was taken, there is one particular aspect of it which has not obtained all the attention it deserves. The government of the United States acted exactly as if the work done in Geneva to date had been transacted in a language utterly unknown to them. Once more, official America remained isolated, impervious to world influences, unable—or unwilling—to learn from the experience gathered by other nations. There were at the time well-meaning and ardent international workers who felt drawn by their offended emotions to attribute all kinds of unworthy motives to Washington. We heard about playing at party football with the peace of the world and what not. Yet without in any way attempting a defense of President Coolidge, which he is better able to do if he chooses, it is hardly necessary to delve so deep in order to deplore his action. The League Commission on disarmament was strenuously grappling with the difficulties of the subject. True, it was not getting on; but, leaving aside the fact that one of its difficulties, perhaps the greatest, was precisely the isolationistic attitude of the United States, the work of the League had already achieved two definite results: the first, to prove that there is no hope of making any headway in disarmament without dealing simultaneously with land, sea and air; the second, to show that disarmament is indissolubly linked up with the growth of international institutions. Both these results were, or should have been, clear to Washington. Both were no doubt unpalatable. But that was not a reason for throwing them unceremoniously overboard.

Nor was that all. For there is no question that the calling of an international conference of five Powers to discuss one of the points which twenty other Powers were already debating with them was, to put it mildly, an unexpected action. There were some Americans at the time who, anxious to help, tried to put the best possible complexion on the singular step taken by their Government. But explanations could not alter the essence of the position. An orchestra is playing Beethoven's Ninth Symphony under the direction of an experienced conductor; another less experienced conductor turns up between two of the movements and suggests that the five principal executants retire in order to perform a Bach Quintet. Surely, love of music can be combined with a better sense of opportunity.

Yet nothing succeeds like success, and if what came to be known as the Coolidge Conference had succeeded all these thorns of reproach would have turned into laurels. Yes. But the fact is that success was impossible. For the Conference aimed at limiting the vessels not dealt with in the Washington Conference and the Washington Conference had succeeded precisely because those vessels were left out of it. It is easy to drive the hollow in a deflated india-rubber ball from one point to another; it is less easy to round the ball up altogether. The Washington Conference was able to reduce or at any rate limit certain types of vessels by allowing the States all freedom to develop their navies in other directions. A limitation of all the navies in all directions is another matter. The Coolidge Conference had to bow before the law which governs all so-called Disarmament Conferences which meet before the political preliminary conditions for their success have been fulfilled. Ostensibly a Disarmament Conference, it became fatally an Armament Conference.

Let it be quite clear that though it took place in Geneva and was even for a time housed in the League of Nations building the Coolidge Conference had nothing to do with the League. The writer was then Director of Disarmament of the League Secretariat and was only invited to the three public meetings which took place during the whole duration of the Conference. But as a sight it was fascinating to the specialist. On coming to grips with the subject every delegation chose its ground regardless of previous attitudes. The Americans, for instance, who in the general Conference had been adamantine defenders of the faith in naval categories, suddenly discovered that the British were most bigoted on this point and, being converted to the excellencies of French logic which they had cursed in the Preparatory Commission, craved the right to apportion their total tonnage as they saw fit. But the most dramatic conversion was that of the British. They had been for years most impatient with the French obsession for security. When the French reminded them of the many invasions which they had had to suffer, their country overrun with foreign troops, their towns destroyed, they listened with respectful boredom and took most of it as political rhetoric. But when it came to cruisers, Mr. Bridgeman in most emphatic terms pronounced immortal sentences which the French loved to repeat. Security, Security above all.

And yet, the French after all could point to a traditional adversary just over the border. But what were the English afraid of? The answer to this question is enigmatic and we should respect enigmas. But any one who saw and heard at close quarters what was done and said during the Coolidge Conference knows quite well that the war which was used as a working hypothesis for the discussion was the Unthinkable War. It was a pleasure to hear Lord Jellicoe who, as the New Zealand representative, was an expert in Channel naval problems, explain how seventy cruisers were an irreducible minimum for England since a hundred and forty cruisers had been hardly enough to save England from destruction during the last war. And still more pleasurable to hear Mr. Gibson, the distinguished American delegate and president of the Conference, argue that if a delegation came to Geneva determined to put forward absolute and immovable claims it was useless to meet in conference at all—which is exactly what everybody had been saying for six years about American delegations.

It is only plain honesty to recognize that Anglo-American relations were never more strained in recent years than they were then. Why should an endeavor to disarm give rise to such heated situations? It seems that a difference in method as to how to do away with armaments should never lead to suspicion and controversy of the bitter character which obtained then. We know of course the key to this paradox: under the vocabulary and gestures of Disarmament, what was at stake in the Coolidge Conference was Armament. The three nations there present, and particularly the United States and Great Britain, were ready for any reduction of *absolute* naval power all round which would result in leaving their own *relative* naval power stationary at any rate and if possible increased. The arguments exchanged in Geneva have no meaning whatever if they have not that meaning. "Your case is a very strong chain hanging from a very weak nail," an international observer said then to one of the British delegates. True, if England did not control the sea-roads she might be starved in a fortnight. But the argument applies to Finland just as well, and, moreover, who wants to starve England? Where is the enemy? And as to the United States, true that having no naval bases dotted all over the world, she would be put in an inferior position if she was forced to build her total tonnage in the form of small cruisers—but in an inferior position towards whom? In what kind of conflict?

The difficulty about this argument is that what is wrong with it is not the case of one or the other of the disputants but the ground on which they both stand. It is—with all respect for the two nations which have put themselves in this awkward position—as if two bootleggers carried on a controversy on the respective forces wherewith they would fight out their claims to supply Chicago with prohibited bliss. Great Britain and America spoke in Geneva thoughts of power in the language of safety. With, however, this all-important difference that England is psychologically entitled to a certain "security-complex" in sea matters as France is on land questions; while it is difficult to explain America's naval policy except as a very human tendency to reap in the naval field the harvest of her financial and political superiority. The difficulty plainly shows the importance of armaments as instruments of policy. It is not so much actually in order to shoot her guns at England that America wants her cruisers; nor to defend her supplies from American cruisers that England is so particular about her superiority at sea. It is because naval preëminence means international prestige; preponderance in the counsels of the world; authority in troubled areas such as China; power to have one's way; political backing to financial economic and commercial penetration.

Such is the reason why a partial attempt at solving

the problem of Disarmament such as the Coolidge Conference can only end in two ways—by sheer failure or by an agreement of a political character apportioning the power available between the parties, i.e., an agreement to pool armaments between the two nations agreeing, which in its turn is only possible when a pool of power of all kinds and particularly of political power has been previously set up between the partners. For let it be said again and not for the last time, the only solution of the problem of disarmament lies in the organization of the World-Community in such a way that power may be used only as the weapon of the World-Community against law-breakers.

Chapter XV

A MASTERPIECE OF THE INDIRECT METHOD

THE KELLOGG PACT

THE Coolidge Conference was sprung upon the world as if the work of the Disarmament Conference did not exist.[1] The Kellogg Pact has been presented to the world as if the Covenant itself did not exist. Dr. Charles Clayton Morrison, one of the prophets of the movement to which we owe the Kellogg Pact hailed its appearance in the following terms: "Mr. Kellogg launched a new idea when he made his offer of a general treaty renouncing war. The idea had taken root in certain circles of American peace thinking but was wholly new to Europe. . . . The fact that America has defined the issue between peace and war in simple unambiguous terms and has chosen peace spells the doom of war. . . . If Christ was standing among us it would be like him to say, 'I see Satan falling as lightning from heaven' . . . It is, we say the natal day of peace. The peace movement has at last been born. There has been no peace movement until now."[2] It should be noticed that the name which finally stuck

1 There was much lip-service paid to it in American official commentaries, but it is the deed that matters and not the word.

2 Quoted by Mr. Kirby Page in "The World To-morrow," New York, May, 1928.

to the Pact is that of the American Secretary of State, though in its intermediate stages it was sometimes described as the Briand or as the Briand-Kellogg Pact. The evolution of its name corresponds to the evolution of its substance—a rather rare occurrence in Anglo-Saxon things. The Kellogg Pact was born in Paris. It owes its origin to that most beneficent and clear-sighted of international workers, Professor Shotwell, of Columbia University. In its inception, it was an offer made by M. Briand to the American people to the effect that France and the United States should agree to outlaw war as between themselves. The next stage begins when the Department of State made the counter-suggestion that the Treaty should not be confined to France and the United States. The French Government grew uneasy. It was all very well to outlaw war between France and the United States but when it came to Europe the matter became more delicate, so delicate indeed that it proved too much for France's legal advisers and the official correspondence of the French Government seemed for a time to cast a doubt on the compatibility of the American suggestion with the principles of the Covenant. What was it that worried France? The United States insisted on outlawing wars of aggression and no other wars; two are the reasons which explain the uneasiness of France: the first that she wanted to be sure that her capacity to fight against a Covenant-breaking State remained unimpaired by the Pact suggested; the second that she wished to keep intact her right to resort to war under any of the residual cases in which the Covenant tolerates it either by failure of the Council to settle the conflict or by the refusal of the losing State to conform with the award. We recognize here the ever-recurring French anxiety to maintain a sound line of legal fortresses round her European status quo.

But why was America so difficult about it all? Why not be content with the French suggestion and limit herself to outlawing aggressive wars? The first answer we find we may as well give in the terms in which it was couched by Mr. Kellogg himself in his address to the Council of Foreign Relations (New York, March 15th, 1928): "My objection to limiting the scope of an anti-war treaty to merely wars of aggression is based partly upon a very real disinclination to see the ideal of world peace qualified in any way, and partly upon the absence of any satisfactory definition of the word aggressor or the phrase *wars of aggression.*" This answer contains two reasons which however are more closely connected than might appear at first sight. The first of them aptly illustrates the fallacy of current ideas on national psychology. How often have we heard about Anglo-Saxon practical sense and Latin theoretical wind? Leaving aside that "Anglo-Saxon" and that "Latin" which are both misleading and irrelevant, and sticking to "American" and "French," who is here not merely in the winds of idealism but in the vacuum of *irrealism?* Is it the French jurist who won't let go the brass tacks of Security or the American Secretary of State who cannot bear to see the ideal of world peace qualified in any way when drafting an actual anti-war treaty to be signed and ratified on our own practical earth? The claim that a universal, absolute and unqualified renunciation of war is embodied in the Kellogg Pact which the Secretary of State makes here implicitly is, with all respect, preposterous and no grown-up person can suggest it in earnest without insult to his audience or injury to himself. That is the honest truth which chancelleries long to speak out but are debarred from declaring out of international courtesy. The "ideal of world peace" *must* be qualified and the "disinclination" to do so in the American Secretary of State is due to the fact that there is only one honest and efficient way of qualifying it, i.e., the organization of the World-Community, a method to which the American State objects.

This brings us to the second reason put forward by Secretary Kellogg to refuse the qualification suggested by the French to the outlawry of war, namely "the absence of any satisfactory definition of the word 'aggression.'" Now this assertion is contrary to the facts, though we asked the reader to give us credit for our opinion till we prove its worth in a later chapter. Thanks to the League of Nations' work there exists to-day a satisfactory practical standard of aggression. Moreover let us observe that whether the border cases are easy to define or not wars may be classed under three perfectly clear heads:

Aggressive wars.

Defensive wars.

Wars to obtain redress of a wrong after all conciliatory methods have failed.

Now, leaving aside border cases and questions of definition, the difference between the French and the American proposal was that the French proposal outlawed the first category only while the American proposal outlawed all but the second, or in other words that while the American proposal outlawed the third category the French proposal did not. This difference however in actual practice *and within the League* would not amount to much. The kind of war in question was no doubt much prized by the French merely as a hypothetical form of defense for the European system. But, given the suppleness of the Covenant and particularly the all but omnipotent mandate which the Council can assume in cases of crisis under Article 11, the chances of actual permissible wars under the Covenant are very small indeed *for Members of the League of Nations.* The matter however presents quite a different complexion if a conflict outside the League or between a League Member and a powerful outsider be considered. Let us imagine that trouble arises between the United States and Japan over the discrimination laws of California. The United States, bound by the second article of the Kellogg Pact, submit the matter to conciliation, but conciliation fails. Japan then refers the matter to the League Council; the United States refuse to let the League "meddle" with it. What then? Three months elapse and according to the League Covenant and to the French proposal for a Pact Japan is free to seek vindication in war. According to the Kellogg Pact, as signed, Japan has no redress whatsoever. The example has been chosen with the United States in the unfavorable light because, according to the Covenant, Japan cannot take an uncompromising attitude since she is bound to conciliate and come before the Council to the bitter end. But the United States remains *motu propio* outside the League and free from the obligations which the Covenant of the League entails. It is therefore evident that the difference between the French proposal and the Kellogg counter-proposal is all to the advantage of the States which are not Members of the League.

This conclusion becomes still more apparent when the two following facts are taken into account:

First, that while a war of self-defense is of course permissible both under the Covenant and under the Kellogg Pact it is in the Covenant severely watched over and regulated by the complicated system of outlawry which Articles 8-20 of the Covenant imply while nothing prevents a State outside the League from waging any kind of war it wishes and calling it defensive. Bad faith, though not to be altogether overlooked, is not the gravest danger here. The gravest danger is wrong-headedness, a stout conviction that "my country is in the right" even in ludicrously wrong circumstances. It is impossible to discuss this point without drawing the reader's attention to the fact that the very nation which suggested the outlawry of war without qualifications should at the same time be waging a war in a foreign country. The Nicaraguan affair may be described in a variety of ways but if the outlawry of war is to be considered as *compatible with that* the idea is less ideal than some American idealists would have us believe.

The second fact to be considered is that the efficiency of the Pact is naturally proportional to the efficiency of its second article whereby the High Contracting Parties agree that the settlement or solution of all disputes or conflicts of whatsoever nature or origin they may be which may arise among them shall never be sought except by pacific means. Now this article implies such a startling alteration in the policy followed by the United States not merely in recent years but under Mr. Kellogg himself, that the natural conclusion to which not a few men and even governments have jumped is that the article does not mean what it says. What, for instance, about the Monroe Doctrine? In a note singularly lacking in political wisdom from both the point of view of the world and the national British point of view, the British Government reserved for itself freedom of action (whatever that may mean) in certain areas of the world invoking the similar position existing under the Monroe Doctrine for the United States. Now the Monroe Doctrine had not been mentioned by the American Government in connection with the Kellogg Pact. It would be a difficult subject to raise without "qualifying the ideal of world peace" which Secretary Kellogg wants to maintain spotlessly unqualified. But there are such things as eloquent silences and despite the indiscreet blurting out of the thing by the British Government, the American Government remained obstinately silent about the Monroe Doctrine. The present writer heard Dr. Clayton Morrison in no less a place than Geneva assert in public that it was the intention of the American Government not to except the Monroe Doctrine from the Kellogg Pact. Such a declaration coming from a man who is counted in both Continents as one of the inspirers of the Kellogg Pact and in general of the outlawry of war deserves the greatest possible attention. It attributes to the American Government so startling a departure from a traditional policy as would seem to require a more positive statement than mere silence even in the face of provocation. Moreover what happens under the black cloak of this official silence? There is only one way of interpreting a silent being: watching his actions. Now the same Secretary of State who has put forward this unqualified ideal of world peace has been actively engaged in renewing treaties of arbitration with a number of powers in which a reservation in favor of the Monroe Doctrine has been introduced now though such a reservation did not exist in the previous form of the treaty.[1] In the circumstances, the inevitable conclusion is that the United States do not mean to arbitrate any question arising out of the Monroe Doctrine, which for practical purposes means any question arising out of events happening on the American Continent.[2]

What is then the value of the Kellogg Pact? First it must be made quite clear that as a pact for the outlawry of war, i.e., as a psychological method for driv-

[1] Treaties have been offered to Great Britain, Japan, Germany, France, Italy, Austria, Hungary, Belgium, Czecho-Slovakia, Poland, Lithuania, Latvia, Portugal, Switzerland, Holland, Denmark, Norway, Sweden, Esthonia, Egypt and Spain. All the new treaties bring in the new Monroe Doctrine reservation. The old treaties renewed have been amended so as to insert this reservation.

[2] The Senate Debates (Jan. 1929) have vindicated this view. The Pact passed without reservations but both Secretary Kellogg and Senator Borah assured the Senate that the Monroe Doctrine remained unimpaired.

ing war out of human possibilities, the Pact is as good as non-existent. Not only in its reservations and interpretations but in its very essence the Pact does not outlaw all wars. It must therefore be considered merely as one of the systems before the world whereby a certain number of wars are forbidden by collective treaty. Viewed in this light the Pact presents quite a different efficiency according to whether it is considered in its effects on League Members or on non-League Members.

In the first case, that is to say the case of the Members of the League the Kellogg Pact closes the gaps in the Covenant just as the Protocol did. But as such of course it only outlaws aggressive wars. It forbids neither defensive war nor League wars of collective vindication of rights amounting to collective defensive wars. These two points are now admitted on both sides of the Atlantic. The Kellogg Pact therefore so far as the League is concerned is a rough and incomplete sketch of the Geneva Protocol which however has practically the same results as far as outlawry of war is concerned.

As to non-Member States the Kellogg Pact is an instrument of moral discipline without any guarantee of actual efficiency. The non-Member State is free to interpret its second article as it wishes and to find reasons for not going to arbitration (for instance American tacit reservation on the Monroe Doctrine). It is also free to interpret the first article of the Pact as it wishes or as it feels compelled to do by its own state of mind at the moment, calling the war "defensive war" or "intervention" or any high-sounding name which may appeal to its public opinion.

It will be noticed therefore that from this first point of view the efficiency of the Kellogg Pact may be considered under two heads: its efficiency in stopping permissible wars which are left open by the Covenant; its inefficiency in stopping "defensive" wars which are efficiently stopped by the Covenant; that is why the Kellogg Pact finally shuts up the ring in which the League Members are enclosed but it leaves non-Member States free to escape from the war prohibition ring through the wide opening of the "defensive" war which *for them* remains gaping.

From another point of view the Kellogg Pact has often been considered as an important step in international politics because statesmen and critics of international affairs have seen it as the beginning of an evolution of the United States of America towards the organized World-Community and the League. The present writer has himself expressed this view during the first period of the international discussion which followed the presentation of the proposal.[1] This argument calls in question the whole genesis and evolution of the Pact from the American side. The Pact was evidently born of the Outlawry of War School. This School, we know, is led by idealists of transparent honesty but who hold strong prejudices about Europe and about the League. Their opposition to political conciliation as distinct from judicial settlement is inspired in noble if, I believe, mistaken conceptions. Theirs is

[1] Article in *The London Times,* April, 1928.

the all-or-nothing attitude about outlawry without qualification. The political machinery tried to satisfy this group and incidentally to reap some international kudos for the American Nation by suggesting the multilateral treaty to M. Briand. But it was evident to any experienced internationalist that such a suggestion was bound to raise all the problems which the Protocol had tried to solve—problems which are not due to European wickedness (wicked as Europe no doubt is) but to the nature of things. The obvious step following the initial suggestion of a multilateral treaty should therefore have been a round-table conference, i.e., the conciliatory international method put at the service of the conciliatory international aim. The idea was of course mooted in Europe. Mr. Kellogg frowned hard. For the chief attraction of his Pact was that America could contribute a magnificent "unqualified" idea to the peace movement—could and did in Dr. Morrison's words begin a movement which had never begun before—without paying a cent in loss of international liberty and independence in its conduct. *The Pact therefore, though aiming at peace and coöperation was transacted by methods of power and isolation.* Hence the maze of speeches, declarations, notes, reservations and silences which obscure its meaning. And on the day the thought was mooted that it might be considered as the first step to further collaboration between the United States and Europe the most authoritative voices in the State rose to put down the error severely. America was ready to sign that she would not go to war unless she wanted and that she would arbitrate whenever she thought fit on the points which her Senate would define (and that is ultimately what the Pact means) but she was not going to give up one inch of her international sovereignty. America thus took back in the spirit what she gave in the letter and in the Kellogg Pact she showed the world a magnificent example of splendid isolation and power in terms of idealism.

The result was felt soon enough. The American President, after having congratulated himself and his nation on the idealism of the Kellogg Pact outlawing war, proceeded to advocate a strong navy to guarantee American defense.

Chapter XVI

THE PRESENT STAGE

TWO important events have occurred in the field of Disarmament since the meeting which the Preparatory Commission held in the Spring of 1927—leaving aside of course the two American experiments dealt with in the preceding chapters. The first of these two events was the arrival of the Russians; the second the conclusion of a shortlived agreement between France and England as to the questions which separated them in the Disarmament debates.

The collaboration of Russia was always considered in Geneva of the utmost importance. This is perhaps one of the most typical examples of the almost magical effect of the spirit of Geneva. No matter the attitude of this or that national government or public opinion towards Soviet Russia—and there is a wonderful variety of such attitudes, some of them more or less picturesque—the attitude of the Community of Nations meeting in Geneva has always been sane; it evinces neither horror, repulsion, fear nor any of the feelings which the cheap and popular press has been fanning in some western countries, nor an undue haste to secure the friendship (and incidentally the concessions) of the new economic Church-State. Geneva remained all through soberly cognizant of the necessity of securing

Russia's coöperation if the constructive work of the League was to be efficiently and successfully carried out.

This necessity is particularly felt in the field of Disarmament. Russia is surrounded by a belt of nations all of which have reasons to fear the Bear's ill moods, and the numerous debates, advisory and diplomatic, which have been devoted to disarmament matters in Geneva bear witness to the creative power of this fear, always manifesting itself in all kinds of reservations, objections, exceptions and special clauses. The absence of Russia from the League organization increased the difficulty to a considerable extent. Behind the veil of absence and silence, the dangers of the Russian Bear loomed larger and many a diplomatic flesh was made to creep as it had not crept since its nursery days. The League, i.e., the Nations in League assembled, have never hesitated in seeking the direct remedy for such evils. Nothing sobers down imagination in a fever as the cold facts of reality. The Commission, the Assembly, the Council solicited Russia's coöperation in all kinds of forms private and public though with a dignity which was not lost even in the face of discourteous replies. As if further to complicate matters a Russian diplomat was murdered by a Swiss citizen during the Lausanne Conference and the murderer, benefiting by a well-meaning Swiss law which demands a two-thirds majority in the jury for condemnation to be possible in murder cases, was set free. This action incensed the Russians who refused to tread on Swiss soil as long as they did not get satisfaction. It is to the honor of the

League and of the Swiss Government that the incident was satisfactorily closed mostly in order to enable Russia to attend the meetings of the Disarmament Commission. Any one acquainted with the state of Swiss feeling towards the Soviets will be able to gauge the extent of the sacrifice consented by the Swiss Government for the sake of the League. Such a sacrifice measures both the international spirit of the Swiss Government and the sense of world responsibility which the Council proved in the transaction of this business. By implication, it measures also the inanity of the Russian contention that the League aims at isolating the Soviet Republic.

Isolated the Russians were and still are, but by their own choice. What is wrong with them is not their doctrine but their method. Who can say that their doctrine, as the end of a slow evolution, would not work as well as ours? But it cannot live when suddenly planted rootless on our ground. The Russians are isolated not in space but in time. They have cut themselves loose not merely from their past but from the present of those who surround them and even from their own national present. They are in a kind of Marxian nowhere and therefore no one can really get at them.

Nor can they get at anybody. They came to Geneva and brought a plan for immediate, general and complete disarmament. When M. Litvinoff, whom I had met years earlier in London before he became a world figure, called on me, he asked me whether the Commission would reject his scheme. "My dear Litvinoff," I answered, "they will do something much worse than that. They will consider it very carefully." The Soviet delegation imagined that they were going to get drama out of the Commission. They were, as most revolutionists, old-fashioned in esthetic tastes, as old-fashioned as newspaper correspondents. If only the Press and its writers understood that present day people are matter-of-fact and want brass tacks! But no. The Press correspondents and M. Litvinoff wanted melodrama. The Soviet delegation's dream was a dramatic presentation of a plan of complete and immediate disarmament by a Bolshevik clad in angelic red and its rejection by a chorus of bourgeois devils clad in Mephistophelian white. (The colors they have changed; we must grant them that.)

The bourgeois devils grinned. They knew too much. The Commission enjoyed a speech by M. Paul-Boncour who, the Commission had perhaps forgotten, is a socialist. M. Paul-Boncour fraternally upbraided Messieurs Litvinoff and Lunacharsky for their schoolboy enthusiasm and inexperience. M. Paul-Boncour who, despite the youth of his eyes, intellect, voice and even years, has persuaded Nature to grant him premature white hair, took advantage of all his privileges at once and smiled with his eyes, scorned with his intellect, caressed while chastening with his graceful and modulating voice and crushed the two Bolsheviks with the experience which shone upon his hoary head. "That is how *we* began, my friends. You bring us nothing new." After the usual adjournment to the next meeting, the Commission had to discuss the proposal whether it wanted or not. The discussion makes excellent reading. The keynote of the debate was provided by Lord Cushendun, who after much preliminary pin-pricking, largely of an irrelevant character, on whether Soviet Russia meant it or did not mean it, proceeded to object to all the vegetables while leaving the meat severely alone. A score of delegations spoke after him. Some were witty, others acute, obvious, jeering, contemptuous—none was convincing. For the fact is that, though there was a case and a very strong one against the Soviet proposal, and though they all knew it or at any rate felt it, no one could put it. In official politics, the truth of truths cannot be uttered. We know of course what this case is. We discussed it in the first part of this book. The reason why immediate and general disarmament is impossible for all but the Bolsheviks is that armaments are instruments of policy; the reason why it is possible for the Bolsheviks is that their policy needs no armaments and would in fact fare better without them. We do not sympathize therefore with the attitude of the speakers who in the committee criticized, jeered and showed their wit at the expense of the Soviets with an undercurrent of distrust in their motives; but we cannot grant to the Soviet the letters patent of international virtue which they claimed for having shown their readiness to disarm at once. Their limbs would be disarmed but not their hearts. Their intentions are bellicose. Only, their war—a class war—needs other weapons.

The discussion therefore was entirely irrelevant and the Soviet proposal was sent to keep company with the Treaty of Guarantee and with the Protocol in the hell of international life, which is paved with good conventions.

But the Soviet delegation presented another draft in which they sought to effect a measure of immediate reduction of armaments by applying the principle that the stronger powers must disarm at a quicker pace than the weaker. In this second draft States are divided into categories according to the size of their armed forces; the first category undertake to reduce their armaments by one-half; the second by one-third; the third by one-fourth; naval armaments are reduced according to the same principle but the number of categories of States is only two; air and chemical armaments are prohibited. This draft was commended by the Commission to the attention of the various governments.

It will be noticed that in presenting such a draft the Soviet delegation leaped over a formidable obstacle—indeed so formidable that the Commission has been paralyzed now nearly two years not merely by it but by the mere shadow of it. This obstacle is the lack of an objective system whereby actual figures of limitation or reduction can be determined. Nothing illustrates the complexity of Disarmament better than the following observation: *the difficulties with which the Commission has been contending all these years are purely preliminary and do not concern the determination of the actual figures to be inserted in the future Convention.* The task which has baffled the Commission is the relatively modest one of drafting a blank convention, a framework without any figures. Thus for instance such problems as the very serious difference between England and the United States on cruisers and that between Germany and France on trained reserves are still pure matters of *quality of armament* to be solved before the far more difficult question of the *quantity* of armaments is approached. From this remark it will be seen that the future of Disarmament is not rosy.

For even when a blank Convention has been drafted by common agreement, the task incomparably the most difficult will have to be faced. Nations will have to come forward and fill up the blanks with the figures of men, material, budgets, ships and aeroplanes which they bind themselves not to exceed without permission of the Council. And it is obvious that then and only then can it be said that the actual business of disarmament will have begun. The Commission is very far indeed from that moment. At present, their work is paralyzed by not a few points of disagreement as to the frame for that picture which is not painted yet. And not the least of their differences as to this frame is that which separates England from America on the matter of cruisers.

The reader is now familiar with the idea which underlies these pages, i.e., that in the absence of an alternative system of policy—which can be no other than coöperative international running of the world—armaments are indispensable as instruments of power and that therefore all disarmament discussions are bound to transform themselves into armament discussions.

No more brilliant and more authoritative confirmation of this view could be wished than the significant incident which excited the western world during the summer of 1928. France and England, the two protagonists of the League Disarmament Commission, could not agree about the principle to be adopted for naval reductions. France said Total Tonnage; England said Tonnage by Categories. The Commission, finding its work blocked by this disagreement, hinted that a direct negotiation between the two Governments would be an excellent occupation during the recess. The two Governments took the hint and presently came to an agreement. The British Foreign Office, eager to cheer up the world, gave the bare news without going into details. But the world, instead of smiling, frowned severely. Italy growled that she knew nothing and would know nothing of it. Germany began to put questions. America was angry. What had happened? "For once that we try to agree," said M. Briand, shrugging his shoulders before the whole League Assembly, "we were not lucky!"

Please note that growls, grumbles and protests began before anything was known of the agreement except that it existed. Now this is most instructive, for it plainly shows that every nation is fully aware of the true character of so-called disarmament agreements. Let these remarks be read in no spirit of suspicion against the motives of either France or England. Both the French and the British Governments sought to further the success of the League Commission by bridging over their own differences, which, they had been told, held the Commission inactive. The cause of the trouble does not lie in the nations but in the material they are handling. In the absence of a universal agreement never to use arms except on collective authority, armaments can only be increased (relatively, which is what matters); they can never be decreased. Hence the growls and grumbles of the others. How were the armaments of these two going to be increased? Against whom? And note the origin of the grumbles and growls: Italy lest her claim of equality with France had gone by the board; Germany lest her insistence on limitation of (French) trained reserves had been the land price of sea concessions made to England; the United States lest these sea concessions had taken a form favorable to the type of cruiser which would strengthen the British navy and weaken her own. And mark the result: *all these fears were justified when the terms of the agreement became known.*

What is the position? One of complete anarchy. The League need not be saddled with any responsibility for it. The League is the only bright spot in the work of disarmament. I mean by "the League" the spirit and the method of international order, law and coöperation as opposed to the spirit of national anarchy, caprice, isolation and unrestricted power. Nothing more outrageously unfair than to attack the spirit of coöperation—for that and nothing else is the League—on the ground that a few Members of the League fail to come up to it now and then; and to utilize such a muddle-headed argument as an excuse to remain outside the League, i.e., outside the spirit of coöperation. The League of Nations, as distinct from the nations of and in the League is responsible for the only two definite results which the work of disarmament has achieved: it has provided the method of work, which is one of continuous hammering at the problem from every point of view and not one of sporadic and fitful attempts at Messianic solutions inspired from on high; it has provided the spirit without which no solution is possible, for it is now evident to all but the mind-deaf that disarmament being not a world-problem but a world symptom, must be cured by curing the world disease which is anarchy and that therefore the spirit of the League is the only possible cure for disarmament.

The work is in suspense. All preliminaries are over. A few definite questions remain open for discussion. They are not being discussed. When one is "solved" between two partners its solution raises a storm. The spirit is not there. It is waiting.

Part III

PROSPECTIVE

Chapter I

THE PROBLEM RE-STATED

IN the first part of this work we have examined the problem of disarmament and the obstacles to its solution from a theoretical point of view: in the second we have reviewed the events which constitute its recent history. The time has come now for harvesting the fruits, if any, of our long work. Can we save an opinion, can we above all save a hope from those ten years of drudgery?

Ultimately our hopes must rise from our opinions. The most pressing need is therefore a clear vision. What is it exactly that we are after? There was once a French schoolmaster who now and then made a point of interrupting his class a few minutes after he had started them off on a problem and when he saw that they all had plunged lustily into their calculations; he then asked them what the problem was about. Very few of them knew. They were all seeking eagerly but they did not know what.

So it is with disarmament. The thing has caught the imagination of all the leading classes everywhere; all want it; all preach it. But where is a clear definite idea of it to be found? Enough has been said here to show that the subject is one of baffling complexity. What with our theoretical disquisitions and our rapid survey of the maze of activities in and out of Geneva, the core of the problem has by now sunk out of sight. Let us re-state it in the light of all that precedes, and try to class the ideas which it calls forth in a proper order and hierarchy.

To begin with, disarmament is not an isolated problem; armaments are one of the features of our present international life. It is therefore hopeless to try to solve the problem of armaments in isolation from the remaining problems of the world. Indeed this idea seems to me to occupy the very basis of the question. As long as it has not been grasped, and as long as it does not impose itself on governments and peoples alike we shall be wasting our time in vain endeavors. We are in the presence of two facts, national armaments and wars, which are but two manifestations of international life in its present stage of development: just as individual armaments and duels are manifestations of national life in a certain stage of its development. There is no question that if wars could be declared unthinkable by decree (or pact) and if armaments could be declared obsolete or illegal by convention the problem could be easily solved. But while duelling and the disarming of individuals had to wait till the national state was strong enough to organize the political and judiciary life of the country, we hear everywhere of great schemes for disarming straight away and for outlawing war by incantation.

Such schemes are simply irrelevant. They have of course their place, and a most useful place too, in the chain of cause and effect which is history. The Russian proposal for immediate disarmament, the Kellogg Pact, sent across the world waves of influence which ultimately are bound to act in the right direction if only because the trend of our present day evolution is irresistibly set in the right direction. But such good effects as they may ultimately have are not inherent in them nor due to their virtues. In so far as such schemes fail to recognize the solidarity of all the manifestations of international life, they are irrelevant, they miss the point.

It is a curious fact that these two proposals should come precisely from the two self-isolated peoples. The United States of America and the Union of Socialist Sovietist Republics (U. S. A. and U. S. S. R.) are strangely parallel in present day history. The fact is so striking that it has been discussed more than once and in a variety of quarters. The parallelism has been based in the common tendency of the two great republics to think in terms of economics and to organize themselves as gigantic workshops—though of course with principles of economics standing at the two poles of opinion. The parallel becomes fascinating indeed when from this plane of home politics it is carried into the wider field of international politics in which U. S. S. R. and U. S. A. occupy strictly symmetrical and similar positions. Both remain outside the League of Nations. Both prefer to pursue a purely national path. The reason is that both are isolated, perhaps by their immensity, from the rest of the world; the masses remain in both ignorance and even enmity towards the European nucleus of the World-Community; their leaders, for reasons strangely parallel (belief in the American gospel of prosperity, belief in the Soviet gospel of communism) prefer this isolation to any commitment or entanglement abroad. The result is a policy which disregards the experience and the findings of the organized world and of course a tendency to imagine that problems can be solved in a simple way. The Kellogg Pact is a gesture purely symmetrical to the Soviet Disarmament Proposal. In fact, had not the Kellogg Pact appeared from the West, the world would have felt conscious of something missing to counterbalance the Disarmament Convention presented from the East.[1] When the Kellogg Pact appeared the symmetry was complete, Russia, after Geneva had been working for four years without her, had joined up from her solitude and was going to tell them how to do it: very simple; you want to disarm, just scrap armaments. And America turned up from her prosperous isolation and, disregarding the Covenant, the Treaty of Guarantee, the Protocol, Locarno, she smiled and said: I am going to tell you how to do it. You want to abolish war? Very simple. Just abolish it in a pact.

Well, the first thing to do if we want to get anywhere is to understand that the problems of the world are all intertwined and that it is impossible to solve any of them by decree or incantation. There is only one way of solving the problem of disarmament and that is by considering it, in the admirable French saying, as *the organization of peace.*

Does this mean that all efforts toward direct dis-

[1] Or vice-versa.

armament should be given up until peace, i.e., a civilized World-Community, has been fully organized? Of course not. The organization of peace is a work of patient evolution and we should wait long if we had to bide our time till such an evolution was over. It may be useful at times to test the progress made in the world organization by exacting from it as much disarmament as it will yield. Moreover, we know that armaments are in themselves a danger and a possible cause of war; it is therefore indispensable to watch them closely and the safest method for watching them is to make them the object of an international convention. Finally there is a double legal reason why the direct method should be tried on sincerely at the earliest possible moment: i.e., that the League Members are bound to disarm in virtue of the Covenant and that those League Members who are at the same time signatories of the Peace Treaties are further bound to disarm in virtue of the preamble to the military clauses of such Treaties.

But, it may be argued, is not all this direct effort going to turn into an effort towards armaments? Have we not laid down that in the absence of a well-organized community all disarmament conferences turn into armament conferences? This most pertinent question can only be answered by going closely into another—and a most important matter—which has remained in abeyance since the very beginning of this work. What are we to understand by "a well-organized community"?

Chapter II

THE ELEMENTS OF INTERNATIONAL ORGANIZATION

AT this point, the observation is bound to be made that we have struck a subject which stands, so to say, on its own legs. The organization of the World-Community should be investigated and pursued on its own merits and not merely as the means whereby disarmament is to be attained. Like the American preacher who advised his folk to be good Christians because that would make them prosperous, or like the Englishman who proclaimed that honesty is the best policy, we seem to be advocating the organization of the World-Community not as an aim in itself but as a means to lesser ends. The temptation is of course strong to leave aside the disarmament scaffolding and to concentrate on the building itself. It must be resisted if only because, though in the heaven of ultimate aims the World-Community occupies a stall higher than disarmament, in the earth of human whims and caprices disarmament is a more cherished child than the World-Community. So that, were it not for the wish to disarm, progress in World-Community organization would be precarious indeed. In short, though the organization of the World-Community should appeal in itself to all reasonable men, we must justify it in terms of disarmament like the preacher with an eye on results justified Christianity by prosperity. We shall therefore remain strictly within the main road of our enquiry. We do not propose to study what a well-organized World-Community should be in an abstract way, but in relation to disarmament. Our question is: What do we require in a World-Community in order to disarm?

In so doing we are not however risking a fall into error. We are by now deeply convinced of the unity of the several problems raised by international life. We know therefore that whichever international problem we choose as a method of approach, the World-Community which we shall be led to outline will always be the same, since in actual fact all these problems of international life are but one.

We can then return with an easy mind to the ground we surveyed when we analyzed the problem of disarmament in search of a solution. We found then that the problem led towards the World-Community not through one but through several avenues. Every one of these avenues will provide us with definite aspects of the World-Community required.

The kernel of the problem we found to consist in the fact that armaments are instruments of power. The way to disarm lies therefore through the evolution which may reduce the efficiency and utility of armaments as instruments of power. It is evident that the first requirement in this respect is the complete renunciation of war as a means to solve conflicts. Nothing can be done until this phase is gone through.

This is not the place to deal with the arguments used against the adoption of a *complete* system for the peaceful solution of conflicts, and we are only concerned with the theoretical possibilities of such a system, i.e., with the internal economy of the problem of disarmament, with what disarmament really implies. If nations do not wish (reasonably or unreasonably) to adopt an absolute, all-round system for the peaceful solution of conflicts, all we say is that their negative implies an assertion of power, and as long as power and not law and reason governs the world, disarmament is impossible.

Needless to say a complete system for the peaceful solution of conflicts does not mean a complete judiciary system. It must on the contrary provide the three forms of settlement generally considered as indispensable if all conflicts are to be covered: i.e.,

A Judiciary, the Hague Court, with compulsory jurisdiction for justifiable disputes,

A system of arbitration for an intermediate category of questions,

A system of conciliation for the most difficult and delicate of them.

In short the first requisite of the World-Community is a system of peaceful settlement of conflicts analogous to that which is set up in the first part of the Geneva Protocol—that dealing with arbitration, possibly developed in what concerns conciliation.

Such a system implies the existence of permanent international organizations not merely of a judicial but also of a political nature. Indeed, our belief in the need of political as well as judicial organs for our

World-Community is but the translation in terms of institutions of our conviction that international life is one and cannot be dealt with in watertight compartments.

But the necessity of a Council and of an Assembly may be deduced directly from the study of the problems of peace. We approach the problem here along another of the avenues which in the first part of this work enabled us to penetrate to the very core of it. We know that most of the causes of war are too elusive to be imprisoned beforehand in the network of judicial claims and principles. We know in fact that the cause of causes is essentially in the nature of a protest against the injustice of Justice; it is the tension developed by the growth of life pulling away from the static conception of the world in which the laws in force were once dictated. Something is needed then to keep its hand on the world's pulse and detect its slightest quickenings in order to guard against possible fevers. And this something must be of an essentially political character since the categories it will have to handle are not yet caked into law. Such is the function of the Council of the League of Nations. The well-meaning but straying critics who reproach it with the defectiveness of its decisions fail to realize that the Council, like all political organizations, lives in the imperfect. Imperfection is the law of action just as perfection is the law of thought (save that the law of thought is more generally disobeyed.) Our system for solving absolutely every conflict by political means would not be complete were it composed only of the Court of Thought, the judiciary organ which decides on matters crystallized enough for thought to handle; it must also comprise a political body to handle imperfectly in the realm of action those conflicts of action too fluid to be seized by thought.

But the political organs of the World-Community, its Council and its Assembly, justify their existence in other no less important ways. We have seen that the kernel of the problem of disarmament lies in the fact that armaments are instruments of power and we have sought to reduce their value as instruments of power by devising an alternative system for the solution of conflicts. Why, however, wait till conflicts occur? Why not prevent them? There are two ways of preventing conflicts. The first is by studying beforehand matters which might eventually lead to conflicts; the second by stepping in as soon as the relations between two or more nations begin to turn awry.

It is obvious that both these ways require the existence of permanent organs of world government. Their activities however must be studied separately. The first category of them, i.e., the study of matters which may eventually lead to conflicts, covers practically every branch of international life. Nor could it be otherwise. The unity of the world meets us at every turning of the road. The Covenant has spread the nets of the League far and wide; it has not spread them far enough. The World-Community must take in hand all its problems as world problems if it is to nip in the bud all its conflicts. Hence the necessity of a far-reaching organization of its technical activities. Such is the justification of the third aspect of the World-Community —a justification made on the strict plane of disarmament and independent of any other form of enquiry which would of course have led us to the same result.

What is the chief aim of the technical organization of the League from the point of view of disarmament? To provide world solutions, i.e., solutions of coöperation and general interest, instead of solutions of power, rivalry and selfish national interests, for the ordinary problems of the world. In this way, occasions for future conflicts are avoided. The most important of these organizations is the Economic and Financial Section. Thanks to its existence, problems of economic rivalry may be turned into problems of economic cooperation and the seeds of future wars gradually removed from history.

The second way in which the political organization of the World-Community may act in preventing conflicts is more especially political. It consists in taking the necessary measures for ensuring that two or more nations whose relations tend to take a bad turn are not left to drift into a conflict. This is precisely the object of Article 11 of the Covenant and in general of Articles 10-20. No other world requirement perhaps points more clearly to the necessity of a political world organization. Life is what it is: no matter treaties, pacts, covenants, promises, standards, there come moments when in certain places certain people let their passion or foolishness take the upper hand. In such cases there must be somebody whose business it is to see:

(a) that the trouble does not become general;

(b) that if possible there is no trouble at all.

Now, no nation or group of nations can or should be trusted with so delicate a task. It is essentially a world task; it must be carried out on a world basis and by standards coming as close as possible to world standards. It is moreover an essentially political task. The point need not be labored. The conclusion is obvious. The Council and the Assembly of the League must be entrusted with such a function. The Covenant is drafted to meet this obvious conclusion.

The essential point to be grasped here is that the effort of the Covenant is concentrated on prevention and not on cure of war. This point has been overlooked by the extremists on both sides: American Anti-Sanctionists and French Sanctionists. While the former have described the Covenant as a military alliance, the latter have denounced it as a pacifist scrap of paper. The truth is equidistant from these two picturesque caricatures.

Let us briefly review the economy of the Covenant:

(a) All conflicts to be submitted to pacific settlement, and meanwhile, no wars;

(b) The Council to watch all movements of a disquieting nature and to step in with discretionary powers of negotiation. No wars with parties that submit to the award under (a); no wars in any case till three months after (a) has failed; yet the power and duty of the Council to take up the matter under (b) even during three months after the failure of (a).

We submit that this system is statesmanlike and of

a nature to prove efficient in the immense majority of cases. War under the Covenant system is a most unlikely event indeed. Why? Because all the obstacles and precautions have been accumulated in the period which precedes war, a period during which public opinion is still undecided and moral factors can exert a powerful influence over it.

The importance of this argument could not be exaggerated. When a conflict is brewing, the public opinion of the nations concerned lacks an authoritative and objective standard. Its own judgment it knows to be befogged by the fumes of patriotic passion; the judgment of the adversary but adds to the flames and fumes; foreign nations may side this or that way and in any case may or may not be reported. Nor is the public opinion of the nations concerned the only one in need of enlightenment. The press and public of neutrals to the conflict stand in need of leadership. That authority and leadership comes from the Council. Needless to say, the world machinery does not always act exactly as its constitution might lead us to expect. Sometimes, the presence of extraneous forces leads to a resultant in a slanting direction. But the beneficent effort has been absorbed in the process. During the Corfu case, for instance, the Council's action was deflected by that of the Council of Ambassadors; and moreover the Assembly, which was then in session, did not meet for several days owing to the fear of public opinion which prevailed in Italian circles. But who doubts that the Corfu case was the triumph of the Council of the League over the Council of Ambassadors and the triumph of the Assembly over the Italian Government?

It is sometimes suggested that in a conflict between great powers the Council will split. But will it? The forces of unity are already strong and they tend to become stronger and stronger with exercise. We may discern in them the Council's esprit de corps, the interweaving effect of long-standing coöperation and last but not least the desire to come up to expectations, for the Corfu case showed eloquently that the world expects the Council to make a clean job of every crisis which comes its way. The only element of weakness in the situation comes from the fact that there are great powers outside the League. Thus the true responsibility for whatever ineffectiveness there is in the League method lies at the door of the nations which remain outside it.[1]

[1] During the first visit which M. Litvinoff paid the League he was invited to meet some of the heads of departments in the Secretariat. Conversation fell on the working of the League. The Russian delegate attacked the Council for its policy and mentioned in particular the solution given by it to the questions of Upper Silesia and Vilna. One of his interlocutors had no difficulty in showing how mistaken M. Litvinoff was with regard to Upper Silesia on which the League, as distinct from the victorious powers, can prove an unimpeachable record of statesmanlike impartiality, but yielded the point about Vilna. Another of the League officials present carried the argument further explaining to M. Litvinoff that the position was as follows: Russia is not in the League; if she was, she would be a Permanent Member of the Council: the Council can do nothing without unanimity; therefore the responsibility for the defective solution of the Vilno, or indeed of any other question on which the Council has proved below the Russian ideal, lies at the door of Russia herself. The burden of this story is that no great power has a right to criticize the League since by joining the League they can, through the operation of the unanimous vote, force the League into the righteous path of which they hold the secret. Great powers outside the League should never mention the League except to show cause why they don't belong to it. This would prove sufficient to keep them busy.

The economy of the League system is thus directed towards the prevention of war. Contrary to what passionate opponents maintain and to what passionate partisans would wish, sanctions are but a relatively small part of the Covenant. The peace system of the Covenant comprises Articles 8-20. Of them only one, Article 16 (and by implication Article 17) touches on sanctions, i.e., on the cure of war. The remaining eleven Articles deal with the prevention of war. This is as it should be. The road to war may be represented as a steep gradient reaching a top after which the road falls rapidly towards hostilities. The point is that the brakes which human good will and ingenuity can devise are almost sure to work efficiently in stopping the chariot of war on the way up-hill, when peoples and governments are still reluctant. The chariot can then still be kept under control. But once the summit crossed which separates the slope of wisdom from the slope of folly, no brakes can be fully trusted, even if they may still work. This is the idea underlying the Covenant. No one who has not grasped it should throw stones at it.

Had it been grasped, a good deal of the ink wasted on the problem of sanctions would have been spared. The problem has been made particularly difficult owing to the French mania for an efficient military sanction system which in its turn has roused the opposition of nations jealous of their unrestricted right to choose when and with whom to fight. For be it noticed the nations which lead the van against the system of sanctions are not so terribly inimical to war and to warlike measures as they would have us believe. The mainspring of the anti-sanctions campaign is the anti-entanglement tendency.

Let us look at the problem with detachment, from a world point of view, free from the security-psychosis and free also from the anti-entanglement prejudice. What is the position? We want to surround our pre-war period with every possible guarantee against war. It is this pre-war period and not the hostilities period we are thinking of. Just as prisons are erected not so much to lock people in as to induce people to stay out, so sanctions must be devised in order that nations should not have to undergo them. The most efficient system of sanctions is that which will never be applied.

Here is a nation which suddenly turns its eyes towards war. Public opinion gradually rises, fanned perhaps by the press. Events evolve rapidly and the day comes when the responsible statesman at the head of affairs must make up his mind. Behold the Prime Minister in the quiet of his Cabinet at a late hour meditating on the problem. He has before him full reports from his military, his naval, his financial, his economic, his labor advisors. He has now turned his attention to the diplomatic position. And at this late hour perhaps an over zealous member of his Foreign Office staff has discovered in a forgotten drawer of a derelict desk an uncut copy of the Covenant of the League of Nations. The Prime Minister's eyes fall on Article 16. All that is wanted is that on that moment Article 16 should have a salutary effect on the mind of the Prime Minister whose country is thinking of war. No one can say that the fear of a full 100 per cent. efficiency of the Article is going to act in 100 per cent. of the cases but this may be said that it is indispensable to maintain the principle of Article 16 in the general economy of the Covenant in such a way that it may act as often as possible and as efficiently as possible to put the fear of the World-Community into the soul of the statesman who is thinking of war.

We are sometimes told: you must not provide for breaches of faith because trust in nations is ultimately the basis of all contracts—of sanctions contracts as well as of others. The argument is puerile. To begin with, breach of faith is not the only nor perhaps the main danger. We must guard against national passion and it is in order to sober down national passion that it is wise to count on some collective method for enforcing the world's peace. But moreover, if in a society of fifty all are pledged, the society can afford to risk the breach of faith from the passionate misbehavior of one of its number. It is true that ultimately the society must rely on the plighted word of its members but there are three degrees of security:

1. The plighted word of one nation.
2. The plighted word of all the nations seriatim and separately considered.
3. The plighted word of all the nations associated in community.

It is obvious to every schoolboy that the security of the last is infinitely greater than that of the second, and the security of the second infinitely greater than that of the first.

Further, it is a curious fact that the same people who object to sanctions are the people who advocate preparedness. In one of those impressive speeches with which he now and then was wont to break his still more impressive silence, President Coolidge put almost side by side the two arguments in apparent ignorance of their incompatibility; [1] he urged that the world should walk in faith after the Kellogg Pact and he argued for the duty of self-defense and the Navy Bill. Now we are in the thick of it. Sanctions means the pooling of self-defense. It means nothing else.

For in the League system of peace the problem of self-defense does not remain unprovided for. It is on the contrary brought in and given its appropriate place. It is a most difficult problem. Left to itself, it would destroy all peace systems through the natural tendencies of all nations to interpret as self-defense every violent action they are led to commit. Prohibition of self-defense is unthinkable. The only statesmanlike and constructive solution which remains is the pooling of the duty of self-defense. Who attacks one associate attacks them all. That this principle raises a host of problems with regard to its application is undeniable. But surely the worst attitude which can be taken towards it is to give up the principle altogether on account of the difficulties which its application raises and to declare that the anarchical right to go to war whenever one feels in a state of self-defense is to remain inviolate.

[1] Armistice Day speech to the American Legion, Washington. 1928.

Since the question of sanctions resolves itself into a question of collective self-defense it follows that the most important problem to be solved in this respect is that of aggression. The favorite argument of the No-Entanglement School is that there is no satisfactory definition of aggression. Thus Secretary Kellogg:[1] "I have not been able to agree to that reservation. My objection to limiting the scope of an anti-war treaty to merely wars of aggression is based partly upon a very real disinclination to see the ideal of world peace qualified in any way, and partly upon the absence of any satisfactory definition of the word 'aggressor' or the phrase 'wars of aggression.' It is difficult for me to see how a definition could be agreed upon which would not be open to abuse. The danger inherent in any definition is recognized by the British Government, which in a memorandum recently submitted to the Sub-Committee on Security of the Preparatory Commission on Disarmament of the League of Nations discussed attempted definitions of this character, and quoted from a speech by the British Foreign Secretary, in which Sir Austen said:—'I therefore remain opposed to this attempt to define the aggressor, because I believe that it will be a trap for the innocent and a sign-post for the guilty.' I agree with Sir Austen on this point. It seems to me that any attempt to define the word 'aggressor' and by exceptions and qualifications to stipulate when nations are justified in going to war with one another would greatly weaken the effect of

[1] To the Council on Foreign Relations, New York, March 15th, 1928.

any treaty such as that under consideration and virtually destroy its positive value as a guarantee of peace."

This argument has been fully answered by Professor Shotwell when he pointed out [1] that Sir Austen Chamberlain had already accepted an excellent definition of aggression when he committed his country to guarantee the victim of aggression under the Locarno Treaties. This definition has been formulated by Senator Capper by merely re-drafting in general terms the ideas underlying Article 5 of the Treaty of Locarno which Sir Austen Chamberlain himself drafted, signed and had ratified by his king in Parliament. Senator Capper's resolution considers as an aggressor the nation "which having agreed to submit international differences to conciliation, arbitration or judicial settlement begins hostilities without having done so." If it is good for Locarno, why not for everywhere?

But of course the discussion is carried on in an atmosphere of hair-splitting objections which is altogether unreal. The point is not definition but conviction. Though regretting to find him on the other side, I confess a good deal of sympathy not with the premise but with the conclusion of Senator Borah's remark: "There is no satisfactory definition of aggression. I have spent hours trying to hit upon one and have concluded that it is impossible to discover a satisfactory formula. It seems to me therefore that the question of aggression and definition must be decided in the light of the particular circumstances at each time of

[1] *New York Herald and Tribune Magazine,* January 8th, 1928.

crisis and that no satisfactory definition can be discovered in advance." [1]

The question of aggression and definition must be decided in the light of the particular circumstances at each time of crisis. That is the statesmanlike and reasonable view to take. But it does not exclude, rather does it imply, three most important requirements to make such an emergency decision as effective as possible:

(1) That the decision be taken by nations in Council assembled and not by each and every one of them on her own accord or following lines of prejudice, alliance or interest.

(2) That a certain number of criteria be defined beforehand if not to bind at least to guide the decision.

(3) That permanent machinery exist whereby the Council and the criteria are brought to bear on the case as soon as possible.

It will be readily seen that the conclusion of all our enquiries is the same, or, better, that all our conclusions harmonize. We noticed how the problem of security could only be solved by pooling the idea of security so that the security of any one nation became the concern of all of them; we noticed also that the problem of disarmament could only be solved by pooling the idea—not of armaments but of the use of armaments, so that, in the admirable words of Professor Hull, disarmament is a world agreement as to the use of national armaments; we noticed how the problem of sanctions could only be understood when it was con-

[1] Quoted by "The World To-morrow," May, 1928.

sidered as the pooling of the idea of self-defense transferring it from the nation to the world so that who attacks one nation attacks the whole world; we naturally find now that the only solution for the problem of aggression is to transfer it from the national to the world plane. But our conclusion here carries important consequences with it. For, when transferring aggression from the national to the world plane, we transform its nature as well as its scope. In the national plane, aggression could be physical and was generally considered as physical; in the world plane aggression is moral. The world, i.e., the community, is based on, nay, *is* essentially law, order and peace. The aggressor is the law-breaker, the order-breaker, the peace-breaker. The aggressor is the transgressor.

Viewed in this light, the analysis of aggression leads us to a consequence similar to that which we observed when dealing with sanctions, i.e., the main point about aggression is that we should organize the World-Community so that it never occurs at all. If we want it clearly defined and, better than defined, clearly understood, it is not in order to make it easier for statesmen to know which side of the fence they must fall when rushing to arms, but so that there is no occasion whatever for arms or even for alarms. We are, let us repeat it and repeat it again, we are concerned with the period of drift towards war, not with war. We are only interested in war events in so far as the definition of national duties in hostilities may act as an efficient deterrent for hostilities ever to occur. Our method consists in creating a state of mind which will class amongst shameful things the refusal of a nation to solve conflicts by peaceful means.

Let us now summarize our conclusions:

(1) Disarmament is a world problem. It can only be solved by the world as the world organized in a community.

(2) This World-Community must possess a Court with compulsory jurisdiction on all questions of a judicial character.

(3) The World-Community must possess a political organization with powers:

(a) to seek the solution of disputes of a non-judicial character by all possible means,

(b) to deal with threat of war and war,

(c) if necessary to lead the world in any action, moral or even physical, against law-breaking nations.

(4) The World-Community must possess a technical organization which will gradually bring under the world control the study and solution of a growing number of problems which are taking on a world-wide scope.

But before we come to a more detailed translation of such a program into actual political terms it may be necessary to review the general position with regard to the practical possibilities of the principles here outlined.

Chapter III

THE UNITED STATES OF AMERICA

THERE is a narrow-minded and wide-passioned kind of type which is unable to take a truth if it dislikes it and which, when unable to disprove arguments, is content with casting doubts on motives. Let no honest man suggest or imagine that this book has been written as yet another effort of League propaganda. That its author is a convinced believer in the League is evident. Why he believes in the League is evident also. But the League is the conclusion and not the origin of his thought. Had his experience of Geneva led him to the conclusion that the League was not necessary or that it was prejudicial to disarmament, the author would not have hesitated to print it here in its appropriate place. Moreover *this League* is not sufficient for disarmament to succeed in any appreciable degree; all the absentees must join and many an important work must be undertaken before a substantial measure of disarmament can be absorbed by practical politics. The league here advocated is one which many a League Member would shrink from. No. This is no work of propaganda. We are not thinking of fostering any particular institution. We are looking war in the face and our conclusion is that we must do a good deal more than we are doing if we want to conjure the hideous thing out of our life.

That point cleared, it is evident that in our opinion the chief responsibility for the stagnant state of disarmament lies with the nations which remain outside the League. No amount of vituperation, invective or self-congratulation can alter the fact. The League is a courageous attempt at solving world problems in a world way and those who remain out of it are badly crippling this effort without contributing any positive alternative of a true constructive character.

We have heard many a so-called reason for the United States to remain outside. There is no reason whatsoever for such a thing. There are explanations of the fact. Of course, the fact is a fact, i.e., a link in a chain of events, the connection of which with preceding facts can be more or less intelligently described. But though the fact may be explained, the act cannot be justified.

The American reader however may say that America has contributed an alternative and a better alternative in the doctrine of the Outlawry of War. Let us then examine this doctrine as a general solution of our problem, now that we have had an opportunity to discuss the first installment of it under the name of the Kellogg Pact.

The outlawry of war doctrine is a red herring, the best meaning red herring that ever navigated the waters of international thought and politics, but a red herring for all that and one most disturbing for the true cause of disarmament. The worst about it is the high standing, the generosity and even the intellectual distinction of its trainers and inspirers. Let us briefly recapitulate the tenets of the school and confront them with our own conclusions:

(1) War must be outlawed as an institution. *All wars* without exception. But self-defense remains. No general guarantees are given of what a nation may come to consider as self-defense. For instance, if Mexico granted Japan a ninety-nine years' lease on a comfortable little bay in Lower California the outlawry of war school does not tell us what would happen. Curiously enough, the outlawry of war school, while allowing self-defense, condemns sanctions. Yet, sanctions, we know, is but another name for collective self-defense. We are therefore entitled to define the outlawry of war school as a party which condemns all wars except irresponsible self-defense; and the Covenant as a system which condemns all wars including irresponsible self-defense, except wars fought after collective self-defense has broken down. The confusion of the outlawry school arises out of an excessive vagueness in the definition of war.

Dr. Clayton Morrison attempts such a definition but although he devotes to the matter a considerable space in his treatise he fails altogether in his endeavor. The fact is that the Covenant of the League of Nations implies such an advance in international law that the progress of its substance makes its wording obsolete. Article 16 should not mention the word war. Surely the true similarity here is between war and duelling, a fact which the outlawrists themselves have not failed to observe but the importance of which they seem to have failed to appraise. War should be defined as an outbreak of hostilities between nations either in defiance of their covenants or else in the use of the rights left them by the Covenant to fight an issue between themselves when international methods for dealing with it have failed to bring about any other solution. An operation whereby the World-Community vindicates the rights of the world peace or the rights of a particular nation which has obtained an award in its favor before the world institutions should not be considered as war. The matter is important not merely in order to clear the confusion created by the outlawry of war school but also because it is difficult to admit in the present state of international law that a Covenant-breaking state should be allowed full belligerent rights. When war is thus accurately defined in the light of the new international law the objection to sanctions falls to the ground. It is true that the favorite argument of the outlawrist remains, namely that the use of violence in international matters whether it is called war or not should not be admitted at all in order thus to eliminate it altogether from international life in a kind of psychological repudiation. But this argument of the outlawry of war school falls to the ground also since all the outlawrists admit an intangible right of self-defense which is also a use of hostilities in international matters and only differs from sanctions, i.e., from international police action, which in our opinion is collective self-defense, in that the hostilities which the outlawry of war school permits may be the outcome of an irresponsible nation while the only hostilities admitted by the Covenant system as international police action must be the outcome of a unanimous international council.

(2) There is going to be a world court with affirmative jurisdiction "with a code of law of peace based upon equality and justice between all nations." This is excellent but alas we are told that "The greater nations know that compulsory arbitration is for them fraught with grave dangers."[1] And moreover "There are some questions which, in the present state of the world, or in any conceivable state of *this* world, cannot be decided by a tribunal of any sort. In the case of the United States we have only to think of tariffs, and immigration, and the Monroe Doctrine, and prohibition, and the allied debts, to see how a meddlesome nation, *under cover of our pledge to arbitrate any dispute whatsoever*, could provocatively precipitate an issue which was none of its business—in any sense which an independent country like the United States would acknowledge—and then demand that we go to arbitration with it." It is difficult to choose the brightest in such a string of pearls. We notice the "independent" nation (there's the rub, independent, yes, not merely in law but in spirit, cut loose, isolated from the commonalty of the world); we notice the imposing list of examples, for they are only examples, of the questions on which the United States would refuse to arbitrate;

[1] These and other quotations, except when otherwise stated, are taken from "The Outlawry of War" by Charles Clayton Morrison, Chicago, 1927.

we observe that the Monroe Doctrine is one of these questions and knowing the admirable elasticity of this expression we begin to wonder whether its scope can be limited even to the vast American continent. Imagine France or Germany suggesting that they would arbitrate everything but European affairs! That is about the effect of the Monroe Doctrine reservation on American policy. True, Dr. Clayton Morrison declares that "the Monroe Doctrine is part of the war system of the United States" and yet with his usual candor and nobility he goes on to say: "We have to protect the Monroe Doctrine by war, but it is war that produces the Monroe Doctrine." A statement that no man with both heart and brain in their right places would care to controvert much as he might wish to complete it. Yet, the very prophet of outlawry excepts the Monroe Doctrine from arbitration and even if he has evolved from his opinions of page 68 to his opinions of page 196, we have every reason to doubt that public opinion in his country has followed him at that pace. Like most physically-quick-moving people, the American people are apt to take their political evolution at a quiet leisurely pace.

We are thus confronted with this somewhat paradoxical situation that the outlawry of war school are opposed to the true and only practical outlawry of war that can be, i.e., a compulsory system for the peaceful settlement of conflicts. The outlawry of war system would appear to be:

1. A judicial settlement of all conflicts provided for in a preëstablished code.

2. No settlement for the remaining conflicts, but wars of self-defense allowed on the unfettered decision of the nation that goes to war.

It is evident that this system can hardly be called satisfactory. The outlawry school shut their eyes to the two following facts:

(a) Conflicts left outside their international code would comprise most if not all the real causes of war. Following the same natural laws which operate in America, every nation would carefully keep outside the jurisdiction of the court its own area of interest and power, its own "Monroe Doctrine."

(b) The latitude given to every nation with regard to self-defense would enable her to get herself into a state of pig-headedness which in her eyes would justify any war as a defensive war. It is useless to talk about relying on good faith and honor. The danger is not in bad faith but in honest, blind passion.

The outlawry school is an international calamity. It is idealistic and must always command the highest esteem in the moral plane. But it has held up the natural evolution of the gravest problem the world has to solve by confusing the issue. In our opinion it is clear:

(1) That as an instrument of outlawry of war, its official suggestions, i.e., the Borah draft resolution and the Levinson draft treaty,[1] are incomparably less efficient than the Protocol and even than the Covenant of the League.

(2) That as instruments for the peaceful settlement

[1] They will be found in Annex, pp. 365 and 368.

of international conflicts they are far more conservative than either the Covenant or the Protocol.

The outlawry of war system does not therefore provide an adequate solution for the first of the requirements of our World-Community, i.e., that there should be a complete system of peaceful settlement of disputes. The first condition thereto is of course that all nations should submit to judicial settlement *all* their judiciable disputes. The step has been provided for in the Covenant and in the statute of the World Court, according to which nations may if they so wish recognize as compulsory the jurisdiction of the Court in all judiciable disputes. The outlawry school condemn the Court on three grounds:

(a) The Court is closely linked up with the League and therefore its decisions may be enforced by war.

(b) The Court is not bound by the body of law.

(c) The Court has no affirmative jurisdiction.

Of the three arguments the first was already answered when we dealt with both sanctions and the problem of definition of war. As a matter of fact we know that war if and when applied to enforce the decisions of the World Court should not be called war and is in any case the most respectable use of hostilities, certainly more respectable than the right of free self-defense which the outlawry of war school admits; moreover the relation between the World Court and the League is only the natural recognition of the fact that all problems of international life are but one and therefore all institutions of international life must be interconnected.

The second and the third of the arguments against the World Court are not altogether correct. Dr. Clayton Morrison himself comments on his own statement as follows:

"Moreover, a judicial body has jurisdiction, that is, the power to summon a defendant to come to court. This principle of affirmative jurisdiction is of the essence of a court of law. For a nation to be free to say, as Austria did when Serbia offered to submit her case to the Hague court, that she would not do so but would take the law into her own hands, is to make a futile mockery of the court. The league court has no more power than the older Hague court to bring to trial any nation that refuses to come. Indeed, the Hague tribunal was no more impotent at Sarajevo than the league court was at Corfu.

"No doubt the optional clause attached to the protocol of the league court, by signing which a nation confers upon the court 'compulsory' jurisdiction in any dispute to which that nation is a party, will arise in the reader's mind to qualify our contention. Twenty-three nations, it is said, have signed this optional clause. I have deliberately omitted to make mention of the fact for the reason that the significance of the fact is utterly nil in respect to the peace of the world. Not a single great power has signed the compulsory jurisdiction clause, and not a single one will do so, as the court now stands. Of the smaller nations which signed it, most acceptances were for limited periods of five or ten years.

"I say the larger nations will not sign it, and I add,

they ought not to sign it. The little nations have everything to gain and nothing to lose by compulsory arbitration, no matter what defects inhere in the constitution of the arbitral tribunal. Lacking in military power to defend their rights in disputes with the strong nations, the lesser nations naturally look with favor upon compulsory arbitration. The greater nations know that compulsory arbitration is for them fraught with grave dangers. They cannot afford to bind themselves to an obligatory settlement of *all* disputes by a court which itself is not bound. To thus confer a roving, irresponsible, blanket jurisdiction on any court of arbitration is to lay one's nation subject to the most unconscionable demands of other nations."

This statement is a chain of unwarranted assertions. To begin with the Court has not "a roving, irresponsible, blanket jurisdiction." The law which it applies is defined by Article 38 of its statute. Dr. Clayton Morrison will find no serious-minded person to agree with him either on this point or on the point that the League Court is an arbitration and not a judicial body. Moreover events have proved him wrong. Germany signed the optional clause, though a great power. Spain has signed it also, though the most powerful of nations after the great powers. The favorite scheme of the outlawry school with regard to the Court is instinct with the same unrealistic tendency which inspires their remaining proposals. Its ideal is codification of international law. Dr. Clayton Morrison pours scorn on the League for its paltry results in this field and goes as far as to quote in contrast Project No. 30

of the Pan-American Union.[1] He fails to notice however that this project was adopted by the Spanish-American Republics as a reaction against the policy of the United States. It is difficult to see how the world can progress towards a better understanding when men of high standing and pure intentions such as the leaders of the outlawry school undoubtedly are can go astray to such an extent. The main point is to have a court and a set of principles to guide its awards; to choose the judges carefully and to submit to its jurisdiction. That it gives advisory opinions to the Council and that it is too closely connected with the League are not arguments which need to be examined here. The question is not why does not America join the Court but why does not America join the League?

It is easy to see that the two short-comings of the outlawry of war proceed from the same source. The outlawrists want to have all the advantages of a World-Community without assuming its obligations; they want to enjoy peace but also to keep unimpaired their sovereignty, what Dr. Morrison calls their "independ-

[1] "The American republics . . . animated by the desire of preserving the peace and prosperity of the continent, for which it is indispensable that their mutual relations be based upon principles of justice and upon respect for law, solemnly declare as a fundamental concept of American international law that, without criticizing territorial acquisitions effected in the past, and without reference to existing controversies. . . .

"In the future, territorial acquisitions obtained by means of war or under the menace of war or in the presence of an armed force, to the detriment of any American republic, shall not be lawful; and that—

"Consequently territorial acquisitions effected in the future by these means cannot be invoked as conferring title; and that—

"Those obtained in the future by such means shall be considered null in fact and in law."

ence." The outlawry of war becomes an efficient proposal as soon as it is completed in both its defective directions by an adequate organization of the World-Community and particularly of its present form, the League. Let us examine this point, dealing at the same time with the objections which the outlawrists raise against the League.

We may observe that the two points are more intimately connected than might be thought at first sight. The area of undefined wars which may be taken as defensive covers precisely the area of undefined conflicts on which nations may not dare to commit themselves beforehand. There is a strict correspondence between the two problems: it comes from the fact that they are both situated in the *political* field. The eloquent preamble which introduces Senator Borah's draft resolution [1] contains the two following paragraphs:

"Whereas we have in our federal supreme court a practical and effective model for a real international court, as it has specific jurisdiction to hear and decide controversies between our sovereign states; and

"Whereas our supreme court has exercised this jurisdiction without resort to force for one hundred and thirty-seven years, during which time scores of controversies have been judicially and peaceably settled that might otherwise have led to war between the states, and thus furnishes a practical exemplar for the compulsory and pacific settlement of international controversies;"

We shall not quarrel with Senator Borah for having

[1] The text will be found in Annex, p. 366.

forgotten the War of Secession,[1] but we cannot let him run away with an argument which blatantly implies that the United States Federation is a mere legal Court. The fact is that the success of the American Federal Court rests on the existence of an all-round federated community possessing:

(a) Common bonds of interest

(b) Common feelings of patriotism

(c) An elaborate political organization more powerful as an executive than any other contemporary government except the Italian.

In view of the gravity of the issues and of the eminence and honesty of the man—for Senator Borah is surely a public man of whom any nation might well be proud—is it too much to ask that such elementary mistakes should be avoided in public life?

The features which Senator Borah forgot in the American community are precisely the features in which the World-Community which we advocate leaves far behind the outlawry of war scheme. For we con-

1 The capacity of American outlawrists for letting American wars slip through their memory is worthy of notice. Dr. Morrison writes: "War as a continuing system, professionalized, prepared for, and ever in evidence, has been relatively unknown in the United States. It has always been difficult for our people to envisage war. It has always been easy for them to envisage peace. I am leaving out of account the developments of the past decade. The perspective in which these statements apply is the long vista of American history within which our traditions took form. International war has been for us only an episode. The Revolutionary War in which the nation was born, and the Civil War by which it was preserved, belong in a wholly different category from wars between nations for the settlement of international disputes. America's experience of such wars was so slight as to leave her tradition unimpaired and her virgin concept of peace uncorrupted." He has forgotten that there is not one nation in Europe which has acquired more territory by war than the United States. The Mexican War suffices to establish the point.

sider it an indispensable part of our World-Community that it should:

(a) Possess adequate political organs,

(b) Aim at fostering common interests and a common world spirit in the world.

When dealing with this matter direct, we pointed out that a political organization was necessary in order to take in hand the causes of war. What have the outlawrists to say about causes of war? "Some, thinking superficially, may be disposed to say that the removal of the *causes* of war would do away with war, without law or court or any other substitute for war. If you could remove all the causes of war, there would be no war. This, of course, is as true as it is impossible. Even if the causes of war that exist to-day were removed, there are bound to arise fresh causes of war to-morrow. Just as in our neighborly and community life there are innumerable causes of individual disputes for the settlement of which courts of justice are necessary, so, as long as there are sovereign nations, there will arise unforeseen causes of dispute among them. And as civil law exists to prevent individual neighbors from 'settling' their differences by force, so international law administered by a court is desired to prevent nations from 'settling' their differences by warfare."

With all respect to Dr. Morrison, who is "thinking superficially" in this business? All the causes of war cannot be removed at one go, but on his own showing, all the causes of war cannot be removed by a judiciary only. We find ourselves again in the presence of Dr.

Morrison's extreme mobility of thought and expression. Here, in this paragraph, he leads us to think that he has removed war altogether by

(1) A declaration of outlawry,

(2) A court,

but he keeps up his sleeve

(1) The numerous cases in which he will not go to court nor to arbitration, i.e., when he will not accept, or when he will reserve for himself the right of not accepting, a peaceful solution.

(2) The right to fight in self-defense and to define self-defense as he pleases.

With this double observation we may dismiss the outlawry of war in so far as it claims to be a constructive proposal. We may find it again on our path as a critical proposal.

What is our solution for this truly crucial question—the removal of the causes of war? The existence of a permanent organization of the World-Community endowed with the necessary machinery for

(a) Forestalling conflicts whenever possible,

(b) Solving them by whatever available means—saving war—it may find at its disposal.

The fundamental ideas to be grasped here are two: the first is that the political conflicts cannot be dealt with by judicial means but must be handled politically; the second, that the moment when a political question becomes a political conflict is hard to find and that as every political question may become a political conflict, the World-Community is entitled to follow all political questions closely if only in order to insure against war.[1] This evident proposition is the point at which our outlawrist friends part company with us. They have a holy detestation for politics and diplomacy. "The illusion that a council of international diplomats invested with armed power to execute their decisions in vital disputes between nations is an organization of world peace, is dispelled when the processes of diplomacy through which such a body works are analyzed. Such an organization inevitably becomes the object of political manipulation by states, or groups of states, to utilize its power for their own special ends. The organization is bound to be inoperative in the most important and crucial matters, because its own power may be so easily divided at the source. In any political league of states there is bound to be perpetual intrigue to secure the aid of the common machinery on behalf of the larger states and of the principal groups of states, and to devise ways by which certain vital issues can be made to wear false masks so that they need not be brought under the jurisdiction of the league. Each great nation, and each group of nations with identical interests, regards the league with favor in so far as it promises to advance the interests of that nation or

[1] We may refer the reader to our opening remarks. Though we have dealt with this aspect of the question from the point of view of disarmament, our conclusion is identical with that to which we would have arrived had we enquired direct into the constitution of the World-Community as an end in itself. We have traveled along the road Disarmament → causes of war → political conflicts → political questions leading up to the conclusion that the World-Community must follow all political questions closely *in order to disarm.* Had we started with the question: what should be the political activities of the World-Community?, our conclusion would have been exactly the same: the examination and solution of all the political problems of the world.

group, and as something to be obstructed in so far as it fails to do so."

But the choice is not between "politics" and "no politics." The outlawrists seem to imagine that under their system "political manipulation," diplomatic intrigue and all the evils which they deplore, and we with them, would disappear. They would do nothing of the kind. We know what the outlawry of war scheme means: judiciary settlement of a small number of questions unlikely to lead to war, no settlement of questions likely to raise the passions, and an unlimited liberty to call any war defensive war. Do they really think their system likely to stop political machinations? Evidently not. Then the choice is between "politics" without organs for the expression of the World-Community and politics canalized and disciplined by the World-Community.

Had the outlawrists consented to study the League at work—which they can hardly be said to have done—they would have felt the immense effect of what is known as the spirit of Geneva. It is childish to expect that nations clubbing together will drop their defects, limitations, interests, selfishness. But the point is that while the pattern of these conflicting tendencies remains the same, something new is added by the mere fact of their union: the League of Nations has a higher moral tone than any of the nations which compose it. And sooner or later this fact is bound to tell.

What is the alternative? The free play of exactly the same forces without the unifying effect of the method, of the continuity and of the foresight of the world organization. And again, we must condemn the outlawry of war as insufficient. It does not realize the very essence of international life. Its mechanism for dealing with life is to the League Covenant what the tribal organization is to the highly specialized organization of a modern state. It waits for conflicts and deals with a few of them. The Covenant aims at keeping all things in hand as they occur and even as they tend to occur.

Let us now sum up our conclusions and the conclusions of the outlawry of war school in parallel form:

The outlawry of war school believe that "the problem of war must be disentangled from all other controversies and, thus isolated, brought directly before the nations for a yes or no decision."

We believe that the problem of (military) war is but the critical or violent form which the problem of permanent war takes now and then; that military war is but the crisis which the gradual divorce between ever-moving life and static law takes on when the tension becomes too strong; therefore we are convinced that war is but a symptom of an international disease or of international growth which cannot be dealt with independently of the remaining problems of the world as such.

The outlawry of war school believe that war can be abolished by outlawing it.

We believe that the world can no more abolish war by outlawing it than men can abolish disease by declaring it illegal.

The outlawry school believe that all that is needed

is a declaration of outlawry and the setting up of a world court with affirmative jurisidiction and a code of international law.

We believe that the system must provide for:

(1) A court for judiciable cases,

(2) A political organization for the remaining cases,

(3) A political organization (which may be the same) to guard against conflicts and if necessary to lead the world against the guilty party—guilt being defined as the transgression of engagements,

(4) A technical organization to solve problems before they degenerate into conflicts.

The outlawry school offer no solution for conflicts of a non-judicial character—the majority of them.

We believe such conflicts must be subject to a procedure such as that described in Articles 11-16 of the League Covenant strengthened by the universal adoption of the optional clause and of some of the clauses of the Protocol.

The outlawry school leave in the dark the question of self-defense—a gap wide enough to admit any wars.

We believe the League system practically outlaws nearly every war and that in any case self-defense under it is made a world affair and no longer left to the unrestricted decisions, whims or errors of isolated nations.

This simple, nay simple-minded panacea—the outlawry of war—holds the imagination of many an American citizen. To begin with it is simple. You outlaw wars and you submit your differences to a court.

What more perfect? This bald form is that under which it circulates and gathers converts. The holes, the gaps, the abysses opened out in it by further elaboration do not appear before the public eye. They are believed to be just slight qualifications of the general principle and not what they really are, its utter negation.

Then the outlawry school enables the American nation to bridge over the gap between its two favorite tendencies: the tendency to isolation (from Europe at any rate) and the tendency to see itself as a leading nation in moral as well as in material progress. There is no question that the ethical urge is an earnest and sincere element in American psychology; hence the implicit demand of the public for moral international leadership on the part of the government. Now the government's task is not particularly easy. They must satisfy the public pride in being "good"; their pride in being strong; their romantic attachment to the no-entanglement advice which Washington is supposed to have given them; their mystical belief in the mystery of the Monroe Doctrine; in these circumstances, is it strange that the government should have adopted this admirable pact which gives everything in a magnificent general public principle, safeguards everything by means of rather intricate judicial-political inferences and enables the United States to remain outside the Covenant of the League?

Unfortunately, the people of the United States have but few opportunities to hear a straightforward statement of the position. The immense majority of them honestly think that the United States are the only peace-loving nation with decent standards of international life. Few realize that their nation bears perhaps the heaviest responsibility for the slow development of international peace. Their absence from the League would suffice to justify this statement. It is sometimes argued on their behalf that they coöperate in nearly all its activities. The observation is correct but irrelevant, for the main point is not movement, work, activity; it is trust, confidence, moral tone. And what is wanted is not merely that the United States should be represented at all the League commissions but that it should assume all the League obligations. The issue has been befogged both by well-meaning fools and by ill-meaning knaves with an argument representing Europe as anxious to entangle America in European wars. "Europe wants your boys again." Such an argument leaves us cold. We at any rate want no American "boys" to come to Europe. We should be delighted if they stayed at home. We should be even delighted if they declined to go to Nicaragua. Our wish is that American boys should not go to war at all in any continent whatsoever. For it is all very well to speak of European politics as squabbles, intrigues and wars. But Europe through the League has salvaged country after country, Austria, Hungary, Bulgaria, Greece, Dantzig, without inflicting any loss of sovereignty on them, any humiliation, any marines, any leases for naval bases; and had a European nation carried out on another European nation exactly the policy which the United States have carried out in more than one Central American country there would have been a grave European war. The reason why the American continent is peaceful is not that the United States have succeeded in maintaining a higher level of international politics in it than in Europe, but that the United States, being incomparably stronger than any other of the American nations, have been free to develop whatever policy high or low they wished, without fear of endangering the peace of the continent.

The obligations which we want America to assume are not therefore so much those of Article 16 as those of Article 10. It is not that we want her as an ally in Europe; we want her as a peaceful nation in America. We do not want her to strengthen League armies for League wars; we want her to strengthen the League's peace by bowing before the Covenant and submitting to the courts.

Nor do we wish in any way either to imperil her material prosperity or to impair her moral prestige. Far from it. The only obstacle to her admirable commercial expansion is the deep mistrust which owing to her imperialistic isolation she is fostering everywhere and particularly in South America; and as to moral prestige she would regain the summits—the highest in her history—which she reached in 1919 if she came forward with truly imaginative proposals for world peace and disarmament.

The responsibility of America is therefore due to the fact that she gives the world a lesson of unlimited and irresponsible sovereignty every day. She does not accept the Court except under her own conditions which fifty-five other nations consider inadmissible; she does not arbitrate except in a few cases and when her Senate has carefully defined the issue; she does not join the League but picks and chooses whichever points she wishes for coöperation according to her own ideals, wishes, whims or interests; she ignores the Covenant and brings forward an alternative scheme as if the ten years of work done by practically the whole of the remaining nations had been the futile cackle of hens. This attitude of "take it or leave it" which America takes, whether for arming or disarming, whether for arbitration or for refusing to arbitrate, whether for defining the Monroe Doctrine or for laying down a no-entanglement policy, this feudal ring which is still to be heard in her voice is the true obstacle on our path. Our American friends do not seem to realize that, in the words of a French poet, the way a gift is given is worth more than the gift, so that such a thing as the Kellogg Pact, ostensibly an act of coöperation, was put to the world in an uncompromising attitude which was deeply un-coöperative, thus destroying by its spirit what its letter meant to convey.

The whole position must be revised from the very beginning if we want true progress in disarmament. I am not—never was—of the opinion that America may be made to glide into the League in a kind of absent-minded way: I hold that the American people must face the issue squarely; that it must realize on the one hand the immense gravity of its responsibility while it remains outside, on the other the full meaning of its obligations if it joins. I believe that the very breadth and difficulty of the true position once it is put squarely before the American nation is of a kind to appeal to its imagination. The American people has a remarkable psychology, a mobility amounting almost to fluidity; a genuine desire for what is good; an enterprising, an almost adventurous spirit ready to experiment with new ideas; and finally a readiness to be led. That is why, though in my opinion the United States is the blackest obstacle on the path towards Disarmament, I believe it to be also our brightest hope.

Chapter IV

GREAT BRITAIN

NEXT to the United States the heaviest responsibility in the slow pace of Disarmament must be attributed to Great Britain. The facts are there and stare us in the face. England turned down one after another every effort made in Geneva. Though her genius it is which made the phœnix-like dove of disarmament rise again from its ashes, English were the leaden arguments which shot the bird dead again when it soared, perhaps too high, in the Protocol. Locarno is to England's credit, up to the moderate point which we have had occasion to discuss in its time. When the League Commission came to brass tacks, the English delegation presented a draft convention obviously inspired in a conservative, not to say a reactionary, estimate of the position. Naval advantages were carefully protected. Budget limitation was refused. Even the most reasonable measure of international supervision was frowned at. A restrictive and even at times a negative interpretation of Article 8 was put forward in order to preserve a freedom of armaments which it is the express aim of the Covenant to destroy. In the matter of manufacture of armaments, England pursues a policy equally at variance with the strict interpretation of Article 8 of the Covenant. The sum total of her state activities in Geneva would be dismal indeed if the work of her distinguished son Lord Cecil were not called to mind in order to restore the balance.

Nor is this all. For we know by now that the work of disarmament is inseparable from the work of the League. We are aware of the one-ness of international life and we realize that it is needless to expect nations to acquire the peaceful turn of mind and the trustful habit while the bigger States follow a policy of power, zones of interest and all the rest of it. Not only must the League develop in all directions, but it must remain the chief political agent for the management of current events. Now, it is painfully evident that Great Britain, which might have had the leadership of the League, as the saying goes, for the asking, has left it vacant and taken in practically every case a line at variance with the best interests of the world.

First as to the development of the League, England has repeatedly made herself the protagonist of that silly movement for so-called League economy which seeks to set a limit to the League budget. Mark this point. The country which refuses to limit her armament budget is foremost in demanding that the League budget should be limited. It is impossible to interpret such an attitude except as a movement to check the growth of the League altogether. For obviously no one can wish the child to grow who limits his expenses to those of the first months of his infant life. This attitude is particularly strange in relation to the economic and financial department of the League to which England owes more than one concrete material advantage.[1] But it is equally deplorable in relation to every other department. The League is one whole and it is as a whole that by fostering the spirit of co-operation it may gradually drive out the spirit of war.

Then, England, at any rate in recent years, has evolved a policy which tends to elbow the League out of the chief problems of the world. There is a curious theory about that the League is a kind of death-bed doctor called only when every other method has been tried and failed. Nothing could be more absurd than a fanatical point of view in this matter. No man in his senses would suggest that if two powers have a difficulty pending and succeed in squaring their difference quickly, they are to be upbraided for not having brought the matter before the cumbrous apparatus of the League. It may even be granted that certain pretty wide, almost world-wide problems such as for instance Reparations, cannot be easily handled by the League as long as the United States is not a Member; but the fact remains that the League should be the chief political machinery for international politics when every question of general interest or a question implying third nations or again a question of principle arises. The distinction is no doubt vague, but so is life. The criterion is not to be found in a set of rules but in a living spirit. It may be frankly said by way of example that the policy of leniency towards Italy in

[1] Such as the recovery of the £12,000,000 loan made to Austria which without the League's own brilliant success in this field later would have been altogether lost.

Albania and worse still the cavalier Italo-English treaty at the expense of another member of the League, Abyssinia, are types of political action which cannot be held to be conceived in the true spirit of the League and that the problems involved would have fared much better had the matter been transacted fully through League channels.

Finally England has remained unaffected by the League in the essential inspiration of her policy which is one of power and world supremacy carried out along the old familiar lines of give and take and balance of power. This statement is so obvious that it needs no elaboration. An example of what it covers might easily be given in reviewing the post-war policy of England with regard to Persia.

The English reader is entitled to argue that no other power has done better. But even if we granted the argument (unfair as it would probably turn out to be towards France and towards Germany) we would take the view that our English reader was too modest indeed. Why limit England's rôle in the world to that of any other nation? Has she not led for a hundred years in social, industrial and political progress? Why not become that world leader for whom the world still looks in vain?

At this point the English reader makes a significant gesture of caution and in a discreet whisper expostulates: "You see, we would lead if we could, but what can we do with those Americans? Whatever we do we can't break with them."

There is no question that the attitude of isolation

and unrestricted sovereignty dear to the American nation is a matter of serious and justified concern in England. A democratic country, she must think twice before committing herself to a line of policy which might bring her into an armed conflict with the United States, for it is evident that her people would only go to war with America if vitally affected by the issue at stake. The position has led to not a few suggestions which we might perhaps discuss here in order to dispose of this point once for all.

The matter of Anglo-American relations may be taken in a number of levels. At the lowest of them, we find the outspoken nationalists on both sides of the water—men who see a war coming and maybe want it in their subconscious depths. They are of course extremely rare. Such a war would be a criminal folly. But that does not mean that it is unthinkable nor even impossible. For it is well to remember first that things drift that way and second that nations may go mad. That things drift that way is the inevitable conclusion to which must come all observers of Anglo-American commercial rivalry. "If I read history aright, we are nearer war to-day than ever before, because we are pursuing a competitive trade policy, and crowding other nations into the background. A policy of this kind inevitably leads to war. . . . So long as you dare to contest the control of the sea with your goods, you are going to have war, as sure as you are sitting in this room. So long as we are proceeding on the lines we are following to-day, war is absolutely inevitable. I do not care whether it is with Great Britain, or some other nation, you are going to have war. . . . Yes, I mean Great Britain, or some other nation whose interests are affected. Great Britain may not herself at the outset declare war, but she will let some smaller nation do that, and then get behind her." So says Rear-Admiral Plunkett, Commandant of the Brooklyn Navy Yard.[1]

It is easy to dismiss the Rear-Admiral; not so easy to dismiss what he says. Now, in the presence of this drift towards war, the wisdom of the masses and of their governments is but a poor dam apt to be burst by a sudden flood of passion. It is therefore necessary to seek some means whereby the calamity may be averted.

Above the dismal level of primal forces under commercial or naval disguise, we find a group of solutions based on the comforting statement that blood is thicker than water. This statement is a truism. Truisms are dangerous things. Generally they are not true. In this case, our truism falls short of truth for even if it be granted that blood is thicker than water, interests and passions are thicker than blood. Be that as it may, the thoughtful Englishmen and Americans who sincerely wish for an understanding between the two nations based on the ties of common origin, may be classed under three heads: at the lower end stand those who advocate an alliance, a kind of English-speaking union for international policy. Their endeavors are vain; for the union they seek, being on too narrow a basis, and not too safe a basis of fact, is bound to remain on

[1] Quoted by W. H. Edwards in "Heading for War," New York, Payson and Clarke, 1928, p. 101.

too low a plane. The basis of race implies the plane of interest and on the plane of interest there is no hope whatsoever of an Anglo-American understanding. English and American interests intersect at too many points: the Panama Canal cuts right across a vital line of communications within the Empire; South America is a market in which both John Bull & Co. and Uncle Sam & Co. meet on terms of keen competition. China is in a similar case. Canada is as much a link as a battle-ground of rival influences. Nor is this impossibility of an Anglo-American alliance on the low plane of material and racial interests to be deplored from the point of view of the world. It would inevitably antagonize the remainder of the world against the Anglo-Saxon group. It would certainly stimulate a movement towards financial emancipation from the pair London-New York; and it would indefinitely postpone the only constructive policy which can save the world from anarchy and war.

A little higher up we find a tendency to buy America out of the naval squabble by granting her special concessions in the maritime law in time of war, i.e., by making her a kind of privileged nation entitled to special rights as a neutral. This suggestion is much to be deplored. It amounts to a bargain with the isolated nation at the expense of the World-Community which it declines to join. In point of fact the world is to-day very much in the position in which the great European monarchies found themselves when the king was strong enough for his writ to be the law for everybody except a handful of unruly barons. In the

World-Community which is gradually emerging out of the feudal chaos of international life there still lingers one big powerful baron, the United States, who refuses to bow before the common law. Another powerful baron, loyally within the law, would then go back on his loyalty in order to conciliate the good graces of the rebel and grant him special privileges to remain free to help whichever side he chose, either the king's troops or the rebel's against the king's authority. The suggestion from the World-Community point of view is inacceptable; from the strict point of view of Anglo-American relations it is of little value for, the matter being put on this low plane of American interests, America cannot give the shadow of a law of war for the substance of a potential superiority in naval armaments.

Higher up again we find that solemn and beautiful idea: "The joint sea-trusteeship of the two great Anglo-Saxon peoples." It is a true mouthful. It may of course mean nothing at all as is often the case with mouthfuls. If it means anything it means that England and America are to take joint responsibility for the peace of the world. But trusteeship calls forth a number of questions. By whom granted? To whom responsible? It is obvious that trusteeship in international matters implies the existence of an organized World-Community on behalf of which the trustees would act. America is not ready yet for this stage. When she is ready, it is not too much to hope that England may be ready for the next stage.

For, above all the insufficient and inapplicable solutions of Anglo-American relations, there is one and only one which would be satisfactory. Union, like sonnets, begins at the end. What is the end which England and America may adopt as common to both? Unless such an *aim* is discovered it is useless to try to find a basis for union in the realm of *means*. Now there does not seem to be any way of conciliating England's interest with America's interest unless the one and the other are lifted above the plane of narrow conflicting rivalry to the plane of coöperation and it is evident that in such a plane the true interests of England and America are identical with the best interests of a peaceful and well-organized world. England with her unrivaled imperial experience and with her masterly use of finance, America with the vitality and the imagination and the public spirit of her great business men could be the joint leaders in this truly magnificent enterprise. On this plane and on no lower one, their union could be both possible and beneficial to themselves and to the whole world.

A general survey of England's other political interests would lead to a similar result. The survival of Great Britain's faith in the navy as her surest shield is one of those cases of over-living forms of thought which were analyzed in the first part of this work. The unaided British navy would have been unable to save Great Britain in the last war. She had to coöperate with one or two dozen other navies and a score of armies. If ever there is a future war the British navy may prove as useful as a howitzer would be in an epidemic. It is a curious fact that those who most stoutly object to the Covenant and the Protocol on the ground that it would put the British fleet at the beck and call of foreigners, are precisely the most prone to argue that Great Britain must have a fleet to meet responsibilities of League action to vindicate the peace of the world. No. Let us repeat here what was said with regard to the United States. It is not the British promise to fight against the aggressor which is wanted but Britain's promise not to fight or threaten to fight when she does not get what she wants. That is the point and no other. And it is inasmuch as Great Britain will advance along this path of law and arbitration that she will help disarmament and peace.

For a nation which has reached the summit of her power, safety is in law and not in force. That truly conservative principle does not seem to meet with as much acquiescence as it might in conservative England. It is useless to argue that whenever she has had an opportunity England has arbitrated, for, even if this were true, the way to strengthen law and arbitration is not by having recourse to them once the pro's and con's have been measured in a particular case and the balance found acceptable, but to acquiesce beforehand in the supremacy of the law. By her refusal to sign the optional clause of compulsory jurisdiction and to accept the principles of all-in arbitration England has cast a doubt on the peaceful way and therefore strengthened the high-handed way. Whether this effect of her policy is in her best interest many of her friends are entitled to doubt.

It should be added that in one or two cases her

actions have gone a long way to complete the ill effects which her omissions had initiated. We have already touched upon the Italo-British treaty over Abyssinia. No amount of explanations will remove the unpleasantness which all sincere workers in the international field must experience when two permanent members of the Council go so obviously behind the Covenant which they are supposed to uphold in order to return to the old game of zones of influence, and in the process conclude a treaty about a third member of the League which they treat as a mere pawn in the game. A still worse case is that of Egypt. The familiar explanation that Egypt is not a member of the League of Nations would be of course irrelevant even if it could not be met by the obvious remark that Egypt is outside the League because England blocks the way. The second argument, that the relations between England and Egypt are not international but domestic, begs the issue. For the point here discussed is no other than the effects on the moral atmosphere of the world in general of the fact that England keeps a whole nation in subjection through the use of sheer power. No one in his senses would expect England to be indifferent to what happens on the flank of her main imperial artery, but doubts may be permitted as to the methods chosen to manifest England's concern and to ensure its *security* at so heavy an expense for another people. Nations whom English public opinion has criticized for keeping huge armies for their security might well retort that the Egyptian case carries the preoccupation for security to a far more objectionable extreme than any which can be shown on the European continent.

Our trouble here is similar to that which confronted us in the case of the United States and the Monroe Doctrine. In fact England herself has drawn our attention to this parallel by linking up the two ideas: that of the Monroe Doctrine and that of the zones in which "interference would not be suffered." This language is heard by others and learnt quickly enough. And as long as the spirit which it represents is abroad in the world, any discussion on Disarmament is a sheer waste of time—with the obvious consequence that thereby the security of the British Empire itself remains in jeopardy.

Chapter V

RUSSIA

RUSSIA is perhaps after the United States and Great Britain the most formidable obstacle for the success of disarmament. In a sense it might even be classed first, for since our diagnosis is that the trouble is due to lack of unity in the world, the existence of a great nation ruled by a kind of "heresy" would appear to be the most serious difficulty of all for the achievement of what is our true aim, namely the establishment of a well organized World-Community. Such is in fact the impression which prevails when world problems are discussed with responsible Soviet leaders. Some of them look upon the League with a hopeless mixture of misunderstanding, mistrust, contempt and a jeering uncompromising superiority. For this type of man, the League is a capitalistic enterprise which aims at enslaving the world proletariat by an efficient organization of the world finance under the usual guise of politics. It is useless to expect any sympathetic attitude from this type of mind. A dogmatic mind, the possessor of final and crystallized truth, the orthodox Marxian, like the orthodox Catholic, is immovable. If you are not with him you are against him. The complexity and the fluidity of nature, the two key features of all historical life, are utterly unknown—

or ignored—by the orthodox. That more is in life than is laid down (the orthodox never dreams) in his philosophy, is a thought which cannot enter his tightly-packed head. All that can be done with him is to leave him till life disintegrates his hard-caked brain with its relentless movement forward.

But there is another type of Soviet man with better qualifications to interpret his country to the outside world. Though not less faithful to the Holy Communistic Church, he reads his Marxian gospels with a difference and he can argue. This type of man has a case. How could we join a league—he says—where we would be in a minority of one, holding views with which no one sympathizes? How could we take our difficulties to a court which applies a law based on capitalistic principles? This voice deserves attention. It bids us notice the difficulty. It does not go so far as to bid us remove it. But the League which—whether its members separately like it or not—is moved by a universal spirit, should endeavor to ease the path of Russia towards Geneva. Universality would be but a vain word if it were to remain limited to a mere physical sense and we should lose all authority to criticize our ancestors' bigotry if we were to ban a whole nation from our community on the ground that their laws for the distribution of wealth differ from our own.

Given the will, the way would not be difficult to find. For after all, the fears of the Soviet are probably exaggerated. The Soviet delegates may have felt a certain amount of "tendency" in Geneva. They should consider it as a natural phenomenon which can be explained objectively by a handful of reasons of the most varied description: a certain amount of social snobbery in an atmosphere saturated with European and American diplomats and unused to intercourse with newly acquired greatness; a survival of somewhat romantic mistrust from the long period during which Russia was the bugbear of all western citizens treated like children by a motherly press; the fears, prejudices and political interests of a ring of frontier nations all belonging to the League and used to presenting Russia before the League as a dangerous or at least as a dark horse; and last but by no means least the reaction of the West against the ludicrous campaigns of the Soviet press itself and the discourteous character of their official speeches and correspondence. But when all is said and done, the League has proved its sincere and honest wish to win the coöperation of the Soviets by refusing to budge from the strict objective merits of every situation regardless of any matters of style and etiquette; so that, despite many a verbal intemperance from Moscow, the Council, advised with true statesmanship by a Secretary-General endowed with admirable coolness, has always maintained a most magnanimous and dignified attitude in its relations with the Soviets.

It is evident therefore that the League has the wish to ease the conversion of the Soviets to true international coöperation. That being so, two sets of problems remain to be solved. The first is that of the legal relations; the second that of the political and economic relations. The first would appear to be the easier of the two. It is certain that Russia could obtain the appointment of a permanent Russian judge in the Hague; this judge would be in a position to advise the Court on all matters on which his country's special law would be concerned. The Court moreover would have jurisdiction on matters of international public law on which it does not seem that the difference in private law which Bolshevism implies would have a considerable bearing; the true obstacle would almost certainly turn out to be one of confidence rather than one of law; and confidence is a matter of life and experience.

As for the political and economic difficulties there might be some trouble at first. Means would have to be devised whereby the peculiar economy of Russia could be linked up with the economy of the rest of the world. The problem, for all we know, may be bristling with difficulties, but if the League's technical organization cannot solve it our answer is that then the problem is insoluble, an answer which would be too pessimistic a judgment on human ingenuity for us to accept. On the strictly political side, Russia would of course be permanently represented in the Council, a position which she might be tempted to utilize in order to spring a few crises on the capitalistic world. The standing difficulty so far as the West is concerned would be the policy of subsidy and propaganda which the Soviets carry on in the world under the thinly disguised organization of the Moscow International. But even in the face of this, perhaps the gravest difficulty of all, the special virtues of the League would triumph, for they result from the inevitable intertwining of interests which gradually develops out of political coöperation, and the Soviets would soon discover that it was to their advantage to let other peoples alone, evolving each along its own national line.

Two points must be borne in mind with regard to the Russian situation: the first is Russia's dependence on foreign finance, the second the dependence of the Soviet system on peace, for it is but plain common sense that what the war brought to them another war would take away. If there is one thing that Soviet Russia cannot afford to risk, it is a war. For these two reasons, and even if we deny to Russian Bolsheviks the pacific tendencies which are normal in every capitalistic or socialistic State, Soviet Russia is on the whole an element of peace in the world which can and should ultimately be absorbed into a world organization for coöperation.

Chapter VI

GERMANY AND HUNGARY

WE have given our reasons why we think that opposition to the status quo does not appeal to us as a serious argument against the strict enforcement of the League Covenant. Yet nothing could be more fatal to the peace of the world than a too rigid attachment to the situation created by the Peace Treaties. During their short life, the Treaties have undergone so many changes that the old-fashioned view about their sanctity has at last ceased to be an argument even in the press of the victorious countries. A reasonable and detached view of the situation would no doubt lead to the conclusion that far-reaching and courageous changes are indispensable in the status of Europe before disarmament can begin to be even a modest reality amongst us. Two are the directions along which the Treaty should be altered: the first is that concerning the disarmament of the defeated States; the second that which concerns territorial adjustments.

(1) *Disarmament of the defeated States.* There is no question that the disarmament of the defeated countries was a war measure dictated by the victorious ones. No one, and particularly no one hailing from a country which escaped the agonies of war, has a right to judge

the disarmament clauses of the Treaty with any degree of severity. Given the psychological premises, these clauses were even generous. But ten years will soon have elapsed and the promise implied in the preamble to those clauses, i.e., the disarmament of all nations, has not even begun to be fulfilled. Germany has every right to feel impatient and to insist that something should be done to justify her own disarmament by getting to business on the disarmament of the world.

The world, however, has two answers. First, that it has been trying these ten years and found the task more difficult than it had anticipated; and then that Germany is not so disarmed as she says she is and as she should be. Germany's retorts to these two arguments are not equally convincing.

If we may begin with the second, Germany's case is not particularly strong. We shall not seek our arguments in the brilliant but perhaps unsound reports of more or less inspired journalists, nor even in the weighty speeches of statesmen, delivered as they may have been on as solemn an occasion as M. Briand's answer to Herr Müller, the German Chancellor, during the Ninth Assembly of the League. Following our own method, the use of unimpeachable material, we shall attach more importance to the tendency than to the facts, since facts are but the definite and ephemeral fruits of the subtler and more permanent tendency; now the tendency may be watched at work by observing that the only military item which the Treaties (rather shortsightedly) did not limit, i.e., the budget, increases steadily in Germany since the Peace Treaty was signed.[1] That money must surely be going somewhere, and as it is budgeted for under the chapter of defense it surely does not go to buying cakes and ale. Germany therefore cannot have a good case to make when she alleges she is disarmed. Nor is it possible moreover to expect that she should be disarmed, considering that she lives in a world of rivalry and that, *granted the premises* which such a world posits as good, Germany has national interests both present and future which she must safeguard by all means at her disposal. It seems to us therefore that when Germany, somewhat hastily, insists that general disarmament must be so to say *paid her* on presentation of the check given her by the Allies in the Treaty, she is choosing a somewhat weak ground for her contention.

But her ground is very much firmer when she chooses to stay under cover of the first argument, i.e., that the League Council has found disarmament far more difficult than it imagined. This argument she can answer in two stages. First as to technical measures, Germany can always show that definite rules for disarmament can be drafted with a tolerable degree of definiteness by pointing to the military, naval and air clauses of the Treaty, so that she can easily dismiss the elaborate technical research of the League or, bet-

[1] Defense budget for the years between 1924-1929:

1924-25	465,750,000	Reichsmarks
1925-26	621,265,000	"
1926-27	658,100,000	"
1927-28	717,154,000	"
1928-29	715,600,000	"

ter still, throw it over to the political side to which it really belongs despite appearances to the contrary. As to the political side itself, Germany has a perfect right to insist that a measure of disarmament should follow up the remarkable spirit of world citizenship which she has shown in suggesting and signing the Locarno Agreements and perhaps better still in signing and ratifying the Optional Clause of the Hague Court. Germany is entitled to such an argument on at least two grounds: that it is not fair that after she has pledged herself to go to the Court in case of crisis she should be surrounded by bayonets and guns; and that the position of inferiority in which she has been placed by the Treaty should cease so that she—along with Hungary, Austria and Bulgaria—should be restored to a position of equality among the nations.

Here again, in our opinion, Germany would be well advised to drop the first argument and concentrate on the second. The fact that her armaments are still a matter for controversy reacts unfavorably on the whole discussion. Her insistence on this argument may be and in fact is interpreted as yet another means used by her for increasing her relative military strength —and let us not forget that in disarmament what matters is relative strength. Moreover there are elements in her political attitude which are still liable to produce a disquieting impression abroad—such, for instance, as the lack of symmetry between her Eastern and her Western policy even in Locarno. In our opinion none of these facts weakens the substance of Germany's claim but it does weaken her position in what might be described as tactical politics and it seems to us that the German case is stronger on the second ground, namely that the psychological position is untenable and incompatible with the League of Nations, since the League is based on equality and the situation created by the Peace Treaties rests on an obvious inequality. On this argument it is evident that the military, naval and air clauses of the Treaty must go.

But of course the world at large cannot afford to let them go for nothing. The world is now painted black save for four nations which are white. Equality can be achieved in two ways: by letting those four nations go black again or by whitening the others. The world's progress demands that the first solution should be rejected. We don't want equality in anarchy; we want equality in submission to the law.

Let us now enquire into the nature of this inequality and see whether it does not suggest a clear way out of it. The status of the four disarmed nations differs from that of the remaining members of the League in two important features: the first is that the armaments of these four nations are limited while those of the remaining countries are unlimited; the second that their armaments are not a matter of national sovereignty but of international concern. It will be seen that each of these two items of inferiority corresponds respectively to the two arguments outlined above: the argument of military inequality is particularly illustrated by the limitations imposed in the Treaty, while the argument of psychological inferiority is more directly connected with the fact that there is a treaty at all.

If then, as is our opinion, Germany should begin by seeking psychological equality first, it follows that she should concentrate on the success of a disarmament convention whatever its actual effect on military force may be, on condition that such a convention fulfill the main aim of Article 8 of the Covenant, which should also be the main aim of Germany's policy, i.e., to transfer armaments from the plane of unfettered national liberty to the plane of contractual obligations and to merge the present League control on four national armaments into a future League control on all national armaments whatsoever.

The same argument applies to the three other disarmed nations. It seems therefore advisable to envisage a future convention of disarmament as the fitting occasion for releasing these four nations from their present humiliating status, not by letting them go back to the anarchy prevailing at present but by devising an international system of contract and control to which all signatories would be bound on an equal footing.

(2) *Territories.* Yet the matter is not one of mere disarmament. The dominant feature of the problem we are discussing is its complexity, and it is the study of this complexity and not the bland ignorance of it which is going to place us on the right way to its solution. It is a curious fact that Locarno has not yielded its full harvest of confidence and security. The reason for this is to be found again in a knot of circumstances some of which may repay consideration:

(a) That nations are not blocks of one mind but

battle-grounds of opinion in which it is always possible to anticipate changes—an observation which applies particularly to a nation in crisis such as Germany is at present.

(b) That Germany, though having consented generous sacrifices in Locarno, has a heavy heart on the whole matter.

(c) That even though the Franco-Germano-Belgian situation may have been eased, there are other situations such as the Germano-Polish and the position with regard to Hungary which remain unsettled and any of which might deeply affect Franco-German relations.

There are in short a number of situations in Europe which are permanent sores and from which infection may be expected to develop sooner or later. The work of disarmament cannot make satisfactory progress unless this fact is recognized and granted the importance which it deserves. The key factor in the situation will be found to be psychological. No territorial reshuffling of Europe is ever going to give satisfaction all round on racial and territorial lines. But what is poisoning Europe to-day is not so much the inherent unfairness of a few definite cases as their unhealthy origin, the fact that the nations which are victims of them can show them to be brands of defeat. Here again, as in the case of disarmament, it is the feeling of inequality that is offensive, not merely to the victims of it but to the spirit of the League which has admitted the victims within its fold.

A series of readjustments of frontiers is necessary if only on this psychological ground. Of course such a suggestion is bound to be received by pundits with the quick fire of their most offensive words. "Madness," "folly," "absurdity," no pebble on the beach will be too hard to be hurled at the idea. Yet, considering what the so-called wisdom of the pundits is doing with the vital problems of European life, we may take courage and insist. Our age lives quicker than the ages gone by, and the Treaties are old and decrepit. We want a Europe based on common consent.

But common consent predicates mutual sacrifice. Germany, Hungary, Bulgaria, Austria cannot expect that the others should meet them on their own ground. They must be ready for an objective consideration of their gravest problems. This is not the place to lay down a complete repertory of what the new Europe should be. Merely as an example of the spirit in which the problems should be approached, it may be useful to put forward a few considerations on the Polish-German difficulty. This difficulty falls under two main heads: Upper Silesia and Dantzig. It is impossible to reach any agreement if Poland is going to insist on the present situation remaining what it is. But it is no less impossible if Germany brings to the debate an uncompromising attitude about frontiers and territories. The guiding light should be that, in a world regulated by law, frontiers need not be taken quite as seriously as in the iron age and that the continuity of a nation's territory is also a dogma lingering from an obsolete past from which we want to break. The exact rights and wrongs of the Polish Corridor affair are a highly technical matter. Whether the races which inhabit this region are Germanized Poles recovering their Polish skin as the German coating is rubbed off, or de-Polified Germans who are being re-Polified by the Poles, is hardly relevant. We suggest that historians, philologists, geographers should receive a well-earned rest and commonsense people get to business. Without any preference whatsoever on the matter, the world should be ready to accept any solution agreeable to both parties. All that is necessary is to realize that the plea that it is intolerable to allow German territory to be cut in two is not in itself sufficient to convince a man of sense. Ulster is cut off from England and Scotland, Corsica is cut off from France, the Balearic Islands are cut off from Spain, and no one suggests that the sea is an intolerable nuisance. There is a whole valley in Spain which can only be reached through French territory. England and New Zealand communicate through the Panama Canal and find themselves none the worse for it. These remarks are not put forward in order to defend the Polish claim to the occupation of the Corridor. They are merely put forward in order to show that the particular claim of territorial continuity should not be considered sufficient either in this or in any other world difficulty. The best solution may still be to abolish the Corridor. It is impossible to know without a thorough study of the ins and outs of the matter. But we must come to this study objectively and not with the idea that the showing of two spots colored with the German conventional color on the map of Europe is enough to justify the absorption of the intervening space.

Such is the spirit in which an enterprising reconsideration of the territorial situation created by the Peace Treaties should be undertaken. Such a work, in spite of its evident difficulties, is indispensable if any serious progress is to be made in Disarmament.

Chapter VII

ITALY—FRANCE

THE Italian nation cannot be said to be particularly fortunate. She happens to be in a mood of militant imperialism when the majority of the nations of the world are getting tired of adventures and would very much like to get down to a quiet enjoyment of the fruits of their past strife. It is true that Italy is not alone on the imperialistic path. As a matter of fact, she saw at the Peace Conference other nations—France and Great Britain, for instance—carve for themselves royal portions of the German and Turkish empires while she was content with what is picturesquely known in Spanish as "beak-syrup" and which Hamlet, amongst other less illustrious people, described as "words." The Italian mood of expansion is evidently felt also by the United States, by Japan and even still by Great Britain. But Great Britain has by now acquired such a mastery at this game that the more she expands the more self-denying she manages to appear in the eyes of an admiring world, while the expansion of the United States is clothed in puritanical respectability and that of Japan proceeds behind a quiet veil of smiling silence. Silence is not an Italian virtue and smiling is no longer the fashion since the land of Mona Lisa became the land of Mussolini. A virile frown and a vociferous assertion of youth are more suitable to this great power in a juvenile state. Europe should watch her *enfant terrible*. Her eyes are greedy—as greedy as those of the greediest children in the world, i.e., those that can be seen on English posters advertising sweets, soups and artificial custards. Juvenile Italy feels an imperial appetite North, South, East and West, and cares little for indigestion. But she has a case. She is growing—less quickly perhaps than a few years ago. She is in the bloom of youth and she feels that her elders have made too much of the opportunity afforded them by her infancy to occupy every part in Europe, Asia and Africa in which she herself would have enjoyed to settle had she been of age. And then, is not she the heir of Rome?

All this sounds formidable enough. But the Italian problem is not perhaps so difficult as it appears on the surface. Italy is not economically in a position to dictate terms. She cannot wage a war without the sympathy of the maritime powers or alternately of the organized World-Community. She has neither the English power for political leadership nor the French power for intellectual leadership nor the American power for economic leadership. Italy will adapt herself to whatever situation is created by a strong movement of world opinion, particularly if, as should be the case, the movement in question meets her requirements so far as is possible within the wider interests of world peace and order.

France is not a nation that need be considered in this survey of obstacles for world organization. All in her genius and all in her present political situation tends to place France in the forefront of what she herself has described as "the organization of Peace." If there is a difficulty to be found in France it comes from her tendency to make the order of the world too rigid, leaving an insufficient margin for unforeseen events and for growth. This tendency is born of both permanent and transitory circumstances. The permanent circumstances are to be found in the French genius itself. In deep contrast with the German genius, which is always in a state of fluid movement forward, the French genius has a tendency to crystallize into solid clear concepts, to "date" events and immobilize history. The very clearness of the French mind is made of this hard crystalline stuff. The perfect thought-out form of her world solutions is in itself one of the forms of this tendency to intellectual immobility. Further, in the present position of the world, France has fully realized that the system created by her last victory can only achieve a certain degree of stability if worked into a wider order embracing, if possible, the whole world. It is therefore difficult to dissociate French advocacy of a world order due to intellectual tendencies and French eagerness to preserve the order created by the victory due to a political necessity.

Though therefore from the constitutional point of view France is not an obstacle but rather a welcome help in the right direction, from the political point of view the world may have to expect considerable sacrifices from France if her constitutional ideas are to incarnate into definite institutions. In fact France may turn out to be after all the country which may have to sacrifice the most. To begin with, her "victory" must go. She has—be it said in her honor—rapidly outlived the first attitude of overbearing triumph, an attitude explicable in the circumstances and before which it is only a duty of international good feeling to bow with respect. Under the wise, nay admirable, leadership of M. Briand she has shown singular moderation in her dealings with her late foes and even with one or two candidates for future enmities. But there remain two important steps for her to take before a true new Europe can be born: the recognition of full equality with Germany and Hungary, particularly in matters of disarmament; the acceptance of the idea that even from the point of view of territorial distribution, the Treaties are no longer desirable, and that a regular procedure of revision should be put in hand by the League of Nations.

Chapter VIII

THE FAR EAST

FOR practical purposes the Far East means Japan and China. The Japanese problem is frankly imperial in character, i.e., the needs to be satisfied are not objective and material but subjective and spiritual. Japan is ambitious and wants to satisfy her ambition. There are four directions along which the Japanese pressure may be felt: Korea, Australia, the Philippine Islands and China.

The expansion of Japan in Korea is now a fact and needs no special comment save inasmuch as Korea may sooner or later create for the imperial power problems and anxieties similar to those which India raises nowadays within the British Empire. The question whether Korea represents a sufficient ground for Japanese expansion is insoluble since the need of expansion of Japan is a purely subjective phenomenon. This need must be taken into account as one of the forces which is shaping the face of the world in opposition to other forces equally respectable. The task of the world consists in preventing the clash of all these antagonistic factors, not in ignoring them.

These remarks apply with particular force to the position in Australia and in the Philippines. It is difficult to feel much sympathy with the Australian claim to exclusive possession of their continent. Their narrow immigration policy which confines the bulk of their immigration to men of British, and in general of Nordic, stock makes their position even more untenable than it would be if they admitted all kinds of whites. For it is obvious that the Australian people will never be able to develop the northern part of their continent. It seems that the hopes of exclusivist Australia are now put in such experiments as the development of air lines which will bring Australians South when suffering from the hot climate of the North, the building of homes better adapted as defenses against tropical heat and even the liberal application of sun-protecting dyes on face and hands. This last method is the most original of all. The question is whether, if Australians are to paint themselves black or yellow in order to develop their continent, the slogan of "white Australia" can still be upheld without some attenuations, however superficial. Moreover, if painted yellow, why not genuine yellow? The very nature of the palliatives suggested shows that the claim is untenable. It is in fact one of those cases in which the interests of the world at large are sacrificed to local interests, or even prejudices, protected by force. For nothing but the British fleet explains that Australia can do what no other people has been able to do in history.

Nor does this mean that Japan should be granted right of immigration in Australia without any more ado. To begin with, the capacity of the Japanese to colonize tropical countries is far from proved. The reverse would rather appear to be the case. Yet the position in the Pacific should be studied, but studied from the world point of view, not from that of this or that state, this or that people. Here again reason and coöperation should take the place of prejudice and rivalry.

In the Philippine Islands the position is entirely different. The Islands are well populated. They are now governed by the United States with sufficient moderation and liberalism to allow local dissatisfaction to express itself though not to meet with sympathy. The United States are pledged in honor to give the Filipinos an independence which they won in coöperation with the United States in their fight against Spain. It has not, so far, honored its pledge. The reason given is that the Filipinos are not yet in a position to govern themselves—an argument which it is as difficult to prove as to disprove, but on which many an independence would have to be withdrawn, including perhaps that of certain American States. But such is not the only nor even the main argument for the attitude of the United States. Leaving aside certain economic factors—some of which might explain the sudden solicitude for the Moros of the southern Philippine Islands evinced of late in certain American quarters—the favorite tenet of those Americans who fight against the independence of the Filipinos is that the Islands would fall the prey of Japan. Now this is seriously to be doubted, for Japan could ill afford the combined displeasure of the United States and of Great Britain, which such an action would certainly provoke. But the Philippines could be easily guaranteed against Japanese ambitions, assuming their existence for the sake of argument, by making the archipelago a fully-fledged member of the League of Nations. True, the independence of Nicaragua has not been secured by League membership, nor that of Albania either. But in the case of the Philippines the moral effect of League membership would be put in operation by the active direct interest of Great Britain and the United States, while in the case of Nicaragua the United States blocks League action and in the case of Albania Great Britain is a discreet but effective collaborator of Italian inroads if only by her passivity.

As for China, the situation is one of the clearest examples of international anarchy which the present age can show. Needless to say, the main responsibility lies at the door of the big powers. Commercial rivalry, diplomatic rivalry, ports, customs, concessions, railways are the true prizes at stake. The vagaries of Chinese administration and justice are the pretext. Civil war could be stopped the moment the powers agreed:

(a) To keep their word not to allow foreign arms to go to China;

(b) To coöperate with China in a truly constructive policy respecting Chinese sovereignty and independence.

The case is clearly one for collective intervention through the League in all its aspects, technical as well as political. Until this course is taken not only will China be debarred from all possibility of peaceful development but the powers will be hopelessly divided by their irreconcilable interests.

Chapter IX

OUTLINE OF A PROGRAM

IF we now look back on the ground we have covered we find that the program of preliminary questions to be solved before disarmament can be a reality comprises:

(a) A thoroughgoing organization of the World-Community having for its basis a universal League of Nations with power to take in hand all the problems arising in the normal course of international life.

(b) A thoroughgoing examination of all present discontents with a view to international solutions on world lines implying perhaps far-reaching changes in existing conditions of law and fact.

Were this program to be taken literally, the indefinite postponement of disarmament would be fatal. In a sense, this pessimistic conclusion is correct. Despite facile speeches to the contrary the world has to make far greater strides along the path of international order and morality before disarmament becomes effective and universal. But of course the actual position is far from being so desperate in practice. History proceeds by evolution, and, in the string of events, aims and means are intertwined more intimately than in our own abstract logic. If we were asked—as well we might be—to give an outline of what we would propose as a practical possible line of development, taking into account both our own views on the problem and the realities as we find them, we would venture to put forward the following:

I. The position of the United States should be the object of fresh consideration and study. Several points ought to be made quite clear:

(a) As long as the United States remains held by her bigoted belief in the two theological mysteries, the devilish character of the League and the heavenly character of the Monroe Doctrine, she is a nation debarred from world leadership. For world leadership implies a clear world vision and the vision of the United States is clouded in the direction of Europe by her anti-League prejudice and in every direction by her truly astounding obstinacy with regard to the Monroe Doctrine. Prejudices yield to no arguments. They are made of the stuff of irrational life and can only be conquered by life itself, i.e., by time. The world must have the wisdom of recognizing this fact, but it must spare some wisdom for recognizing its consequences also—the main of which is of course that the United States cannot lead a world which she does not see freely. Until the great Republic of the West has cured herself, the world must turn somewhere else for leadership.

(b) The United States has become a country with world-wide interests. It is estimated that her financial stake in Europe only is equivalent to the wealth of seven of her own States. In addition, she has considerable financial and economic interests in Asia and in

South America. In fact, the United States is to-day the only power whose material interests abroad are on the same scale as those of the British Empire. Whether they are bigger or smaller would probably turn out to be a highly technical matter without much practical importance.

(c) This country so deeply "entangled" financially and economically is also morally entangled owing to her truly admirable vocation for world service. Every one even slightly familiar with American life knows where this international virtue originates. The United States is, with England, the country of public service. Her wealthy men have inherited from their English ancestors the sense of social duty which is perhaps the main strength of the English aristocracy. Her middle classes are also richly endowed with this vigorous impulse towards social work. The incomparable record of the United States in generous international service is but the extension of such a national virtue to the international field. The names of her great foundations—Rockefeller, Carnegie, Guggenheim and others—the record of their world-wide schemes of charity, the long roll of the distinguished men who have given their unstinted collaboration to League of Nations enterprises, last but not least the excellence of some of her institutions for political study—such as that admirable Foreign Policy Association—suffice to witness to the creative capacity of the United States in the field of world affairs.

(d) As a consequence of the three preceding observations it may be pointed out that the present inability of the United States to take a position of leadership in the world may only be transitory. She has everything a leader should have: a wide and generous spirit and a big powerful body. Her shortcomings are in the nature of mental troubles which are curable and should be cured. Her objection to the League of Nations is but a mental aberration in a country which is itself a league of States; her belief in the Monroe Doctrine is an obsolete dogma which the growing dissatisfaction of the nations which it offends may help her to discard. We have every right to hope, perhaps without undue optimism, that this double line of evolution has now entered into a phase of reasonable acceleration.

If such is the case it seems that the world organized in the League should coöperate in the evolution of the United States towards that freedom of mind which she must conquer before she can take her leading position in international affairs. What form should this coöperation take?

In our opinion no concession should be made to the United States which implies a retrograde step on the path of international evolution. The statement is self-evident. It is nevertheless frequently sinned against. Three cases might be quoted here by way of illustration:

There are people who advocate that the Members of the League should accept the conditions which the United States put forward for their acceptance of membership of the Permanent Court of International Justice and particularly that the Court should not give advisory opinions to the Council on questions in which the

United States would declare to be concerned. This means depriving the world of an invaluable method of peace administration. The obvious course is to wait till the United States have reached a sufficient stage of international development to join not merely the Court but the League.

There are people, particularly in England, who advocate that the United States should be given certain guarantees of non-interference with their trade in time of war. We have already dealt with this, in our opinion, dangerous proposition. It means that League Members would go back on the present stage of the world which tends towards the abolition of neutrality.

Finally when Judge Bassett Moore resigned from the Court there were people—and most sincere and well-meaning people too—who suggested Mr. Hughes as his successor. Mr. Hughes was appointed. It was, in our opinion, a most deplorable choice. Had the United States joined the League of Nations, no happier choice could have been made then for the post of American Representative on the Council of the League than Mr. Hughes. But the prominent ex-Secretary of State, the chief representative of the United States at the Havana Conference, should never have been elected to a judicial post at the Hague. The transformation of the Hague Court into a political body must be resisted at all costs, and not even the advantages to be derived from the popularity of Mr. Hughes' name should have counterbalanced the higher claims of the institution in itself. There is no lack of eminent judges in the United States who would have added their own judicial prestige to that of the Court. But the choice of Mr. Hughes is typical of the tendency to transform what should be the higher aim into a means for political advantage in negotiation, and this tendency we consider to be dangerous even when well-meaning.

The right and proper way is to consider the League in itself as more precious than the collaboration of the United States. Therefore, the right method is for the Members of the League to insist that all world matters must be transacted through the League. This view is not put forward in any fanatical spirit. Far from it. Let us be quite clear on this point: if it was proved that the scrapping of the League meant universal order and peace, we would gladly scrap the League. If it was proved that any real world problem could be usefully dealt with outside the League, we would gladly agree that it should be so treated. But we are convinced—and we hope our readers are by now fully convinced—of two things:

(1) That the problem of world peace can only be solved if a world organization exists.

(2) That no world problem can receive adequate treatment except in the appropriate setting which such a world organization affords.

In these conditions we must deplore the lenient tendency of some States to let the United States discuss world problems with them outside the League; not because it is bad for the League—we are not concerned with the League, nothing can kill it; it will survive many a nation—but because it is bad for the problems themselves and bad for the United States.

Let us put forward two examples. With one of them we have already dealt in substance. We want to take it up again here from the point of view of procedure. The United States was allowed to put her reservations to the World Court before the several Members of the League as if the League did not exist, and though the reservations were discussed in Geneva by a committee of Members of the League which dared not call itself a League Committee (there were even people glad of the fact that owing to momentary difficulties accommodation had to be found at the International Labor Office) the League Secretariat was not allowed to answer the Government of the United States, and the separate Nations answered separately as if they had never heard of the League. This procedure was highly disingenuous and apt to favor the preposterous opinion which many a misguided friend of the League in America is heard to put forward that the Court is not at all a League Court connected with the League. The Court is a League Court. It is *the* League Court. And when the United States joins it she should be fully aware of the fact that she is joining the judiciary of the League of Nations.

A second case in point is the procedure chosen in connection with the Kellogg Pact. That M. Briand should offer Mr. Kellogg a Franco-American pact, well and good. But once Mr. Kellogg made the proposal multilateral, and particularly as soon as he made it universal, the right and proper answer for M. Briand should have been: "Admirable, Mr. Kellogg. Come to Geneva and we shall talk it over in the proper place for world things to be discussed." Had this course been taken, the Kellogg Pact might have been the beginning of great things. Of course Mr. Kellogg might have refused. But whether he had refused or accepted the problem would certainly have become clearer, either by showing that the United States was not ready to enter fully into the implications of her own idea or by showing to the United States that it was indispensable for her to adopt the idea with all its implications in order to make it at all substantial. At any rate the world would have spared itself the curious sight of Senator Borah urging acceptance of the Navy Bill for increasing the American Navy in order to secure the passage of the Kellogg Pact for the outlawry of war.

In short it is not by wooing America that America is going to be won. It is by fighting gallantly against the dragon of her prejudices. America is a romantic lady and will be moved by courage. But whether the policy is good for conquering America or not the League Members are in honor bound to follow no other, for surely it is on the face of it absurd to impair the spirit of the League in order to conquer a new Member.

II. The nation best placed to assume the leadership of the movement of world construction is Great Britain. She must lead or she must drag. If she does not fall in with a movement, she blocks it. If she falls in, she must lead.

Every allowance must be made for her hesitation. The splendid achievement of the British Empire was created by her under the old system of international struggle for life. Her genius is particularly fitted for a competitive world. It is but natural that she should remain attached to a phase of world evolution which for all practical purposes corresponds with the acme of her success and might indeed be described as the English era. There is moreover in the new spirit a call to world comradeship which is almost directly antagonistic to her deep insularity. Yet, despite such serious obstacles, the new spirit is one which should appeal to the English genius. England has a rich experience of coöperation and her long history as an imperial power has allowed her people to develop both the universal sense and the sense of government on a vast scale.

The British Empire, moreover, is rapidly evolving towards a loosely knit association of nations. Such an evolution, if left to itself, so to say, in the open, might end in total disruption—signs of which are apparent to the wary eye of the English statesman in more than one quarter of the globe. Held, however, within the framework of the League, the evolution of the British Empire is sure to develop along smooth lines acceptable both to the metropolitan country and to the Dominions, present and future. And it is evidently to the advantage of Great Britain to strengthen the outer ring while the fatal forces of history are at work making the inner ring, if not weaker, at any rate more elastic.

There is moreover a more tangible argument. Amateur statesmen are still discussing whether Great Britain is or is not in Europe. Every schoolboy knows of course that the British Isles are an integral part of the

Continent. Some of these schoolboys are apt to forget it later, particularly when they specialize in strategy and join the Committee of Imperial Defense—which explains that the Channel Tunnel Scheme should have been rejected time and again by that august body. But the fact remains that Great Britain can only be absolutely certain of her life if her communications with France are secure. Now this means that Great Britain must guarantee European peace at all costs, and, as the grave problems of Europe are but one problem, it follows that Great Britain has a first-rate, nay, a vital interest in maintaining order in Europe. In so far as the United States and Japan command a sea power commensurate with her own and, in the case of the United States, capable of a formidable development in case of war, Great Britain is also committed to a policy of peace in Asia and in America. In fact, the policy of power is for Great Britain obsolete. She still remains faithful to it, partly through inertia, partly through sentimental attachment, but sooner or later she will be bound to realize that the course of her ship must change.

Such are the reasons which give substance to the opinion that Great Britain may soon lead the world in a true League policy instead of acting as the most powerful of the brakes which are slowing down the movement of the League machinery and threaten sometimes to put it altogether out of gear.

III. Led by Great Britain the League Members must all agree to a system for the peaceful settlement of all disputes on the lines of the arbitration clauses of the Protocol. This system would comprise:

(a) The signature of the optional clause without reservations,

(b) Arbitration and/or conciliation of all other disputes without exception,

(c) A criterion of aggression adapted from that defined in the Locarno system.

It is indispensable that this program should be prepared and adopted as an all-round convention on the basis of the League, not only because a general treaty affords a better guarantee of good legal and diplomatic work in the drafting and linking together of the obligations assumed, but because the main effect to be sought is moral and moral effect is deeper when the World-Community acts as such than when the sum total of its members act separately even in the same direction. A perusal of the memorandum whereby the British Government communicated to the Council its disapproval of the Protocol would show that Great Britain can claim no unanswerable objection to a system of the kind here advocated. Let it be understood that the system would deal with political disputes but not with political problems, a point to be treated hereafter.

The scheme would aim above all at security. It would amount to a method for guaranteeing the world against war. It should stand separate from disarmament and concentrate on the precautions to be taken in the prewar period. Its basis should be Articles 11-15 of the Covenant. The Council under Article 11 should consider itself under permanent obligation to watch disputes and not to allow them to develop without as early a reference as possible to one or other of the methods for peaceful settlement.

This scheme should comprise a series of international agreements covering:

(a) An agreement organizing the financial organization which would enable the Council to come to the help of a nation attacked or under threat of attack, on the lines suggested by the Finnish Government and studied by the Financial Commission of the League of Nations.

(b) An agreement organizing the air communications of the world on an international basis in order not merely to secure the best possible commercial efficiency of air lines but particularly to remove all danger of misuse of air lines for military attack.

(c) A similar agreement organizing chemical industries on an international basis in order to remove all sense of mistrust due to the possibility of using chemical industries in a surprise attack by poison gas.

The scheme should also provide for a more complete organization of the League with regard to the use of the articles of the Covenant in the prevention of war. In particular the League Council and Assembly should take a more positive attitude with regard to Articles 18 and 20, which are devised in order to guarantee that no treaties or alliances, in fact no international stipulations, can be concluded in the future or even may remain in force when existing if they are contrary to the spirit of the Covenant.[1] Machinery should be set up to

[1] Article 18. Every treaty or international engagement entered into hereafter by any Member of the League shall be forthwith reg-

deal with this matter in an effective way. The Council should publish a yearly report on the treaties registered in the Secretariat within the year, explicitly taking responsibility for them in this connection. This procedure would suffice to ensure that the treaties in question were in harmony with the Covenant of the League. Other similar developments in connection with the Covenant might perhaps be studied and incorporated in the scheme.

IV. In order the better to fulfill this task, the Council should consider itself as the political leader of the community constituted in the League. We are aware of at least two tendencies against this view:

—That which would have the Council wait till things settle themselves outside it or till they become too grave to be allowed to drift any further;

—That which tends to substitute for the Council small inner groupings of powers, known to the gentlemen of the press as the Big Three, the Big Four, the Big Five, etc.

istered with the Secretariat and shall as soon as possible be published by it. No such treaty or international engagement shall be binding until so registered.

ARTICLE 20.

1. The Members of the League severally agree that this Covenant is accepted as abrogating all obligations or understandings *inter se* which are inconsistent with the terms thereof, and solemnly undertake that they will not hereafter enter into any engagements inconsistent with the terms thereof.

2. In case any Member of the League shall, before becoming a Member of the League, have undertaken any obligations inconsistent with the terms of this Covenant, it shall be the duty of such Member to take immediate steps to procure its release from such obligations.

Both these tendencies seem to us to miss the main point. The main point is that we are studying how to get rid of armaments, therefore, how to put reason instead of brute force in international relations. The policy of drift or of outside diplomatic development means that the weak are left alone to argue it out with the strong until they are either cowed into submission or enraged into revolt—in which second case presumably, the Council would step in. As to the policy of the Big Three, it openly rests on power and it sends down the slopes of international society a daily lesson of international ambition. There are people whose philosophy leads them to the view that this, let us call it, system of world ambition and power is an element of progress in the world; others who, without going so far, shrug their shoulders at criticisms of it, exclaiming "Yes, but what will you have? There it is." These people are entitled to their opinion. But *they must not come forward as advocates of disarmament as well.* All that is claimed here is that if we want disarmament and therefore a just peace, the government of the world must rest on the Council of the League as the Council of the League and not in meetings of members, and that political problems must be taken in hand by the Council as a matter of course and before they become political disputes.

The difficulty of the absence of the United States should not be exaggerated. It is ridiculous to suggest that all but two nations should feel paralyzed by the remaining two. If the members of the League had been as convinced of the supremacy of League methods as they ought to be, they would certainly have carried with them the United States and Russia. The point has been fully dealt with under No. I above. There is no question that, if all the members of the Council were determined that the Council as the executive of the conscious and organized World-Community must take responsibility for the business of the world, means would have been discovered whereby the United States and Russia would have coöperated with them.

The truth of the matter is that the big nations represented in the Council have found America a convenient stick to beat the League dog with. Every nation which wanted to run its own pet business on the old anarchical system of secret compacts secretly arrived at found in America's absence a convenient pretext. And this fact, that the United States has been the most efficient though unwilling accomplice of every bit of reactionary international work done in the world since the League's inception, should be a matter for bitter thought for the numerous phalanx of American idealists.

We consider an active Council of the League as an indispensable element in the creation and fostering of security. The world must feel that its business is well in hand. Such a transformation of the life of the Council would make the convention on arbitration and security here advocated a living thing instead of yet another solemn paper. The Council having thus proved a new spirit would have assumed sufficient authority for attempting the next task in the true preparation for disarmament.

V. We refer to a series of systematic agreements in order to re-cast the status of Europe on a basis of mutual consent. We have already discussed the reasons which force us to the conclusion that in a Europe split by the bitter memories of defeat and by the fears bred by the insecure gains of victory, disarmament is a vain hope. We do not however claim that Europe should be thrown into a kind of diplomatic melting-pot—for which there would be no lack of heat. Here, as in all this chapter, our concern is rather with the spirit than with the speed of the work. Europe would soon realize that a new wind was blowing if only it did blow. Nor is it our business to suggest detailed solutions for which, moreover, no preconceived rules, principles or prejudices, should be set down, since solutions are bound to be empirical. All we wish to put on record is that the work is necessary, that it is possible, given good will, and that the League organization is fully capable of dealing with it in a fair and impartial way. A difficult work, no doubt. A work of years, certainly. But a work with a hope in it and not a hopeless and incompetent drift. Method, continuity and courage: the virtues which should make the League.

VI. The Council having thus become a really active leader of world polities, it would be in a position to deal effectively with other than European affairs. We have said why we are not impressed by the so-called obstacle of America's absence. *America would have believed in the League if the League had believed in itself.* The League must be up and doing and America will then look up, for America knows power when she sees it. Take the Chinese question. Is it not a shame that such a situation should be allowed to drift by nations which claim that they are organized in a community and at the same time try every one of them to steal a march on the others with an eye on markets and ports? How statesmen can bleat disarmament at dawn while howling trade-war at dusk is one of the mysteries of our baffling age. This unseemly sight must cease. Stop the bleat or stop the howl. We are grown-up men and fear not a return to the savage contests of yesterday, if returns there must be. But it is against human dignity to continue this silly make-believe. There is no reason whatsoever for keeping the Council of the League busy with enquiries about the transportation of the blind and the protection of the youthful maiden—a species as rapidly becoming extinct as the old diplomat so full of fatherly solicitude towards her. The Council should meet for something more substantial. In every corner of the world there are dangers brewing. The Council must take the world in hand. People keep complaining that there is no security, no moral disarmament. On the day the world would feel itself governed, security and moral disarmament would be in our hearts. We should not have to wait till the Council had finished its task. The task is permanent and unfinishable. We should feel the impulse, the spirit, and the effects on the world would be instantaneous.

VII. It goes without saying that the political work of the League would have to be carried out in close touch with a far-reaching economic development of its activities. There are many international problems but only one international life. To hide one's head under the sand has become obsolete, even for ostriches. It is time to face difficulties boldly and to solve them intelligently. A policy which consists in paying eloquent lip-service to disarmament while severely frowning at every technical method of study whereby rivalry may evolve into coöperation must be roundly denounced as both hypocritical and mischievous. *The League must grow in all directions if it is to succeed in any one of them.*

A brisk pace in technical studies must set in. The League has in its constitution a sufficient number of brakes to spare us any fear of its exceeding any speed limit and the problems of the world—health, labor, economic and financial relations, communications—grow at a quicker pace than our best endeavors to grapple with them. The world must feel itself governed in its material as well as in its moral and spiritual life.

VIII. Once the Council has justified its existence by showing signs of understanding its responsibilities, the work of Disarmament will proceed in an atmosphere of more hopeful optimism than has been the case hitherto. The convention on security and arbitration which should be signed and ratified without conditions would have paved the way for a disarmament convention. A feeling that a certain number of political problems were well in hand would also help. The removal of the sting of defeat from the soul of Europe would ease many a situation. There should be moreover no pressure exerted to reduce figures. For the first stage, figures should not matter very much. What should matter is:

(a) That there should be a contract, i.e., that armaments should cease being a purely national concern in law when they obviously are an essentially international concern in fact;

(b) That there should be an institution incarnating such a contract, i.e., that the League should possess an organization entrusted with the duty and the power of keeping its hand on the pulse of the world and of reporting the slightest tremor of armament fear.

We therefore advocate a convention of limitation of men, material and money, duly supervised by an international commission responsible to the League Council. This convention should be set up on the basis of Article 8 of the Covenant, i.e., it must be perpetually binding save for revisions every ten years. The case of non-Member States could be met by drafting two separate instruments: a convention of limitation of armaments proper, which could be signed by all; and a protocol of application and supervision of the convention which would be signed by the League Members. Complaints against non-Member States could be brought before the League Council by means of machinery similar to that of Article 17 of the Covenant. As publicity would in any case be the only sanction for Members as well as for non-Members, the procedure would be equally efficient for all.

IX. It will be noticed that sanctions do not come into this picture at all. We believe the problem is sufficiently dealt with in the Covenant. Considerable progress might be made, however, in removing misunderstandings if the wording of the Covenant were revised in this connection on the lines suggested in a previous chapter, i.e., by defining international action against aggression or against Covenant-breaking States in general as a new and original state of international law different from both war and blockade. The consequences of the Covenant in international law must be borne with courage and a positive sense of their value. Neutrality law and blockade law must be adapted to a new situation, and the error which consists in thinking of an entirely original international phenomenon in terms of old international phenomena such as war and blockade must be removed from our discussions. The change might be far-reaching. It might even go as far as denying belligerent rights to a law-breaking state, whose true status should be analogous to that of piracy.

X. Though the rhythm of the development here outlined might be, and probably would be, slow, there is no reason why the leading States should not accelerate it by courageous and creative statesmanship. There is at least one direction in which such statesmanship might be forthcoming. In order to discover it we might ask ourselves which is the particular kind of disarmament which might be undertaken with the least amount of risk for the nations which would sacrifice the most? It is evident that the answer to this question points to naval disarmament. For the two biggest naval powers in the world, namely Great Britain and the United States, are incomparably more powerful than the others also in one other element of international power, namely finance. Moreover naval disarmament, provided it is not used as a card in an international game, could be undertaken with a relative facility apart from land and air disarmament. It is true that, as has been stated in other chapters, the method has been tried unsuccessfully owing to the opposition of other naval powers. But it has been tried in the wrong spirit. What is required in order to succeed is a far more imaginative and a far more courageous scheme of disarmament by example. The method of disarmament by example has been denounced, probably rightly, if and when it was put forward as meaning that a nation should immediately proceed to cut down its own armaments without any more ado. This is of course beyond the realm of practical politics. But there does not seem to be a similar objection against a disarmament by example consisting not in actual immediate disarming but in a suggestion of actual immediate disarming on a definite courageous and imaginative plan. For instance there seems to be no reason why the two great naval powers should not unite in suggesting to the world the total abolition of navies within a relatively short period of years together with the disarmament and neutralization of all the narrow sea passages. Such a proposal entailing, as it would of course entail, the total abolition of submarines and mines would in our opinion if anything rather increase than decrease the sea-power of the great sea-faring nations. It would moreover constitute a formidable stimulus to the development of disarmament and peace in the world. An organization of sea-police, either on the lines of the Soviet suggestion or on other lines to be agreed upon, would of course be necessary.

Such a far-reaching change in the organization of the world could not of course take place in a very short number of years. We would refer the reader to our remarks in the first part of this volume with regard to the organic character of armies and navies. The disappearance of a naval organization from countries such as England, in which it is one of the oldest limbs of the body politic, would be equivalent to a surgical operation, and would require most delicate handling. Here again, therefore, it is not with speed that we are concerned but with spirit. But, even with the full conscience of the gravity of the proposal, we are of opinion that if Great Britain suggested to the League and to the world that she was ready for the neutralization and de-militarization of the seas and narrow passages to be achieved within a definite number of years, however long, she would not reduce her actual power over the world—a power which is mostly financial, political, historical and racial—she would still remain the most formidable nation on the water, she would give the world the greatest lesson in international statesmanship since Wilson presented the Covenant to the Paris Conference and she would tremendously increase her moral authority in the world.

Chapter X

CONCLUSION

THE several items of this program are not suggested as necessarily linked up in time. Opportunity must always be the omnipotent and capricious fairy of life. What is suggested, in fact what must be emphasized, is that success in disarmament is impossible unless a new spirit is felt in world affairs. New, though the spirit wanted has already moved the world and assisted at the birth of the League of Nations. Pundits, practical men, wiseacres, have been busy since then pouring—oh, not cold water—tepid, deadly tepid stuff over our imagination and soul. "You must not break the back of the League," they say, it is too young." And meanwhile they deprive it of food and of spirit so that it may not grow. We are not cranks. We are no "enthusiasts." We are as cold-blooded as any political old hand and as "hard-boiled" as any financier. We do not advocate the League because it is a religion; we advocate it because it is the only reasonable way to solve a definite problem, the terms of which can be put clearly to every man and woman with senses to observe and sense to judge. We believe that no business man would "run" his business as the world is run to-day, letting every one of its departments steal a march on every other one, allowing them to work in utter lack of coöperation in a spirit of enmity and distrust. We do not advocate holiness. We advocate sense. We bear no grudge to the out-and-out imperialist and militarist. We are not where he is but we know where he is. He believes in progress by selection. He belongs to a school of thought which is plausible and whose views deserve respect. But we consider as the pest of the present age the best-of-both-worlds individual, whether of the sheep or of the fox variety, the person who goes about feeling like Bismarck and speaking like Jesus Christ. To him we say: Get out of the way.

Get out of the way, we say, for we mean business and you don't. We do not want to suppress or abolish war. We would suppress or abolish nothing. Our work is not negative and destructive; it is positive and creative. We do not want to destroy war. We want to create peace.

For peace is no negative state which turns up through the mere absence of war. Peace is not going to come about by mere bleating. The work of peace is hard work, the hardest work of all. For we shall not obtain a state of peace unless we keep in check the herd of wild beasts which we harbor in our individual and national heart—the tiger of which Mr. Baldwin spoke with his usual candor, yea, the tiger and the dog as well, and the swine also, not to forget the donkey, in charge of utterance—all the zoo which is in us must be kept vigorously in leash every day and everywhere. Like the price of liberty, the price of peace is eternal vigilance, but also eternal activity.

A hard work for every day. The world is not going to conquer peace and then sleep on its laurels and roses; for the instincts of war are ever alive and so the reasons of peace must be ever awatch. A point which peace-bleaters usually forget, for they see peace as a rest between men, while peace is the organization of men for the fight against the devils of war by coöperative means. No institution, no coöperation; no cooperation, no peace.

Nor is it possible to rely on fear of war, for fear never stopped man at the gates of folly. And moreover, the folly of war usually begins with exhilaration, just as the delirium tremens of the drunkard is born in the delights of the first frothy cups. Easier, ten times easier to drift into war than to defend peace against the ever-recurring attacks of the war disease. The world must know that if it wants peace it must work hard for it.

But it is a glorious fight. First because it is creative. How paltry the ideal of those so-called statesmen who see no higher than the commercial balance of their little world province! The greatest masterpieces of statecraft are awaiting, uncreated, in the divine imagination. They are awaiting the great hands able enough and worthy enough to manifest them to a world groaning with fear and expectation. Will the great hands appear? Small hands are busy everywhere, small crooked hands, grabbing right and left for what they can get, unaware of the one-ness of the world, impoverishing themselves by what they acquire. While the world waits for the great hands of the creative statesman big enough to realize how small his country has suddenly become.

The truly great statesman will want to create peace. He will want also to save the world from the catastrophe which lurks in the awful future if the spirit of wisdom does not light upon us. In a world grown smaller by man's new conquests—ether and air—nations with power multiplied by science move at quicker and quicker speeds, all eager or selfish gain, all intent in following their own orbits unaware of the other nations rolling equally intent in their own orbits also; while the eastern and southern continents, leavened by a western ferment of activity are seething with deep discontents, brewing future upheavals yet ready for future reconciliations. The races of man have come to live at closer distances than ever in past history. Let those nations hearken whose power is made of the subtle and immaterial stuff of good will spread widely through oceans and continents. Let them meditate whether it is in their interests that the world should learn examples of material power from the apex of our international society. The races yellow, brown and black and white are all alive with a new ferment, ready to evolve towards strife and death or towards coöperation and life. Peace there must be by an ever-reiterated act of will and reason. For if men do not deliberately walk towards peace they will drift into war. And then the unfortunate races of man may still give a new and sinister meaning to the poet's beautiful verse:

> "Yellow, and black, and pale, and hectic red,
> Pestilence stricken multitudes."

ANNEX

RESOLUTION INTRODUCED IN THE UNITED STATES SENATE, FEBRUARY, 1923, BY SENATOR WILLIAM E. BORAH

Whereas war is the greatest existing menace to society and has become so expensive and destructive that it not only causes the stupendous burdens of taxation now afflicting our people but threatens to engulf and destroy civilization; and

Whereas civilization has been marked in its upward trend out of barbarism into its present condition by the development of law and courts to supplant methods of violence and force; and

Whereas the genius of civilization has discovered but two methods of compelling the settlement of human disputes, namely, law and war, and therefore, in any plan for the compulsory settlement of international controversies, we must choose between war on the one hand and the process of law on the other; and

Whereas war between nations has always been and still is a lawful institution, so that any nation may, with or without cause, declare war against any other nation and be strictly within its legal rights; and

Whereas revolutionary war or wars of liberation are illegal and criminal; to wit, high treason; whereas, under existing international law, wars between nations to settle disputes are perfectly lawful; and

Whereas the overwhelming moral sentiment of civilized people everywhere is against the cruel and destructive institution of war; and

Whereas all alliances, leagues, or plans which rely upon war as the ultimate power for the enforcement of peace carry the seeds either of their own destruction or of military dominancy to the utter subversion of liberty and justice; and

Whereas we must recognize the fact that resolutions or

treaties outlawing certain methods of killing will not be effective so long as war itself remains lawful; and that in international relations we must have, not rules and regulations of war but organic laws against war; and

Whereas in our constitutional convention of 1787 it was successfully contended by Madison, Hamilton, and Ellsworth that the use of force when applied to people collectively, that is, to states or nations, in the execution of a judicial decision, is unsound in principle and would be tantamount to a declaration of war; and

Whereas we have in our federal supreme court a practical and effective model for a real international court, as it has specific jurisdiction to hear and decide controversies between our sovereign states; and

Whereas our supreme court has exercised this jurisdiction without resort to force for one hundred and thirty-seven years, during which time scores of controversies have been judicially and peaceably settled that might otherwise have led to war between the states, and thus furnishes a practical exemplar for the compulsory and pacific settlement of international controversies; and

Whereas an international arrangement of such judicial character would not shackle the independence or impair the sovereignty of any nation, and would not involve or affect the right of self-defense against invasion or attack, such right being inherent and ineradicable, but should not be a mere subterfuge for the traditional use of war: Now, therefore, be it

Resolved, That it is the view of the senate of the United States that war between nations should be outlawed as an institution or means for the settlement of international controversies by making it a public crime under the law of nations and that every nation should be encouraged by solemn agreement or treaty to bind itself to indict and punish its own international war breeders or instigators and war profiteers under powers similar to those conferred upon our congress under Article I, section 8, of our federal constitution which clothes the congress with the power "to define and punish offenses against the law of nations"; And be it

Resolved further, That a code of international law of peace based upon the outlawing of war and on the principle of equality and justice between all nations, amplified and expanded and adapted and brought down to date should be created and adopted.

Second. That, with war outlawed, a judicial substitute for war should be created (or, if existing in part, adapted and adjusted) in the form or nature of an international court, modeled on our federal supreme court in its jurisdiction over controversies between our sovereign states; such court shall possess affirmative jurisdiction to hear and decide all purely international controversies, as defined by the code or arising under treaties, and its judgments shall not be enforced by war under any name or in any form whatever, but shall have the same power for their enforcement as our federal supreme court, namely, the respect of all enlightened nations for judgments resting upon open and fair investigations and impartial decisions, the agreement of the nations to abide and be bound by such judgments, and the compelling power of enlightened public opinion.

MR. S. O. LEVINSON'S DRAFT TREATY TO OUTLAW WAR

We the undersigned nations of the world hereby condemn and abandon forever the use of war as an instrument for the settlement of international disputes and for the enforcement of decisions and awards of international tribunals, and hereby outlaw the immemorial institution of war by making its use a public crime as the fundamental law of nations. Subtle and fatal distinctions between permissible and nonpermissible kinds of war are blotted out; the institution of war is thus outlawed, as the institution of dueling has been outlawed; but the question of genuine self-defense, with nations as with individuals, is not involved in or affected by this treaty. In order to provide a complete and pacific substitute for the arbitrament of war, we hereby agree to take immediate action for the equipment of an international court of justice with a code of the laws of peace, based upon equality and justice between all nations. With war outlawed and the code approved and ratified, the court shall be given jurisdiction over all purely international disputes as defined and enumerated in the code or arising under treaties, with power to summon in a defendant nation at the petition of a complaining nation and to hear and decide the matters in controversy. We hereby agree to abide by and in full good faith to carry out the decisions of such international tribunal. The judicial system thus established, being a complete substitute for the outworn and destructive war system, will enable the nations to adopt far-reaching and economically vital programs of disarmament.

INDEX

C